PTSD Self Help

Transforming Survival Into A Life Worth Living

By A. E. Huppert

Lora,

What a pleasure meeting you.
Everyone deserves a life worth
living, don't you think? Join
me!

Peace,
A.E. Huppert
p. 263

Produced by:

FriesenPress
Suite 300 – 852 Fort Street
Victoria, BC, Canada V8W 1H8

www.friesenpress.com

Distributed to the trade by The Ingram Book Company

TABLE OF CONTENTS

Disclaimer..vii

Author's Message To The Reader...............................xiii

Introduction..1
   The Tree Of Life..*1*
   Is This Book For You?...*3*
   Supply List...*7*

How The *PTSD Self Help* System Is Organized 9
   Four Seasons...*9*
   Three Key Concepts..*10*
   Three Key Action Steps..*12*
   Three Practical Application Guides.......................*13*
   Three Levels of Engagement...................................*13*
   One Story: What You Can Look Forward To
   —Annmarie's Story...*14*
   Practical Support...*16*

Season Of Hope—Part I: 19
   Planning For The Journey..*21*
   How Long Will It Take?..*24*
   Addressing Anxiety and Depression......................*26*
   Counting the Cost...*33*
   Three Key Concepts..*37*
      Concept #1: PTSD is Normal.............................*37*

Concept #2: Normal is What Works *49*
Concept #3: Work Your Strengths *62*
Three Key Action Steps *65*
   The First Step: A Healing Commitment *65*
   The Second Step: Taking Action *68*
   The Third Step: Changing Your Mind *69*

Season Of Hope—Part II: 77
Packing For The Journey
Tools for Your Backpack: *79*
   The InnerAction Journal *80*
   Enlightenment *95*
   An Emergency Plan of Action (EPA) *101*
   HomeWork *105*
   Toy Box *106*

Season Of Renewal 109
Recruiting Your Healing Team: It Takes A Community
—And One Day, A Nation *111*
How A Healing Team Works *112*
Recruiting a Mental Health Professional *115*
Getting Your Spouse on the Team *123*
Choosing a Healing Partner *124*
Choosing A Chiropractor *129*
Choosing a Massage Therapist *134*
Recruiting A Nation To Care *139*
The Origins of PTSD Stigma and Rape Culture *141*
Overcoming A Rape Culture: Be A Change Agent *145*

Season Of Transformation: 155
Let The Journey Begin! *157*
A Word About Marriage *158*
A Word About Medication *160*
Scheduling Time *166*
Sacred Healing Moments -
Planning Time for Rest & Recovery *171*
HomeWork *183*
Staying The Course: Decision-making
& Unplugging From Triggers *189*
Healing, Religion & Spirituality *205*

Spirituality *216*
Collaborative Healing Activities *221*
Body Armor: Why You Need A Massage *222*
The Center for Hope & Renewal:
PTSD Transformation for Survivors & Families *249*

Season To Enjoy A Life Worth Living: *253*
Trying On The New You! *255*
Life After Healing *259*
Freedom and Vulnerability *263*

APPENDIX A: *267*
Practical Application Guides *267*

APPENDIX B: *269*
Summary Of Exercises *269*

APPENDIX C: *271*
Resources For A Dynamite Trip! *271*

Work with A. E. Huppert *274*

About the Author *277*

DISCLAIMER

Always consult your health care provider about your particular case and obtain full medical clearance before practicing yoga, exercise programs or any other physical/mental healing activity. The information provided in this book, related blog, website and other material (information) is strictly for reference purposes only. This information is not a substitute for medical advice and is not to be used in any manner for the diagnosis and/or treatment of any medical, mental or surgical condition. If you suspect you have a medical problem, consult your physician or a qualified health practitioner.

The information provided herein is also not to be used in any manner as a substitute for the direct guidance of a qualified exercise instructor, medical or mental health provider. Always practice yoga, exercise and other wellness programs under direct guidance of a qualified instructor or facilitator. Practicing wellness activities under the direct supervision and guidance of a qualified professional can, but is not guaranteed to, help avoid injuries. Not all yoga, exercise or other wellness practices are appropriate or suited for every person. Practice yoga, exercise and other wellness programs at your own risk.

The publisher, author, editor, illustrator and distributor collectively and severally disclaim any liabilities and assume no responsibility for injuries or any other loss that may result from practicing yoga, exercise or other wellness activities associated with the information in this book. The publisher, author, editor, illustrator and distributor collectively and severally disclaim any liabilities and assume no responsibility for injury in connection with any information provided in this book, related blog, website, and/or other material. The publisher, author, editor, illustrator and distributor all make no representations or warranties with regard to the completeness or accuracy of this book, related website, any linked websites, DVDs, or other products represented herein.

For my Healing Partner, armor bearer and soul mate

Rebecca Ann Cooper

Between stimulus and response there is a space. In that space is our power to choose our response. In our response lies our growth and our freedom.

−Viktor E. Frankl

AUTHOR'S MESSAGE TO THE READER

Many PTSD survivors suffer years of disappointment in traditional on-the-couch psychotherapy; three months worth of twice weekly visits was enough for me. Because of my negative experience, I didn't return to the PTSD healing journey for ten years. However, I eventually found a holistic approach to healing to be the most beneficial. Through this, I finally started listening to my intuition and began integrating other activities that weren't focused solely on my mind, as I couldn't stand having my brain picked at anymore! Surprise—these other activities opened a back door to healing my mind.

Before I learned how helpful a holistic approach to healing PTSD could be, the body symptoms were excruciating, wearing me down physically and emotionally—never mind the mental symptoms. I was so distracted by the pain I was suffering and how miserable I felt that I didn't make any connection between the intrusive thoughts, unwelcome memories, and what had happened to me during my lifetime.

Does your life sound like this (or some version of it)?

Here's some of what I was dealing with: not wanting to go anywhere without knowing where the nearest bathroom was; intense jaw pain and tension (affecting not only the ability to eat but also the ability to hear); migraines that began with a slow darkening of vision, result-ing in an entire day spent in an unlit room, nursing an implosion of the brain that would make me puke until I passed out; grinding my teeth during those rare nights of sleep; loss of hair; limited mobility and chronic aching of the shoulders; a weakened immune system, resulting in susceptibility to viruses and colds; frequent episodes of tachycardia (an excessively rapid heartbeat), sweating and an unexplained sense of impending doom; digestive disorders, including heartburn, acid reflux, a burning stomach, hiatal hernia, diarrhea, hemorrhoids, and feeling like my guts were literally going to drop into the toilet bowl; unexplained nerve pain, making areas of the skin painfully hyper-sensitive to touch; a really screwed-up menstrual cycle, beginning every twenty days with severe cramping, clotting, and an abnormal amount of blood loss—often lasting for ten days, leading to anemia (or having all the nasty symptoms with no bleeding at all); unexplained "eruptions" of staph infections on my fingers and toes.

Yeah. Fun times—and that was just the physical part. After my first visit to the emergency room for a mental breakdown (when I was twenty-five years old), I did my best to bury what was coming up in my mind. As a result, the effect of the crimes committed against me erupted in my body. That got my attention. Unfortunately, I didn't yet understand the dynamics of unhealed trauma, so I traveled down more than a few rabbit trails before confronting PTSD head-on at the age of thirty-five.

Giving up my career as a felony trial paralegal with the prosecuting attorney's special assault unit was part of the fallout from the physical onslaught. Leaving was bittersweet; it was there I'd discovered I was a crime victim. One day, I added up all the possible charges that could have been filed against sexual predator number two (there were four in my life) based on the memories I still had of the incident. A quick tally of the hash marks revealed thirty-two counts, ranging from indecent liberties with a minor to rape. That ranked up there with some of the most heinous crimes I helped prosecute. Thirty-two. That number never left my mind. My transformation had begun, and there was no stopping it.

Always the optimist, I chose to take a different view of why, only five years in, I needed to leave a career I had studied so long and hard to enjoy. The truth was that PTSD was killing me. Oh sure, to my husband and anyone else with whom I closely worked, it was obvious that my ailments were stress-induced. I was the only paralegal to nine attorneys and was working on one of the most high-profile death-penalty cases our county had seen in a long time. Without a doubt, stress was killing me slowly. However, it wasn't just the huge caseload that was the cause of my stress: what neither the people around me nor I realized was that I was still suffering from trauma related to a series of events that began when I was seven years old and continued until the year I turned forty (I'm grateful that it ended. For some, I know it never ends).

In those early years after leaving my career, I told myself that I just needed a break. Owning my own business seemed like a good way to be able to set my own schedule, and since I'm a fan of working smarter, not harder, I capitalized on my talent for guiding people in a practical way, and started a life coaching business. In the late '90s, life coaching had not yet become popular, and the term "coach" was just starting to catch on in the business world.

But I didn't want to plug in to the professional world; I wanted to reach the stay-at-home mom with a four-year degree who was living in the shadow of her husband. You know the one: she's given up everything to raise a family and support a husband, only to wake up one morning to realize she doesn't remember who she is. I brought a few other women on board and trained them to focus on their natural, relational abilities, supplemented their experience with solid, factual understanding, and connected with our lost clientele to deliver quick, three-month transformative experiences. We did well. We helped a lot of people. We felt good about ourselves and the impact we were having in our community. However, we weren't making money.

It would take a couple of business name changes and redefining our focus over a period of seven years for me to admit two things: One, I suck at the small things of business; two, my ideas are ahead of their time. But I'm great at marketing! Out of this world at innovation and visioneering (usually five to seven years ahead of the curve)! Spectacular at delivering value! Yet I stink at the minutiae that a growing business needs in order to flourish. Plus, our nation was on the verge of near financial collapse, and I could sense it coming.

I closed down Character Development Coaching (turned Life Navigation Concierges) just in time to avoid the 2008 financial disaster. By now, I had multiple degrees and certifications, and had experienced a number of life-changing programs, ranging from The Pacific Institute to Landmark Education (a descendent of Est) to SGR (an off-shoot of

The Secret) and ten years of dedication to the Christian church. I was ravenous for knowledge; my personal library of more than 500 self-help books, all of them read cover to cover, is proof of this. Deep within myself, I was trying to unravel the mystery of how and why the early events of my life were haunting me. If I could understand how and why, maybe I could break free of the effects. Why not help a few folks out along the way?

It seemed selfish to keep all that knowledge to myself, especially since I was finding answers. I spent a lot of time in front of audiences as a motivational speaker, in classes as an instructor, and in groups as a facilitator, although it took a number of years to break away from being asked to share my abusive history. Whenever I shared what had happened to me, I always followed it up by delivering practical steps for alleviating the pain and suffering I had known. I had thousands of letters, notes and messages from people who were thankful for the advice and found success of their own. Even so, I felt inauthentic; the shadow of PTSD following me, and I still had unanswered questions. By this time (the early 2000s), my second marriage was falling apart, I was rapidly approaching a second nervous breakdown, and my church had abandoned me. After my life blew up for the second time, I learned that most of my physical symptoms were directly related to how anxiety shows up in my body. PTSD, being an anxiety disorder, was the root cause; however, it was a little-known program called Attacking Anxiety and Depression from a small organization in the midwest that was instrumental in setting me on the path that would save my life. The practical advice given in the fifteen-week, home-study, recovery program gave me the relief I needed to begin making pivotal decisions toward healing—the most important of which was finding a mental health professional.

I wasn't hung up on degrees or titles when it came to resourcing myself with whatever I needed to make sense of the chaotic world my life had become. To me, normal was what worked. Period. If it didn't work, it or he or she was outta there! Fired! People didn't like that very much. As a result of having been abandoned to the ravages of men for most of my life, I was used to starting over, breaking bonds, and unfortunately, being disappointed. So, after three close encounters with suicide, walking away from relationships that were toxic (either because of the nature of the relationship or because certain individuals didn't agree with the recovery methods I embraced) was easy. My heart became hardened toward people who wanted me to be someone they thought I should be. I still have no tolerance for it, even if my heart is softer.

The look on a person's face when you say, "I've found belly dancing to be really helpful in healing childhood sexual abuse," is priceless. It's true. I've tried a lot of unorthodox activities. When a person's life is on the line, they have permission to do just about anything they see fit in order to reclaim their life. Belly dancing, along with karate, equine-assisted psychotherapy (EAP), and afternoon "play" dates are just some of the out-of-the-box activities that circumvented my intellect to bring me the healing I so desperately needed.

Child sexual abuse inflicts a unique kind of trauma in that it not only annihilates a person's sense of security and trust, but also rapes their very soul. Karate, my first experience in anything even remotely connected to self-defense, was key in teaching me that I could choose to no longer be a victim. Beyond giving me confidence that I could defend myself should someone sneak up behind me in a dark alley, my body taught me, through karate, that another's malevolent intentions can be diverted to my benefit. Similarly, belly dancing was also an effective tool. By using slight, intricate movements limited to specific parts of my body, I learned that there were whole regions of my body that I had ignored to the degree that those areas were numb. Pilates and yoga taught me how to control the chemical surge brought on by adrenaline; through their unique breathing techniques and a devotion to building strength in the core muscles, these practices helped my mind let go of its panic-stricken reactions. I began to experience balance and flexibility in my body, resulting in the belief that I could find inner balance and flexibility in my daily life, too.

Sometimes you have to do something practical and active in the natural realm to see change happen in the mental, emotional and spiritual realm. One hundred percent of the time, the change I saw was a shift in my perspective, how I was thinking about symptoms, and the story I was telling myself about how child sexual abuse was limiting me. Consequently, with PTSD safely eight years behind me, I now believe that choosing to fully engage in the healing process can be the doorway to the most profound personal transformation you'll ever experience. That's what happened for me. I know it will happen for you. I'll show you how.

INTRODUCTION
THE TREE OF LIFE

The self-help method I developed and advocate for in this book finds its foundation in two metaphors. Carl Jung, a student of Freud and himself a famous psychologist, introduces us to the first. He used a metaphor of a growing tree to describe an actively healing client. When a tree, naturally growing taller and fuller while its roots spread out wider and deeper into the ground, encounters a large stone or other obstacle, does it try to shove the stone away or demolish it? No. The roots just continue growing, embracing the obstacle and moving on.

The stone may have postponed or delayed the tree's growth for a while, but no stone, no matter how large, can stop the tree from growing. Stones in the way of tree roots symbolize obstacles to personal growth— things like an internal emotional conflict (such as loving and hating the same person) or an external stressor (such as a traumatic experience). Certain emotional conflicts are never eliminated; they are outgrown. Metaphorically speaking, pushing away or cracking stones encountered by the tree's roots is a deeply-entrenched and ineffective approach to mental illness that is shared not only by society, but also by many mental health practitioners.

Just as stones surrounded by tree roots become part of the tree, people can integrate and grow beyond their trauma, with their roots moving far past the stones in their path into new territory. A person can redirect the powerful energy generated by the trauma to their benefit, using it to pursue goals of their own choosing. Trauma, the core component in developing Post Traumatic Stress Disorder (PTSD), can become a vital part of a person's life, just as the stones support and strengthen the root structure of the tree.

The second metaphor is my own interpretation of the healing journey. It has been said we are sojourners, travelers in this world and when it comes to walking the pathway toward transformational healing, it is one that is personally challenging in every way. Let's imagine together.

The place where you've been living has become a desolate wasteland. Out of desperation, you decide to set out on the pathway others before you have taken—never to return. Beginning this journey is filled with uncertainty and fear. Others have sent back reports of the beauty and richness of reaching a place of healing, cheering you on to freedom; however, instinct tells you the trip will not be easy. You wonder if you'll have what it takes to make it to the other side alive. You've loaded your backpack with supplies to sustain you and keep you on course. You know the general direction in which you will travel and have seen images of your abundant destination, but each step along the path is an unraveling mystery, a sometimes treacherous stumble or breath taking relief. At times, darkness reduces your visibility to only the few feet revealed by the light you shine at your feet. Other times, clear vision reveals hopeful vistas and motivating sights. One thing is certain, the journey requires all of your abilities—physical, mental, emotional and spiritual—in order to make it safely to your destination.

The all-at-once treacherous and breath taking pathway is your own transformational healing journey; a journey you set out on as a last resort to escape the pain of past trauma. You are free to detour from the path as you wish in order to gain personal insights, but decide there is wisdom in continuing along the path's general direction. Just as you would be sure to head out on a hike with a good pair of boots and a map, this book becomes the "boots" that will carry you and the map that will guide you to your destination. The solutions introduced here are supplies and tools you'll use in concert with your brain—the back-pack in which you carry every single meaning you've given to events in your life. Before you know it, you are using not just your brain but all of who you are to travel this amazing path and find yourself whole, complete and restored at the journey's end. You will carry with you always the skills you learn and abilities you've honed on this healing journey. Whereas desperation thrust you upon this initial pathway, before long, you are climbing mountains of your own choosing.

By now, you've been struggling with the debilitating effects of PTSD for awhile. You understand the havoc it can wreak in your professional life, your relationships, and your own peace of mind. There's no need to convince you that getting rid of PTSD for good would be a miracle! A Godsend! A huge relief! So, in this book, you won't find a rehash of depressing symptoms designed to convince you to help yourself. You and I are focused on one thing only: moving ahead toward healing your PTSD.

IS THIS BOOK FOR YOU?

Strengths-based mental health professionals who are Post-Traumatic-Stress-Disorder-savvy are hard to find—not impossible, but for someone in the throes of full-blown PTSD symptoms, it can be extremely difficult. Combine this with the overwhelming number of people being diagnosed, limited professional resources and the challenging financial circumstances of our times, and we have a recipe for an epidemic of biblical proportions.

With demand high and resources low, self-help methods are one way to get started on your healing journey. You're probably looking for self-help alternatives because you:

- Can't afford traditional therapy

- Don't have adequate medical insurance

- Have had a bad experience with an agency, therapist or counselor

- Are having to wait a long time to see a professional

The fact that you're interested in self-help methods is a good sign that you're on your way toward healing. Did you know one hundred percent of survivors with PTSD feel victimized by the original traumatic experience? Heck—that's the nature of PTSD! Because the traumatic incident was out of your control, it feels like someone or something acted upon you. This sensation can keep you paralyzed and is a key element in a PTSD diagnosis. The idea that you are ready to help yourself (even in small ways) is the beginning of a paradigm shift that will grow into a strength that will heal you.

In *PTSD Self Help: Transforming Survival into a Life Worth Living*, I reveal step-by-step details of how I overcame more than half a lifetime of living under the burden of Post Traumatic Stress Disorder (PTSD). We'll take the journey together, starting at the very beginning. First, you'll wrap your mind around the possibility of healing. Then, you'll begin to develop a Healing Plan and a Healing Team. Along with easy activities and lifestyle changes, you'll start feeling better fast! Next, I'll introduce you to ways you can enjoy your new life, never to return to the fear-driven existence you endured while in the grip of PTSD. Finally, you and others reading this book, will join together in a *PTSD Self Help* group on Twitter, Facebook or Instagram, where you can share your experience, ask questions, or encourage one another.

CAUTION!

However, there's one more thing. *PTSD Self Help* comes with a warning label. There are two cautions:

1. Self-help methods must be used in collaboration with a high-quality mental health professional ... eventually.

2. Beware of individuals who claim to have PTSD expertise—do your homework.

The nature of PTSD drives survivors into secrecy and isolation. This is a dangerous place to reside. As much as you might like to ignore PTSD's symptoms in the hope that they will go away, they won't. Although you will gain much-needed relief from implementing lifestyle changes, there comes a time when self-help isn't enough.

Unlike a cold that can be remedied with rest and fluids, PTSD requires the assistance of a very unique professional, someone I call a PTSD-informed, strengths-based mental health professional (MHP). In the chapter *Season of Renewal: Recruiting Your Healing Team*, I'll define this professional's qualifications, teach you how to form a healthy collaboration, and show you how to find a professional in your area. At last, you can know with confidence what to expect! With *PTSD Self Help* in your back pocket, you can design your own plan for overcoming PTSD. Best of all, you can heal at your own pace, beginning whenever you are ready. Transforming survival into a life worth living is as easy as going on a journey—all it takes is commitment, planning and action. Once you're underway, moving smoothly from point A to point B is not how healing from PTSD works; it is not a linear process. However, there are clear seasons you can expect to move in and out of, or occasionally return to, over the course of your journey. Much like the growth of a tree, you'll revisit each of the four seasons many times over the course of your entire PTSD healing journey. No two traumatic incidents are alike, and neither are the survivors who experience them, so the details of each season will be different for every survivor. Generally, if you actively participate in *PTSD Self Help*, you can expect the following:

SEASON OF HOPE: PLAN & PACK

In this first season, you're preparing for a journey. It's a mystery how long you'll be traveling this path, but you can be sure that any journey undertaken with planning and preparation will bring you to your destination quickly and safely. *Season of Hope* will show you what it takes to wrap your mind around walking away from PTSD forever, and introduce you to action steps as you begin preparing for the journey. But wait! Don't wave good-bye to the *Season of Hope* entirely. You may pass this way again to repack with new tools you've discovered along the way, and reorganize your plan to continue moving forward as you gain in confidence and healing.

SEASON OF RENEWAL: RECRUITING YOUR HEALING TEAM

One of the biggest illusions PTSD presents is a feeling of separation—separation from your body, loved ones, helpful professionals and a normal human experience. This sense of separation is heightened if your country is barely functioning with a broken healthcare system, has a medical culture where specialists work independently instead of collaboratively, and where patients have limited access to their own medical records. During this important season, you'll interview and recruit seven key members of your Healing Team, and with their help, coordinate the team's efforts in moving yourself toward feeling better fast. Without realizing it, you'll be actively traveling the path toward healing while creating your Healing Team. Helpful questionnaires, exercises, guidelines and online resources to connect you with qualified professionals will bridge the gap between your past efforts at seeking help and this new, final push toward reclaiming a life worth living. One key task you'll complete is the creation of an Emergency Plan of Action (EPA), a step-by-step instruction guide for what to do during a healing crisis. Once again, don't wave good-bye to the *Season of Renewal*. You may find yourself adding additional members to your team after experiencing the next season, a *Season of Transformation*.

SEASON OF TRANSFORMATION: LET THE JOURNEY BEGIN!

By the time you reach this season, you've done the preparatory work of committing to the healing process, created an Emergency Plan of Action (EPA), developed a Healing Team, and adjusted your schedule to accommodate the difficult work you are now fully engaged in. On the other hand, maybe you've read the material about commitment, recruited professionals for your Healing Team, and have thoughts in mind for moving forward at some later time. Either way, during *Season of Transformation*, you'll really engage the *PTSD Self Help* method and continue to gather information, learn to act on your intuition, and follow through with advice from your Healing Team. Tools such as HomeWork, the InnerAction Journal, the Toy Box and Enlightenment will help you along your way. Since life never stops happening, *Season of Transformation* will become your constant companion; however, you'll notice times when actively engaging in healing activities will slow down to make room for other life events. Don't mistake the occasional subtlety of this season for inaction. Like plants in Autumn and Winter, there's a lot going on under the surface in preparation for Spring, but the growing never stops.

SEASON TO ENJOY A LIFE WORTH LIVING: TRY ON THE NEW YOU!

Toward the end of your PTSD healing journey, physical symptoms and emotional roller-coaster rides are few and far between. However, something new presents a challenge: vulnerability. The heavy burden of PTSD symptoms has lifted, and a new strength emerges through knowing you can face and process the meaning of flashbacks or intrusive memories should they arise. The entire world seems new, beautiful, and even a bit intimidating. No longer driven by old ways of coping, survivors often struggle with re-entering their lives as a whole, feeling individual. This is the point of no return. You have a choice: retreat back into what is comfortable yet painful, or learn how to enjoy the vibrant life you've travelled so far to find. *Season to Enjoy a Life Worth Living* will help you adjust to living as a whole person through suggestions that can help you re-enter life without returning to unhealthy coping habits. Presenting lifestyle recommendations and ways to celebrate what you and your Healing Team have accomplished, this advanced season will introduce you to a new beginning and the life you were intended to live.

Are you ready to reclaim the life that was intended for you? It'll be a strange, occasionally painful, yet wonderful trip. You'll need a few supplies.

Supply List

No one undertakes a journey without packing a few necessary items. Here's a list of items you'll find useful in order to fully engage in *PTSD Self Help:*

- Binder or other folder for print-outs and hand-outs

- Journal and/or sketchbook

- Fancy pen, colored pencils, crayons and/or markers

- Blank paper (include a few extra-big pieces)

- Access to the Internet

- Comfort items, such as a blanket, pillow, stuffed animal and/or cozy pajamas

- Uplifting and/or calming music

- Wellness items, such as a high-quality Omega 3 & 6 supplements; epsom or other bath salts; calming teas, like chamomile or Yogi Tea's

Bedtime; healthy comfort foods

- Candles, scented sprays and/or aromatherapy oils (don't forget the diffuser!)

- A special, private space to designate as your "safe zone"

- A basket, box or other special container to hold all your Toy Box and Emergency Plan of Action items

- Calendar, day planner or smartphone reminder for scheduling appointments

HOW THE *PTSD Self Help*
SYSTEM IS ORGANIZED

Trauma occurs by experience; therefore, experience (what I call experiential learning) can heal trauma. In a nutshell, you'll make preparations for what could be the final healing journey of your life; then, you'll recruit others to help you along the way—people who will also rejoice with you when you reach your goal. Near the end, you'll finally participate in activities that will create healing experiences you can build on in order to re-wire your brain to let go of the past; and finally, you'll be guided into a plan for living the rest of your life free from the grip of PTSD symptoms.

PTSD Self Help is established on a foundation of four seasons that you'll return to throughout the healing process. Each season embraces the following three concepts, three action steps, three guides, three ways to engage, and one story. Let's get a brief overview of the *PTSD Self Help* system:

FOUR SEASONS

Because you've picked up this book, your healing journey has already begun, and there's no stopping it. Your mind and body are ready to heal from PTSD when you finally find yourself in a place of safety in your life. When everything should be going right, that's when symptoms gain momentum, moving you towards resolving what has been left undone by trauma. From this point, with a little planning, your life can begin moving more productively toward healing. Without planning, your life can become a train wreck waiting to happen. That's why the success of *PTSD Self Help* is established upon four healing seasons, each building upon the next. That makes this one of those books you can't skip around in. It's important to begin at the beginning and work the process through until the end, in order to transform, not seek a quick fix (of which there are none, by the way). The seasons are:

Season of Hope: Plan & Pack

Season of Renewal: Recruit Your Healing Team

Season of Transformation: Let the Journey Begin!

Season to Enjoy a Life Worth Living: Try on the New You!

THREE KEY CONCEPTS

Throughout each healing season, we'll reinforce three key concepts. These concepts are foundational *ah-ha!* moments that'll turn your thinking around and make your efforts at overcoming PTSD successful. If you experience challenges, blockages or stalls in the healing process, return to these three key concepts. They'll come to your rescue! They can be summed up in three statements:

1. I am normal.

2. I will do what works.

3. I already have what I need.

CONCEPT #1 - PTSD IS NORMAL

If this is the first time you've heard someone affirm that PTSD is normal, you probably have a sense of relief, quickly followed by the thought, *Wait a minute—there's nothing normal about the way I'm feeling and acting.* But it's true: PTSD is a normal response to an abnormal amount of stress. Period. This first concept will introduce you to the reality of what happens inside your brain while under the influence of PTSD. Then, you'll understand how your brain is working double time to keep you safe, why you haven't been able to control it (until now), and that feeling guilty about your behavior is making it worse. Are you capable of walking on a broken leg as if nothing is wrong? No. Repeat this central thought whenever you feel out of control: *What is happening within me is a normal response to an abnormal amount of stress; I AM NORMAL.*

CONCEPT #2 - NORMAL IS WHAT WORKS

Traumatic events are *not* normal, but what your brain does to protect you *is;* your brain has worked to keep you alive, although at a very high cost. Work smarter, not harder (or longer)! Use the unique way your brain learns to clear your pathway toward healing. Do what works; don't waste your time, money or life waiting for something that doesn't. Don't let anyone else's insecurity keep you from having what is rightfully yours—a life.

You'll meet many people on your healing journey. Be prepared: some people, although they've been with you for a long time, will surprise you with their opinions of how you're handling the healing process, what you're doing to gain relief, and why you're dedicating yourself to do whatever it takes. Hopefully, the people you meet and those closest to you will admire your courage, cheer you on and be amazed by your dedication. When others treat you with anything less than dignity, respect, and compassion (because of PTSD or your commitment to heal from it), they're hiding behind their own ignorance. This is called stigmatization, and it's wrong. Remember this basic concept: *I will do what works.*

CONCEPT #3 - WORK YOUR STRENGTHS

Trauma taps into our instinctive ability to protect ourselves, often depending on coping skills learned in childhood that, unfortunately, aren't very helpful in our adult lives. However, what you were drawn to as a child can hold clues about how to heal as an adult. Combined with skills and abilities you've developed while growing up, childhood methods of self-soothing and processing strong emotions can actually accelerate the healing process—which means, when it comes to healing from PTSD, you can confidently say: *I already have what I need.*

Revisit each of these concepts as you work your way through *PTSD Self Help.* You can relax knowing you'll be reminded of these key concepts throughout the four healing seasons.

THREE KEY ACTION STEPS

It's one thing to wrap your mind around the idea of getting over PTSD; it's quite another to actually do it. The key is in doing something, anything, every single day to move you closer to the freedom you so dearly need. You won't see the entire pathway of your healing journey until the end; for now, the steps right in front of you are clear, and they are all you need. Here are three important first steps that are sure to set you on the healing path:

THE FIRST STEP: A HEALING COMMITMENT

You don't need me to tell you that PTSD is wrecking your life. You wouldn't be reading this if it wasn't causing problems at work and in your relationships. How painful will it need to get before you make the commitment to rid yourself of PTSD forever? Is it possible that you're getting a bigger payoff from limping along with PTSD than you *think* you would without it? If you're tired of living in fear of the next time PTSD will raise its ugly head, tired of looking over your shoulder year after year wondering when the next breakdown will be, tired of losing friends and family because you just can't get over it, then you're in the right place, and you've picked up the right book. *PTSD Self Help* will not only walk you through what it takes to make a commitment to see your healing through until the end—it will give you hope and confidence that you can walk away from PTSD forever.

THE SECOND STEP: TAKING ACTION

PTSD symptoms often leave a person feeling stuck, paralyzed, or unable to advocate for their own best interests. Taking small actions each day will move you closer to being symptom-free. It's not the big actions (like going to the doctor or taking time off from work) that get you the best results; it's the small, everyday actions that matter. They build up your confidence and strength to step out toward those big, important actions. No matter what you choose to do to move you closer toward healing, just be sure to choose something—whether big or small—every single day. *PTSD Self Help* contains practical suggestions for small actions you can take daily.

THE THIRD STEP: CHANGING YOUR MIND - HOW YOU'VE CREATED THE WORLD YOU LIVE IN

Is it possible you are contributing to the pain of PTSD? It's not only possible, but likely. Beliefs are emotionally charged meaning we've attached to information delivered through our senses; these beliefs are the reason for the flood of chemicals our brain produces to get us to take action. If the beliefs you have about healing, trauma, or PTSD are infused with fear or guilt, you'll be getting in your own way and setting up obstacles to your goal. This step will equip you with practical how-to strategies on achieving those all-important paradigm shifts (also known as *ah-ha!* moments) which can ease the pain associated with PTSD symptoms.

THREE PRACTICAL APPLICATION GUIDES

Throughout *PTSD Self Help,* you'll see special formatting (called *guides*) that contain helpful information that supports what you're reading. Packed with relevant insight from industry experts, the latest scientific studies, and leaders in human effectiveness, these guides present the right advice at the right time—much like having a life coach by your side as you read. These guides can be recognized by the following:

Thinking Things Through will provide you with practical how-to tips for making sense of the beliefs you have connected to your symptoms, the originating trauma, and healing methods.

Weighing the Evidence offers brief factoids about healing from PTSD that you can compare to your current state of belief.

Making Sense of . . . debunks myths, deconstructs difficult concepts, and demonstrates how to make *PTSD Self Help* concepts work for you.

THREE LEVELS OF ENGAGEMENT

Throughout *PTSD Self Help*, you'll be challenged to take specific action toward your healing in ways that take into consideration where you're at on the healing pathway, what healing season you're in, and any fatigue you may be experiencing. However, in *Season of Transformation* you get serious about putting your boots to the path, so you'll find three levels of activity to choose from. This way, you can choose from easy to more challenging activities based on your daily energy levels, emotional strength, or financial resources. One day you might be *All In!* while the very next day *Be Gentle!* will be more appropriate. However you choose to engage is up to you—but be sure to choose something.

Be Gentle! suggestions are easy, low or no-cost activities developed as action steps which can be taken when uncertain or wrestling with a healing crisis.

I'm Open! suggestions are moderate activities for the person who is willing and able to take on a little more challenge.

All In! suggestions can (but not always) include intense activities designed for the person dedicated to completing the healing journey as quickly as possible, without limitations on cost, location, or time commitment.

One Story: What You Can Look Forward To—Annmarie's Story

Survivors who have achieved a measure of recovery from PTSD are some of the most gracious, caring, and authentic individuals a person will ever meet. You're becoming one of them! Wise people throughout history have carried heavy burdens of pain at some point in their lives; if you're grappling with the debilitating and emotionally painful effects of PTSD, you have the unique opportunity to awaken to a deeper wisdom and empathy than most ordinary people.

How can you know what it means to give freely of yourself unless you've had parts of your identity taken away? To really experience the joy of choosing to show your emotions, choosing to treat another with compassion, or choosing to sense the beauty of an autumn afternoon requires a long walk through very dark places—and often, it means being repeatedly disappointed by others.

Freedom from PTSD begins by making a decision to heal. The pain of who you are pretending to be finally becomes greater than you can continue to bear. After years of putting on an everything-is-fine face, you become aware of your tremendous burden by recognizing the relentless cycle of relationship departures, physical illness, financial struggle and escapist thoughts (e.g., suicide, isolation). Finally, you can reason *The pain I might face in order to become who I was intended to be couldn't possibly be any worse than the pain I am experiencing now.* Awakened to this new possibility, your healing begins.

Some time after your decision to heal (the timing is different for every survivor), a beautiful and amazing thing will happen: the dark, oppressive belief that says *If you engage your pain, it will never end* suddenly disappears. The mental fatigue and physical pain that's bombarded and overwhelmed your senses of taste, touch, smell, sight and hearing for so long simply lightens. I call it one of PTSD's gifts. One day, healing stops being such hard work. It actually becomes exciting and full of wonder. It's as if the storm has passed, and you can get busy cleaning up the damage and start building something new. Nothing you do and no relationship you have is ever seen the same way again—nor is it taken for granted.

Many survivors describe the awakening PTSD healing brings in this way:

> For the first time in how long? Years? If ever? I'm appreciating things I didn't take much notice of before. Things like the trees and my pets, the way the sun feels on my skin—you know, really simple things. I can read a book just for fun. I can sit in the warmth of an Autumn sun. I don't ever remember enjoying these things, allowing them to nurture and feed my soul. I've woken up. If this hadn't happened, I'd still be asleep, walking around in a living nightmare. For the first time, I feel alive.

Like waking up from a bad dream or recuperating from a long illness, you will still be recovering, fatigued by the stimulus of your environment. You've spent a long time numbing yourself, remember? However, the dread of surviving through each day is replaced by a richness and depth you never dreamed possible. Plus, your stamina is building. Whether you are already on the road toward healing PTSD, or have just recently picked up this book, this is one of the many gifts you have to look forward to.

When I was going through the healing process, I was frustrated by the self-help and recovery books that gave examples from people's lives. Although it can be helpful to see examples from all walks of life, I always wondered, *Do these people have anything in common with me other than the fact that they've been diagnosed with PTSD? Did any of these people make it to the end of the healing process? What other challenges did these people have? Were their challenges anything like mine?*

PTSD had robbed me of a normal life, and with suicide on my mind, what I really wanted to know was whether or not anyone made it through the healing journey alive. The examples given in many recovery books are only Polaroid snapshots, frozen moments in various survivors' lives. The examples didn't answer my question. In fact, that scary voice in my head repeatedly told me that the examples were the *only* shining moments in those survivors' lives, and that they were living miserably, struggling to continue to survive every day. I don't want that for you, so instead, I've chosen to tell you one story—mine.

Instead of snippets taken from the lives of lots of people, I've included beginning-to-end glimpses of one young girl's journey from trauma to freedom throughout this guidebook, so you can see how all of life works together to move us toward peacefulness, our natural state of being.

PRACTICAL SUPPORT

In the age of social networking, we've found it easy to hide behind our computers and smartphones, pretending everything is all right. Using three darlings of online interaction— Facebook, Twitter and Instagram—*PTSD Self Help* has established a community of sojourners walking the path of healing beside you. You can connect with others to share your healing experiences or just watch from the sidelines to encourage yourself that you're not alone. *PTSD Self Help* makes it easy to find encouragement and support 24/7. Just follow the hash tags #PTSD_SelfHelp. On Instagram you'll see people sharing their *PTSD Self Help* journey of healing through pictures. Try Twitter for short snippets of conversation, suggestions and encouragement. Visit the *PTSD Self Help* Facebook page, www.facebook.com/PTSDSelfHelp for inspirational quotes, resource sharing and friendmaking. *PTSD Relief TV* on YouTube (www.youtube.com/user/PTSDSelfHelp) offers video resources like interviews, inspirational shorts and educational how-to's in alignment with *PTSD Self Help* concepts. Ultimately, you can find everything you're looking for associated with *PTSD Self Help* on our website www.PTSDSelfHelp.com

Consider joining or starting a book club based on working through the method contained in *PTSD Self Help*. You'll likely find others on Twitter or Facebook who are implementing *PTSD Self Help* concepts and suggestions. Why not join them and share your wisdom, your *ah-ha!* moments, and your healing journey? Everyone needs companions sometimes.

Are you ready to get started?

SEASON OF HOPE—PART I

PLANNING FOR THE JOURNEY
WRAPPING YOUR MIND AROUND HEALING

Healing PTSD is hard work. Period. No sugar coating here. No quick-fix promises. Without you, it won't happen. Makes sense, doesn't it? After all, if you had a run-of-the-mill illness that needed medical attention, you'd have to participate in the process outlined by your physician for you to become well. You'd have to get yourself to the doctor, tell him or her what's up, listen to their advice, then follow through with applying that advice.

Or you could choose not to do any of that.

What would the result be? You'd still be sick and miserable.

Of course, none of the suggestions in this book add up to much without *you* in the mix. Since PTSD manifests six months to (you fill in the blank) years after the original trauma, there's been plenty of time for you to form habits of thought—ways of thinking you don't even recognize—that could get in the way of healing. If you've experienced secondary wounding or stigmatization, you understand what it's like to have roadblocks preventing you from getting the help you need. Would you wound or stigmatize yourself? Of course not!

At least, not intentionally.

Thinking Things Through: Post Traumatic Stress Disorder

What do you believe? Professionals from a multitude of practices have varying opinions about what constitutes PTSD, but you're living it. Is it something you're trying hard to ignore? Are you tired of trying to outrun it? What *is it*, anyway? Living everyday life blown about by the winds of your thoughts and emotions, your reactions, desires and aversions without any deeper sense of yourself creates a continuous low-level unease, discontent, boredom or nervousness—what author and spiritual teacher Eckhart Tolle refers to as a kind of background static. This is a common state of being for most of Western society. Add to that the effects of a major life challenge, threat, or loss (whether real or imagined), and a habitual resistance to or denial of *what is* results. This resistance to the current reality of what is taking place within you and your environment makes PTSD possible.

Are you ready to walk away from PTSD? Before you take your first steps, set yourself up for success! To give yourself the best shot at healing, make a commitment to yourself. Agree that first, you'll make a plan to heal; second, when you're ready, work your plan for all it's worth! Did you know you can start now by wrapping your mind around what healing means to *you?* There are many opinions out there, but when it comes to your own healing journey, only your opinion counts. What does successfully healing from PTSD look like to you?

- Not having nightmares and being able to sleep

- Remembering/forgetting the trauma

- Getting off medication

- Feeling plugged back into life and relationships

- No more flashbacks

I chose to set my sights on getting rid of any physical symptoms connected to PTSD and being able to process any unknown triggers/ memories without spiraling out of control. I figured if I could have that, then I could live with anything else PTSD chose to leave behind. And guess what? PTSD *did* leave some things behind. Wonderful things.

Weighing The Evidence: The Financial Cost of PTSD

Michele Rosenthal, host of the radio show *Your Life After Trauma,* cites the Sidran Institute's statistics about the economic burden of PTSD— and it's not a pretty picture.

The annual cost to society due to the effects of anxiety disorders is estimated to be significantly over $42.3 billion, often due to misdiagnosis and undertreatment. This includes psychiatric and non-psychiatric medical treatment costs, indirect workplace costs, mortality costs, and prescription drug costs.

More than half of these costs are attributed to repeated use of healthcare services to relieve anxiety-related symptoms that mimic those of other physical conditions.

People with PTSD have among the highest rates of healthcare service use, and present a range of symptoms, the cause of which may be overlooked or undiagnosed as having resulted from past trauma.

Non-psychiatric direct medical costs, such as doctor and hospital visits, amount to twenty-three billion a year; the largest component of the societal costs are due to anxiety disorders, including PTSD.

Oh, and what about veterans and active-duty military? According to Expedition Balance, a non-profit organization staffed by veterans to help other veterans cope with PTSD, the Rand Corporation released a report (2008) specifically about military personnel deployed to Iraq and Afghanistan. It put the economic impact of PTSD (including medical care, productivity and suicides) at four to six billion over two years. They go on to say that these numbers are growing every day. And without early intervention, diagnosis and treatment, the cost to our economy will skyrocket.

As a result of living in flight/freeze mode for more than twenty-five years, my adrenal system was fried. It's been the last thing to recover, not something I'm happy about, but I've learned to adjust. My career as a writer has made that adjustment a joy! Clear and healthy boundaries are now a part of my new life, meaning that I'm not a doormat anymore. Loving, vibrant, positive people surround me; the neg-heads and haters, as my son likes to call them, are gone.

But best of all, I'm not afraid.

No more looking over my shoulder, waiting for the next PTSD trigger to steamroll me into oblivion! I've accomplished the measure of healing I set out to achieve and then some. With that in my back pocket, I have the confidence to do anything. You will too.

How Long Will It Take?

Before PTSD set in, your amazing brain captured every sensory aspect of the traumatic incident. Like a crystalized snowflake, each thing you smelled, saw, heard, touched, perceived, tasted, thought, or felt emotionally at the moment you experienced the trauma was frozen in time. It was your mind's way of encapsulating the horror, containing the confusion and protecting you from a life-threatening event. Over time, your mind invented creative ways to keep you from experiencing anything remotely similar to the original trauma, but not always successfully.

Why? Because the mind was so detailed in crystalizing the event, it can't avoid bumping into any number of sensory elements resembling that original event over your entire lifetime. These are called triggers. When you bump into these triggers, it results in PTSD symptoms. Trust me—making your environment "behave" by forbidding friends and loved ones to trip your triggers doesn't work. Triggers are everywhere! It would be impossible for anyone to avoid potentially setting off the multitude of triggers connected to your traumatic past. Furthermore, if you're actively healing from PTSD, what bothers you one week might not bother you the next. However, asking a friend, family member or spouse to temporarily refrain from certain behavior can be appropriate, given the right circumstances. *PTSD Self Help* on line will show you how to ask and when.

Making Sense of . . . Triggers

Did you know that traumatic memories are stored differently in the brain from other memories? When images of the traumatic event, feelings, sounds, smells or other bodily states associated with the event pop up to the surface of your daily living, you can be confident you've encountered a trigger. Triggers could be described as something that arises in the present that not only reminds you of a past event, but also causes you to feel the feelings associated with that past event. We call the present moment event a trigger because it is the catalyst for a cascade of emotional and sensory memories. That's how traumatic memories are different from other memories—they're linked, chained if you will, to emotional and sensory replay. Also, triggers can even happen with traumatic events about which you have partial or total amnesia.

Healing from PTSD is the gradual thawing of that crystalized snowflake, unlocking the sensory clues inside. Just recognizing those clues for what they are is often enough to dissolve the power they have over your mind and body. For this reason, the length of time it will take for you to reach your personal vision for healing from PTSD is unknown. However, you can be sure that for every day, week, month or year you put off healing and addressing the effects of PTSD, is one more day, week, month or year of running from something you can't quite put your finger on.

Set yourself up for success by keeping these thoughts in mind:

- I am headed toward healing.

- This is not a race: there is no time limit.

- I will do what I can today and leave tomorrow alone.

- I don't have to remember, I just have to listen to what my mind/body is telling me.

- The more attention I give to healing and communicating, the sooner I will be well.

ADDRESSING ANXIETY AND DEPRESSION

By nature, PTSD is an anxiety-driven condition—after all, the word "stress" in the term *post-traumatic stress* is there for a reason. But have you considered just how much you might be contributing to this major element of PTSD? We all have an inner voice that prattles on throughout the day, commenting on what we experience. You might be surprised to discover that much of what that voice tells you can be aggravating PTSD symptoms, such as:

- Flashbacks

- Trigger responses

- Muscle tension

- Panic attacks

- Depression

- Digestive problems

Need convincing? I did. At my lowest point of suffering, I still needed to be sold on the idea that I was contributing to my misery. After having lived for such a very long time with the aftereffects of victimization, I couldn't help but continue to think that my physical, mental and emotional ailments were happening to me as a result of some outside force I couldn't defend myself against. Although it would take years to overcome the victim mentality introduced to me as a child, my first step toward eliminating PTSD from my life was to turn and face myself.

Annmarie's Story

I was in my thirties when I finally realized that the initial trauma that induced my PTSD happened when I was about five years old, at the hands of a pediatrician. Before I had come to that realization, I had always assumed that sexual abuse had entered my life at the age of ten; I had been the victim of a sexual predator, a pedophile who had married my great-aunt. From that tender age forward, I couldn't shake the pervading sense of feeling dirty and broken; later, it was no surprise to me when the first boy I showed interest in overpowered me one afternoon, raping me on the floor of my living room. We were fourteen years old.

Raped again at eighteen by another extended family member, then married to a man who was emotionally, psychologically, and (at times) physically abusive, I was on the fast track to a total meltdown. I felt like some unseen force kept luring me, like a magnet, into the orbit of some very sick individuals, with the false promise of being heard, seen, acknowledged, even loved.

My second marriage, this time to an alcoholic, was no exception. Who could blame me for the victim mentality I had embraced? At every turn, something that seemed outside of my control was acting upon me. I had learned to react to others' intentions, powerless to act on my own behalf. Finally, I had to admit the common denominator in this disastrous lifetime of an equation was me. And so began my journey to reclaim a life worth living, one that was intended for me from the beginning.

Admitting I was making the situation worse was easy, once I paid attention. Next came the guilt I felt for treating myself so poorly. Combined with the barrage of physical symptoms and emotional roller coaster rides, it didn't take long for me to become seriously depressed, sinking into the quicksand of pity for being such a burden on others, having my behavior make the people I loved most miserable, and feeling exhausted enough to begin taking unnecessary risks, like not wearing my seatbelt while driving, or not looking out for traffic as I crossed a busy street.

Since *PTSD Self Help* is about healing from PTSD in a practical, empowering way, the first thing I recommend is getting a grip on your inner dialog. I chose a fifteen-week, at-home program to recover from anxiety; it was very helpful. Right away I began feeling better physically. Learning how to counteract my inner critic gave me the clarity and strength to ask for more help.

Still need convincing?

One of the first exercises I did to see whether or not I was part of the problem instead of the solution was the one shown below:

Hello, Ego. Who Asked You?

Find yourself a small notebook or pad of paper (and a pen!) you can carry with you at all times. Another option is to become familiar with using the notes feature on your smartphone. Choose three days during which you will conduct your experiment. Put on your scientific observer hat and vow not to allow yourself to judge, critique or form an opinion about your results. Simply dedicate those three days to recording the information you witness. To get a feel for how you speak to yourself both at work and at home, choose days that include a Saturday and/or a Sunday.

Thinking Things Through . . . The Ego

There's been a lot of psychobabble about the ego over the centuries. Whatever your beliefs are about whether it exists or not, it's a good idea to "know thy enemy," or at the very least, understand how this active part of your mind could get in your way. Here are some common manifestations (though it is by no means a complete list). Would you listen to your ego if you recognized that this is what it is doing?

- A questioning aspect capable of asking questions but not of perceiving meaningful answers

- A strong sense of belief versus actually knowing

- Giving to get

- Comparing

- An "us and them" mentality, or a sense of separateness, division

- Judgement or labeling

- Busy-ness with nonessentials

- Preoccupation with problems set up to be incapable of solutions

- Harsh thinking about the body, its vulnerabilities, and "unacceptable" impulses

- Fearful thoughts, including guilt, suspicion, callousness, detachment, disbelief, etc.

- Analyzing

- Focusing on error and overlooking truth or selective perception

- Independent of any power except its own

- A sense of fear about the success or failure of God, a higher power, or something bigger than yourself

- A preoccupation with or sense of dread about the concept of time

Never accord the ego power to interfere with the journey. —A Course in Miracles

---

The evening before you start your experiment, place your note taking material next to your bed. In the morning, before you step one foot out of bed, right when you become really aware that you're waking up, *listen.* What is the first thing you say to yourself? Write it down in your scientific evidence log. What is the next thing you say to yourself? Write it down.

Once you get the hang of it, be diligent over the next three days to write down any statements, comments, observations or opinions your inner voice/ego makes. It's okay to just jot down what I call the *Inciting Statement.* An Inciting Statement is the first thing said before a flood of conversation begins bouncing around in your head. What you'll discover is that as soon as you start observing that inner voice, it will quiet down, hiding in the shadows, so to speak. But it won't stay quiet for long! That inner voice is used to running your life and can't resist speaking up. What's important is to capture the initial statement and tone of what is being said. What is said afterward is the inner voice/ego's way of distracting you. Above all else, don't get into an argument with your ego. You'll lose. Remember, you are conducting a scientific experiment, and are operating as an observer only.

After conducting this experiment, I was shocked to hear what I was saying! I would never have said those things out loud, and certainly not to my child. So why was I surprised at how crappy I felt, considering the horrible way I was talking to myself? Here's a sample of what I wrote down the first five minutes I was awake:

- Great. It's gonna be another crappy day. (after noticing it was raining outside)

- You are so fat! (walking past the bathroom mirror)

- Don't bother. Nothing can hide how fat you are. (looking into the closet)

Nice, huh? That first morning was a little shocking, but the results of the experiment had piqued my interest. *What else am I telling myself throughout the day?* I wondered. Even worse was the intent I heard behind the words. To be honest, I didn't need to do the exercise for the entire three days. After day one, I was convinced. I was definitely contributing to the mean, scary thoughts I was having. And guess what? That was one thing I could do something about.

Weighing The Evidence . . . Visual Motor Rehearsal

Denis Waitley, counselor to Apollo astronauts, Fortune 500 executives, Olympic Gold medalists, and Super Bowl champions, developed a program for NASA called *Visual Motor Rehearsal* and was asked to introduce it to the U.S. Olympic teams beginning in the 1980s. Here's how it worked:

"Using this program, Olympic athletes ran their event—but only in their mind. They visualized how they looked and felt when they were actually participating in their event. The athletes were then hooked up to a sophisticated biofeedback machine, and its results told the real story about the value of visualization. The neural transmitters that fired were the same that actually fired the muscles in the same sequence as when they were actually running on the track! This proved that the mind can't tell the difference between whether you're really doing something or whether it's just a visual practice."

Now, think of the damage being done by allowing your inner critic to run rampant. Then, consider that a certain amount of intrusive thoughts and memories, sometimes called flashbacks, are initiated by chemical responses in the brain—certainly outside of your control once they've begun. Learning new ways of coping with triggers and flashbacks can minimize and even eliminate the adverse effects of the biochemical aspect of PTSD. Not to mention, learning new ways to use your inner dialog with an intention toward healing can fast track your healing process. Remember, as Mr. Waitley says, "If you've been there in the mind you'll go there in the body." Is it any wonder the physical symptoms of PTSD are so debilitating?

Anxiety and Depression Programs

If you're struggling to keep your head above the waters of depression, and if every day is a fight to stay connected to the people and things you love, you'll find it helpful to pause in your focus on PTSD and address the coping skills you're using that could be weighing you down with depression. You use what you've got, right? But when what you use doesn't work or makes matters worse, it's time to find new answers. Consider participating in an anxiety and depression recovery program to give yourself new tools to use and some immediate successes to build your confidence before you dive right in to attacking PTSD. Engaging an anxiety and depression program, whether online or in a group setting, will help you learn about:

- Internal and external causes of anxiety

- How to stop panic attacks

- Negative vs. positive dialogue

- Overcoming fears

- The effect of "should-ing"

- How diet affects anxiety

- Tolerance levels

- Becoming more assertive

- Putting an end to "what-if" thinking

- Letting go of guilt

- Obsessive, scary thoughts

Don't know where to find information about anxiety and depression programs in your local area? Not sure what books are worth reading on the subject before you invest ten or twenty dollars on them? Never fear! Google is here! Just key the words "anxiety," "depression," and "programs," (along with your city and state) into the search bar at Google. com. You'll be amazed at how much helpful information comes your way. Take time to read comments and ratings to find out what people are saying about the various resources; then do another search. This time, key in all the same words, but include a word or two, such as *criticism, feedback, positive* or *negative press.* This will turn up individuals' blog posts about the program, as well as consumer complaints to the Better Business Bureau. Plus, you can always visit the *PTSD Self Help* website for links to programs that could help! That way, you can make an informed decision about meeting your needs.

Thinking Things Through . . . Stigmatization

Have you ever been told that seeing a shrink is for crazy people? Hopefully you've never encountered someone so blatantly ignorant and discriminatory. However, is it possible that the effects of such a statement have impacted the way you think about caring for your mental health? Cultural ignorance about the nature of the connection between our mind and body adds unnecessary guilt and burden to the person seeking to overcome PTSD. Maybe you've heard statements that are just as damaging, such as these:

"What's wrong with you?"

"You're just too self-absorbed. Get outside of yourself and think of others for once."

"You don't have anything to be depressed about!"

Don't let the ignorance of others keep you locked away in a prison of guilt, shame or despair. There is a way out! And you have the key. It's as easy as changing your mind about what's right for you today. And guess what? What's right for you today may not be what's right for you tomorrow, and that's okay. You have the right not only to change your mind, but also to do whatever it takes to reclaim a life of wholeness.

COUNTING THE COST

No journey can be undertaken safely without counting the cost of making the trip. If you were taking a solo backpacking trip into the wilderness, you'd give some thought to how long you'd be gone, if you could take time off from work, or how your absence would impact your family. So, what are the costs of walking away from PTSD? And I'm not talking about money.

Annmarie's Story

For better or for worse, in sickness and in health. I had every reason to believe those vows when I took them. What I didn't count on was the power of addiction, the depth of emotional wounding or the ramifications of the Law of Free Will that governs us all. Twice I chose spouses who, when facing the uncertainty of my PTSD diagnosis, abandoned those vows and the safety I had hoped they would bring. The first time, it was blatant. We were sitting in upholstered chairs across the desk from the psychiatrist who had been assigned to me by emergency room staff after my first nervous breakdown at age twenty-five.

"Jim, why are you here? Do you want to work with Annmarie on your marriage and her PTSD issues?"

"Nope."

Just like that. The end.

The second time was different, and just as sad.

"Mike, please. Will you stop drinking? I need you to remember the conversations we have and the promises you make. Besides, I feel unsafe when you're drunk, and I'm exhausted trying to keep myself together for our son. I need your help."

"I'll cut back."

It was then I knew that I couldn't compete with his mistress. I knew I would lose the battle against his alcoholism, but I was determined I would not lose the war for my soul.

To each of my previous husbands, I am grateful. They helped me unearth strengths within myself that I never believed existed, strengths that would have stayed dormant had I chosen men who took those vows seriously. I also learned a valuable lesson: each and every one of us has the power to choose. From a young age, my power had been taken from me, overruled by adults much stronger than I was. I learned by reaping the harvest of others' choices that I, too, had the power to choose. I learned that others' choices had been made without regard to their effect on the lives of people around them. I learned that choices could be made with love in mind - love for myself and love for the paths others have chosen. Mike and I discovered that PTSD and alcoholism weren't listed in the fine print of our marriage contract, leaving it open to renegotiation. Ultimately, he chose to embrace his lifetime of alcoholism. In good conscience, and as a matter of self-preservation, I could not.

During the years in which I was raising my son, my first husband, Jim, his new wife, Stacie, and I found a way to establish a working relationship dedicated entirely to our son's health and welfare. However, even our best efforts at making the transition between our homes for visitation couldn't make up for my child's need to be influenced and loved by his father on a daily basis. I learned there are things that mothers can't teach their sons about being a man. Ultimately, although it came at a high cost, some of that cost having been paid by my son, it was in the failure of marriage that I got my *yes* and my *no* back.

I'll help you out. Start here first: What is your vision of successful healing? Can you see yourself free of debilitating physical symptoms, enjoying holiday gatherings again, or feeling loved and connected to your partner or spouse? Hold that vision in the back of your mind and know with confidence that wherever your healing journey takes you, you're heading in the right direction. Step by step, we'll get to that place of healing together. Now, here comes the price tag.

PTSD deeply affects every aspect of a person's life. What may surprise you is not everyone will be happy about you healing . . . maybe not even you. Since PTSD develops over a period of six months after a traumatic incident, there is plenty time for attachments to develop to things like:

- Special treatment received from loved ones

- Having an excuse for (you fill in the blank)

- Hiding behind a diagnosis

- People who reinforce unhealthy relationships or a victim mentality

And guess what? I'm not just talking about your attachments. You may very well be attached to some of these beliefs and more! Others may hold attachments to your PTSD diagnosis, too. Count the cost of removing these attachments not only in your life, but also in the lives of others. It may look like this:

- Will the mother of a veteran struggling with PTSD still receive the same special attention from her friends at church?

- Will your spouse suddenly be held accountable to participate in family activities now that you don't use PTSD as an excuse for avoiding BBQs?

- Will your friend still hang around if you refuse to buy in to her belief that there's just nothing you can do to change the past, and that you just have to get over it?

- Will you have the courage to end relationships if it means getting well?

Be prepared. Healing cannot be achieved without the help of loved ones, friends and qualified professionals. Because they're human, it's possible that they may unknowingly seek their own best interests and hinder you in achieving your goal. Consider the following:

- If you no longer need special treatment, what does the person helping you do now?

- How does your freedom from excuses make others have to hold themselves accountable?

- When you no longer want to be viewed as a victim, will people in your life who have an attachment to your neediness still be around when you're healed? Will they allow you to be the whole, healed and confident person you've worked so hard to become?

As you consider your vision of successful healing, think about how you want to feel in your relationships both when they're going smoothly and when they aren't. Giving thought to this will help you identify positive, supportive people you can count on. When you walk away from the effects of PTSD, your life will be different, and may contain different people than when you started. This truth is one of the biggest obstacles to healing. Are you ready and willing to do whatever it takes?

THREE KEY CONCEPTS

Now that you have a vision for what it will be like on the other side of PTSD and have counted the potential cost of getting there, let's continue putting down a good root system for that tree we talked about earlier. Because healing is more like a marathon than a sprint, you'll want to continue careful planning by understanding the three concepts that'll serve you well throughout your healing journey.

Concept #1: PTSD is Normal

PTSD is a normal human response to an abnormal amount of stress.

Once, I heard an analogy that brought the truth of that statement home to me. I never forgot it. It went something like this:

> Have you ever cut yourself? With so many knives out there, it's likely you have and more than once. Maybe it was just a close call, leaving behind nothing more than a red mark on your skin. Another time, you may have really done it up good, blood gushing everywhere, stitches. But I'll tell you what. In either of those incidents, had the blade been very sharp and the power behind that blade strong enough, there would be some real damage, possibly even cutting off your finger. How injured you were came about because of the sharpness of the blade and the force behind it, not because

of the toughness of your skin. With enough force, even rhinoceros skin wouldn't protect you or your precious finger, and anyone else in the same circumstance would experience the same thing.

Who you are as a person, the degree of your character, or your level of moral commitment has little to do with how PTSD or its symptoms, no matter how severe, can come to be a part of your life. Instead, the symptoms and their severity come as a result of the intensity and duration of an extremely stressful event. Subjected to enough stress, any human being has the potential for developing full-blown PTSD or its symptoms. Without a doubt, a person's beliefs and values will affect their reaction to and interpretation of the stressful event; however, people do not develop PTSD because of some inborn weakness in their personality, character or faith. Trauma changes people, plain and simple. The way they were created doesn't make them candidates for trauma.

YOU REALLY CAN'T HELP IT: BIOLOGICAL CHANGES ASSOCIATED WITH PTSD

Often biological changes occur during a traumatic event. These changes are part of the way we are designed as humans; they include adrenaline (fight or flight) or noradrenaline (freeze) surges, depression, addictions and/or compulsions acted upon as forms of self-medication. The changes occur in the chemical functioning of your brain, resulting in symptoms you feel in your body through the five senses. Because these biological changes make their way into your body's system via mental pathways, like etchings on glass, it takes some amount of effort to create a new pathway. It is as if your brain were stuck sending these chemical responses down the same old pathways. Consequently, you may have times when, against your will, you feel as if you're still living under the conditions of the original traumatic event. You may know logically that you're safe, but on a biochemical level, your body is screaming, "It's still going on! Can't you feel it?" Sadly, many people—especially people of faith or those striving for some level of perfection—conclude that they're failures for being unable to control their reactions.

Weighing the Evidence . . . Flashbacks

A flashback is a sudden, re-emergence of a traumatic memory as a vivid recollection of sounds, images and other sensations associated with the traumatic incident causing the person having the flashback to feel as if they are reliving the event in the present moment.[1]

This means you may see, smell, taste, hear or feel some aspect of the trauma. You may or may not loose your sense of present reality. Flashbacks are not a sign that you are crazy, but rather that your mind is ready to heal. Some aspect of the traumatic material saved deep within your brain is trying with all its might to reach the surface of your awareness. A flashback can last only a few seconds to several hours. Rest and recovery time is usually required to regain a sense of stability and an awareness of present reality.

Earlier I asked, "Would you be any more able to walk on a broken leg?" Traumatic events happen; unfortunately, most occur at the hands of other human beings, often when innocent bystanders (such as people doing their everyday jobs, or someone in the wrong place at the wrong time or with the wrong person) happen to be in the mix. Given the rise in violence over the past decade, the risk for PTSD to develop is very high. Science has looked into the possibility that the more quickly a person exposed to a traumatic event can get to a mental health professional (preferably a trauma specialist), the more likely it might be that they can help keep PTSD at bay. But just seeing a therapist one time, or even more than a few times, isn't proving to be enough. Just like breaking a leg and rushing to the emergency room where the doctor can set it straight, provide some protection from re-injury (with a cast), and monitor the healing process, a person exposed to a traumatic event requires the same quick intervention to prevent PTSD symptoms from developing. A skilled trauma specialist can help "set thinking straight" by providing other perspectives of the incident and the survivor's reactions, thereby minimizing or eliminating guilty feelings. Over a relatively short period of time, a licensed mental health professional (MHP) can also equip a survivor with healthy coping skills to overcome the

---

1 Gale Encyclopedia of Medicine

immediate discomfort associated with a traumatic experience, consequently "protecting" them from secondary wounding or re-injury. However, I believe there's more to getting well than paying a visit to the emergency room, as in the case of our broken leg.

Making Sense of . . . Mental Health Professionals

Not all therapists or counselors are alike. It's important to partner with someone who has an understanding of how Post Traumatic Stress manifests not only in behavior, but also in the body. Additionally, locating a professional whose philosophy is in alignment with the idea that you have strengths, skills and natural abilities can mean the difference between a rewarding journey toward healing and a train wreck waiting to happen. To learn more about choosing a strengths-based, PTSD-informed mental health professional, see *Season of Renewal: Recruiting Your Healing Team.*

Usually some active form of physical therapy is required to get the atrophied muscles (a consequence of having been in a cast for a long period) moving again. It takes time and practice to rebuild stamina and strength. Likewise, high-quality mental healthcare combined with active, experiential learning can do more for staving off PTSD than choosing to only spend time on the therapist's couch. Staying connected to an MHP ensures that the healing process steadily progresses, especially as the mind lets go of the urgency to react and assimilates new-found safety.

So what happens when a person doesn't get help quickly? It is likely you already know the answer to that question, or you wouldn't be reading this book. PTSD symptoms begin to take hold almost immediately; without proper medical intervention, a diagnosis of full-blown PTSD can be made in as little as six months after a traumatic event. Psychology and science are just now waking up to the urgent need to prevent PTSD and are still debating whether quick mental health intervention is helpful. If you experienced trauma sometime prior to the 1980s, it's likely the psychological advice would have been, "Don't talk about it." Slowly, the concept of talk therapy made its way into the realm of PTSD treatment; now, survivors are sick of talking about it, whether to their MHP, their physicians, their employers, or their support/therapy groups. They are tired of retelling the events of their trauma or simply stating the fact that they're a survivor over and over again. Clearly, the system is broken.

Annmarie's Story

It wasn't until 2003 (thirty-six years after my parents first consulted a psychiatrist on my behalf) that I found the kind of help I needed to wake up from the PTSD nightmare. Being semi-abducted at the age of ten (a story for another book) when I was raped, fondled and photographed, was the red flag that sent my mother to the experts for advice. In 1978, the popular philosophy surrounding the treatment for childhood sexual abuse was "don't talk about it." It was believed that reliving the traumatic event would compound the mental and emotional duress of the victim/survivor. We know now that this couldn't be further from the truth. Thanks to the prevailing method of the time, I remained relatively silent about what happened during those two weeks in a remote cabin deep in the aboriginal woods of Punzi Lake, Canada. As you can imagine, I learned that when bad things happen to you, don't talk about it. So, when I was raped repeatedly over the next thirty-plus years - even in my marriage - it was a burden I kept to myself.

At the beginning of taking control of my healing journey, I urged my then-husband to participate with me in marriage counseling as an attempt to develop a place of support for him. Simultaneously, I worked independently with my own therapist, and we sought to establish a partnership with someone who could help us with our marriage, once I was on the mend. The marriage counselor's response to me on our first visit, after disclosing my abusive background and active pursuit of healing from PTSD, could have been a death blow, had I been in a deeper, more treacherous state of suffering:

"Annmarie, you've got a problem, and it's ruining your marriage. You need to find someone to help you with your disorder, your PTSD problem."

No, shit, I thought. That's why I came to see you.

Weighing The Evidence . . . Healing Childhood Sexual Abuse

The days of asking children to remain silent about abuse they've suffered are thankfully in the past. As a matter of fact, the International Rescue Committee (IRC), in partnership with the U.S. Department of State, the United Nations Children's Fund (UNICEF) and the Bill & Melinda Gates Foundation have dedicated resources toward developing a program model of care (called the Theory of Change) and have set guidelines for implementing the model of care for child survivors of sexual abuse across humanitarian settings.

The Theory of Change proposes that children can be supported in their recovery and healing from sexual abuse with child-specific, compassionate and appropriate care and treatment; it also outlines key elements of care and treatment, but more importantly, the knowledge, skills and attitudes required for health and psychosocial service providers to be able to offer such care. Humanitarian settings often present difficult obstacles to providing adequate care for children. How much more effective could we be in providing the resources and support for children right here at home if we made the implementation of a program model of care, such as the Theory of Change, a nation-wide top priority?

For more information about the Theory of Change and to download a copy of the International Rescue Committee's PDF—*Caring for Child Survivors of Sexual Abuse* —visit the *PTSD Self Help* website at www.PTSDSelfHelp.com.

The nature of PTSD originates in a person's victimization—in other words, having been acted upon, either by circumstances or other people outside of their control. It stands to reason that undoing the damage caused by trauma should include an active process of "doing" specific activities that support a survivor's sense of being in control, especially when it comes to their recovery. That's why I feel just getting yourself to an MHP after a traumatic incident isn't quite enough. The saying "Time heals all wounds" is only partially correct. Healing from a traumatic incident requires an incubation period of sorts, a length of time (different to every survivor) where the brain is permitted to isolate the incident. Then, with periodic monitoring by an MHP, debriefing (when the time is right) combined with cognitive restructuring, and healing activities and skill development, one can begin to move the survivor toward wholeness.

As if witnessing or experiencing a traumatic event weren't difficult enough, Western psychology and medicine are at odds about how to best help survivors. By understanding that our mental health care system is only now beginning to address PTSD, and your body's automatic response to danger is stuck in overdrive, you're hopefully beginning to see that you really can't help the way you're feeling and, to a certain degree, the way you're behaving.

ACCEPTANCE AND SURRENDER TO THE PRESENT MOMENT

There comes a time during the PTSD healing process when, in order to move forward on your healing journey, you'll surrender to the events of the past as they occurred. However, when your emotional pain has woven its way deep into the fabric of your being, you'd rather escape from it. It's this tendency to avoid the fear-pain cycle that perpetuates a state of chronic Post Traumatic Stress. This state of avoidance manifests as extreme exhaustion and eventual immune system fatigue, wearing down the body's ability to protect itself. Think of the various sensory aspects of each traumatic event that's occurred in your life as a beach ball. As you stand in the shallow end of the pool of your life, you try with all your might to hold down below the surface as many of the beach balls as you can. As you can imagine, eventually it becomes futile. The only way to disrupt the fear-pain cycle is to deflate the beach balls. In other words, the only way out is through.

BEING THE OBSERVER

Eckhart Tolle, in his book *The Power of Now*, gives an excellent description of not only how to implement acceptance and surrender to the present moment, but also how to implement the *PTSD Self Help* technique of being the watchful observer assigned with the task of recording flashbacks and/or triggers.[2] Here's my take on what he had to say. Trauma is a deeply distressing emotional shock. Translation? Painful.

---

2 Resource: Tolle, E. (1999). *The Power of NOW: A Guide to Spiritual Enlightenment*. CA: New World Library.

Judgement becomes so clouded, it can seem as if there's no way out of the pain cycle. But that's just it. The pain is a cloud, a fog hiding something else—the way out! The only way out of the fog is to walk right on through it. So, when pain in the form of grief, fear, dread, loneliness, whatever it is, shows up, give all of your attention to it—the feeling. Don't give attention to thoughts of the person, event or circumstance surrounding it. Face the feeling, then with everything you've got, let it in, feel it. Allow it to move through your body. Don't allow it to take up residence in your mind. Feel it! Don't think about it! Don't start weaving a story about it. Later, you can express it if you have to.

Allowing a story to arise about the pain makes you feel sorry for yourself or compels you to recite your story over and over to others. This only creates a victim identity and keeps you stuck in suffering. As you give your complete attention to what you feel and stay away from labeling it, be intensely alert. You're already well versed at this heightened state of awareness (called hypervigilence). It's just been mis-directed, so work with what you know! At first it will seem dark, terrifying, and you'll want to turn away. Stay present. Remind yourself that they're feelings bringing helpful information. Pay attention with your whole being—body, mind and spirit. Full attention brings full awareness. Full awareness brings full acceptance, which is surrender to the reality of the present moment.

The acceptance of suffering, which is to face deep pain by allowing it to exist, is a lesson in a kind of death. When you've died this death, there's nothing that will stop you from taking on the whole world, because you realize there is nothing to be fearful of. It was all clouds and fog.

> And when this perishable puts on the imperishable and this, that was capable of dying puts on freedom from death, then shall be fulfilled the Scripture that says, Death is swallowed up [utterly vanquished forever] in and unto victory.—Isaiah 25:8 (NIV)

Thinking Things Through . . . Fight, Flight or Freeze

At one time or another, most of us have heard about the concept of fight or flight, but have you considered that an equally acceptable response to a dangerous or life-threatening event is something called the freeze response? In the animal kingdom, some animals, such as lions, fight when presented with a threat. Other animals, such as horses, run for their lives, fleeing from imminent danger. Yet other animals, like the opossum, roll up in a ball or flop over on one side, feigning death to trick their potential killer into believing they're already dead. The human mind, however, is created with the ability to draw upon any one of these three responses to a traumatic event. A cascade of the chemicals adrenaline or noradrenaline showers the brain, triggering it to send signals to the rest of the body. In the case of adrenaline, the brain shouts, "RUN FOR YOUR LIFE!" or "FIGHT TO THE DEATH!" However, in the case of noradrenaline, the brain shouts, "QUICK! PLAY DEAD!" What does a noradrenaline surge look like? It can look like this:

- The victim of a crime passes out, faints, falls asleep or blacks out, depending upon the method of attack

- Immediately after an attack, a victim has a hard time staying awake or has an overwhelming need to sleep

- Long after an attack—sometimes for years later—a victim can experience chronic muscle tension (often called "body armor")

Other symptoms of a noradrenaline surge include:

- headaches

- nausea and vomiting

- high blood pressure

- difficulty feeling rested

- profuse sweating

- paleness

- skin that is unusually cool to the touch.

The good news is you can minimize many of the negative biological effects, and at the very least, you can learn to anticipate and prepare for— rather than panic in response to—PTSD-related reactions. Anticipating and preparing for PTSD reactions is what *PTSD Self Help* helps you accomplish.

The symptoms of Post Traumatic Stress Disorder are not "in someone's head" or a play for attention. Rather they are aftereffects of an event or series of events severe enough to profoundly alter a person's thinking, feelings, and physical reactions. —Aphrodite Matsakis, PhD[3]

Most of the aftereffects experienced by a survivor are entirely appropriate responses to a seriously life-threatening event. The emotional and biochemical shifts are what caused the survivor to respond in a manner consistent with taking measures to save one's life. However, those same aftereffects are no longer needed or useful in a relatively safe world. In fact, if you are a survivor, allowing those aftereffects to continue "rescuing" you unnecessarily could be harmful.

For these reasons alone, I encourage you to cut yourself some slack. Don't be so quick to embrace guilty feelings. Some people take on a sense of responsibility for the traumatic event. Others feel an overwhelming sense of guilt because of their reactions in the days, months and years afterward. These feelings will surface. Allow them to have their say, then encourage them to move on. They can be miry bogs that trap you along the pathway of your healing journey.

Annmarie's Story

As an only child, I spent a lot of time playing alone, and I learned to create imaginary worlds to entertain myself. During the early stages of my healing journey, I came to realize that my imagination was what had saved me each time I experienced trauma. At first, I felt guilty that I hadn't done more to protect myself. I didn't run away, fight off my attackers or even cry out for help. Didn't that make me an accessory to the crime? Did my lack of response in some way give permission to my attackers? Once I understood how the mind and body respond to pain and traumatic scenes, I was able to let go of the guilty feelings. Keeping

---

3 Resource: Matsakis, A. (1996). *I Can't Get Over It: A Handbook for Trauma Survivors*. 2nd Ed. CA: New Harbinger Press.

my mind in the present moment and out of the twilight world of imagination, however, proved to be much more difficult.

There came a point in time where I sensed that if I didn't get professional help soon, I was going to lose myself in that twilight world and not make it back. I had started slipping into flashbacks, intrusive memories and the make-believe world I had created as a little kid. I was doing it so often, I was starting to not be able to control it. Worse, I was beginning to prefer "checking out" over the reality of my circumstance.

Once, a friend of mine was pressuring me about my strange behavior, asking questions I couldn't answer about my up and down emotions, hot and cold attitude or on and off commitments. Suddenly, I just floated away. Off in the distance of my mind, I could still hear my friend asking questions, but I wasn't responding. I was off in a strange but comforting place, and I wanted to stay there . . . forever. My friend told me later that I had walked over to a long, floor-to-ceiling window that looked out over the woods, rested my forehead on the glass, began rocking side-to-side, repeating in a whisper, "I can't, I can't, I can't." An hour or so later, like waking up from a nap, I found myself curled up on the kitchen floor in front of that window, with my friend across the room staring at me with genuine fear.

What is PTSD? Do I Have it?

Maybe you haven't been diagnosed, but suspect that you might be struggling with PTSD. Or maybe you were diagnosed with PTSD, but it was a long time ago. Spending a few minutes investigating the possibility with a licensed mental health professional (MHP) is the only way to know for sure. Furthermore, documenting an official diagnosis can be beneficial in obtaining support, should you need it at any time during your healing journey. The *Diagnostic and Statistical Manual of Mental Disorders* is a book that helps mental health professionals make an accurate PTSD diagnosis. Often abbreviated as DSM-IV or DSM-5, the manual receives periodic revisions or updates. In this case, the Roman numeral four indicates the 1994 publication, and the Arabic numeral five, the most current diagnostic revision, published May 2013. You may also see a current revision abbreviated as DSM-IV-TR, which indicates a July 2000 revision of the descriptive text pertaining to some disorders.

The official definition of PTSD found in the DSM-IV identified acute

PTSD as occurring within six months after the traumatic event and delayed-onset PTSD as occurring any time later than six months after the event. The new DSM-5 eliminated the distinctions between acute and delayed phases, and acknowledged the development of PTSD symptoms as early as one month after the trauma; however, clinicians still acknowledge the possibility that delayed symptom onset may not occur sooner than six months after the event. Once the timeline of symptoms has been established, the DSM-5 further requires a person to meet the following seven criteria:

CRITERION A

Exposure to a traumatic event involving actual or threatened death, serious injury, sexual violation (e.g., direct experience, witnessing in person, learning of a violent or accidental death of a close family member or friend, first-hand repeated or extreme exposure to details of a traumatic event—though not through media, unless work-related).

CRITERION B

Re-experiencing the trauma as dreams, flashbacks, intrusive or spontaneous memories.

CRITERION C

Evidence of avoidance behavior (e.g., numbing of emotions, distressing aspects of memories, thoughts, feelings and/or unrest at being in situations that remind you of the trauma).

CRITERION D

Negative thoughts, moods and/or feelings (e.g., a persistent and/or distorted sense of blame, reduced interest in others and the outside world, inability to remember key aspects of the event).

CRITERION E

Physiological hyper-arousal evidenced by insomnia, agitation, irritability or outbursts of rage, as well as aggressive, reckless or self-destructive behavior.

CRITERION F

The symptoms in criteria B, C, and D persist for at least one month.

CRITERION G

Vocational abilities, social abilities, or other important areas of your life have been significantly affected by the above symptoms.

Remember, this information is only a guide. A licensed, PTSD-informed mental health professional is the only one who can determine if you are struggling with PTSD. But don't worry! Coming up in *Season of Renewal: Recruiting Your Healing Team*, I'll walk you through the process of finding the right MHP for you. For now, I only want you to understand these three things:

1. The aftereffects of trauma are a normal part of how your mind and body tries to protect you.

2. These aftereffects are the consequence of chemicals produced by your brain—something you can't control.

3. Eliminating or minimizing the intensity of aftereffects can be achieved once new coping skills are learned—something you *can* control.

CONCEPT #2: NORMAL IS WHAT WORKS

When mental health professionals toss out a diagnosis of PTSD, they often fail to explain to their clients how trauma affects a child's development or an adult's ability to cope. Whether the original traumatic experience happened when you were young or old, you can expect to have a season during which you'll return to being the person you were just before the trauma occurred. In other words, you'll start over (developmentally and emotionally) where you left off (at the time of the trauma).

Annmarie's Story

Strange thoughts and emotions bombarded my mind at the most inappropriate times - while coaching a client, making love, while sitting in church. They were strange in the sense that they were the thoughts and feelings of a ten-year-old. Finding me shrouded with a blanket over my head, sitting in a corner or inside the bedroom closet, was a common occurrence. It wasn't possible for me to just lay down and go to sleep at night anymore, and my love of books was crushed by a sudden inability to focus long enough to read. Oh sure, I could still read, but it sounded like blah blah blah in my head. I couldn't understand what I was reading, much less apply it to my circumstance. This made the reading material prescribed by my therapist impossible to digest. My Healing Partner was dedicated to helping me find a solution. We paid a visit to the local library where I checked out beloved books from my childhood; Dragon Song by Anne McCafery, and How the Camel Got His Hump by Rudyard Kipling were two of my favorites.

The evening routine went like this: After dinner, I watched either light-hearted television or had a candlelight soak in the bathtub with either salts or cider vinegar. Then I went off to bed for either a foot or full-body massage; then I'd take supplements, which included supportive herbs for my adrenal system. Next was a long listen to one of the children's books which my Healing Partner would read to me. At just that right moment, when sleep seemed impossible to resist any longer, out went the lights, and on went the headphones for a thirty-minute relaxation routine. At some point, my Healing Partner would reach over and rub my ear. That's all it took until my usual three am waking time.

It was very unsettling to be a ten-year-old girl trapped inside a thirty-something body while trying to function in an adult world. Until I began studying the debilitating dynamics of PTSD and came to understand its tendency to bring a person back to the developmental state they were in at the time of the trauma, I thought I was losing my mind. I feared being institutionalized. But I was compelled to do whatever was necessary to bring relief to my overactive mind and throbbing senses.

During this season of re-developing, I was married and had a teenaged son. At first, some of the things I did to soothe myself, I did in secret. I felt silly and ashamed; worse, I didn't trust my family to understand. After awhile, keeping the secret felt as bad as the symptoms I was trying to overcome. Slowly, with the help of my Healing Partner, I allowed my family in on what I needed to do to feel safe and comforted. I stopped caring what other people thought about how I was helping myself. This was a battle for my very existence, my life, my soul. Looking back, I wish someone would have told me that it was okay, that sometimes in order to move forward, you have to make what seems like a few steps backward.

For people who've experienced their first trauma as an adult, this isn't much of a revelation. However, you can be sure many subtle coping mechanisms used prior to the traumatic incident could become greatly exaggerated. You might even acquire some new, rather interesting ones.

For people whose first traumatic incident occurred during childhood or even infancy, you may be surprised to discover yourself wanting to revert to self-soothing and comforting habits you had as a child. This "re-developing" in adulthood can be especially confusing, first to the survivor, then to loved ones.

Notice I'm talking about first traumatic incidents. Often, a later trauma can unearth unresolved issues you haven't thought about in years. For this reason, healing from PTSD is an opportunity to deal with *all* the baggage you might be carrying around. Consequently, choosing to undertake PTSD healing becomes a sort of "all or nothing" decision. So, how about an example or two?

Let's say you're a woman who was molested as a young girl (meaning that someone of influence engaged you in at least one age-inappropriate sexual interaction). You decided to enlist in the military, and, as a result of your service, experienced a number of horrible things. Back home, you are actively participating in traditional therapy along with extra self-help healing activities. You begin to feel drawn toward engaging in things you used to do as a child to feel safe, like cuddling a teddy bear or rocking yourself to sleep.

Or how about a metaphor, such as a frozen lake? All of your life's traumatic experiences are locked in the ice, and have been for a long time. You don't mind sitting where you are on your frozen lake. Life is predictable. One day, something or someone cracks the ice; the crack begins to fracture the ice, and the fissure is racing its way toward you. You realize that safety doesn't lie in maintaining your predictable life— after all, the possibility of falling through the ice presented itself far away from the original fracture point. You begin to scramble, doing whatever it takes to save yourself before the fracture grows long enough to plunge you below the surface.

These examples describe the events leading up to a "regression" toward things that help your mind feel safe enough to undertake the healing process. The fact that PTSD symptoms are even surfacing at all is a clear indicator that your mind is ready and able to take on the challenge. So, there is no need for fear; simply lean on your Healing Team, which you'll learn about in the chapter *Season of Renewal*, and do whatever it takes to press forward.

Thinking Things Through . . . Are You Closed or Open?

Do you think PTSD is a life sentence? How do you feel about being called disordered? Have you locked yourself into thinking help looks a certain way or comes wrapped in a certain package? Albert Einstein, the genius Nobel Peace Prize winner and the greatest scientist of the twentieth century, had something to say about our thought process when it comes to understanding problems in our life:

"Problems cannot be solved at the same level of awareness that created them."

This means that in order to solve problems, we need to change our perspective. How can this be done if we have already made up our mind about the answers to these questions and more? Being willing to consider that it's possible there's more information out there, something yet to discover, or that you may not have all the answers is the beginning of unlocking the verbal prison you've created for yourself. Try opening up your perspective with thoughts like:

I'm right where I need to be at the right time.

What will life show me about myself today?

I've made it this far; I'll just keep going, one day at a time.

Regardless of when the trauma happened, the method (and timing) survivors choose for their healing is their decision alone. Don't let anyone, including professionals or family, embarrass or shame you for doing things that help you feel better (Of course, be wise in this area. Abusing drugs, alcohol, money, your body or someone close to you is never a healthy choice).When it comes to a life or death decision about healing from PTSD,"normal" is what works.

Here are some examples of things adults have used during a temporary season of regression to help them cope with flashbacks, recover from healing activities, or just to take a break from PTSD:

- Cuddling a teddy bear

- Hiding under a blanket

- Taking a nap

- Laying in the sunshine

- Having a children's book read to you

- Sucking a thumb/pacifier

- Drinking from a baby bottle

- Being held or caressed

- Taking a bubble bath

- Sleeping with clothes on

Weighing the Evidence . . . Secondary Wounding

Sometimes, doing "whatever it takes" to heal can expose survivors to secondary wounding. In short, secondary wounding is when someone the survivor has turned to for assistance or revealed their PTSD struggle to responds negatively. Some measure of mental preparation for the possibility of moments like secondary wounding will go a long way toward a successful PTSD recovery, since people are the most important part of healing from PTSD; however, they can also do more harm than good.The devastating effects of ignorance and insensitivity can take many forms, resulting in secondary wounding experiences. Many PTSD survivors report that secondary wounding is often more painful and devastating than the original traumatic event. Survivors with PTSD already struggle on a daily basis with numerous challenges to their self-esteem. Secondary wounding[4] intensifies these challenges, and impacts their resulting emotional, physical and psychological symptoms.

Secondary wounding can be committed by anyone to whom the survivor turns for assistance or reveals their PTSD struggle to, such as:

- People close to the survivor (friends, family, spouse, or children)

- Institutions (religious, legal, medical, or assistance-related)

- Caregivers (mental health professionals, doctors, parents, healing partner or teachers)

Secondary wounding occurs by responding negatively to the survivor's account of the trauma, the magnitude of its aftereffects, the meaning to the survivor, or its impact on the survivor's life in one of the following ways:

- Disbelief – doubting or distrusting

- Denial – refusing to believe

- Discounting – dismissing or minimizing through comparisons or outright statements

- Blaming the survivor – on some level, suspecting the survivor deserved it

- Stigmatization – judging the survivor negatively for normal reactions to the trauma, efforts to heal or long-term symptoms

- Denial of assistance – withholding necessary, expected services based on a personal or procedural judgment of the survivor's need or lack of entitlement

Survivors respond to secondary wounding by going through an

---

4 Resource: Matsakis, A. (1996). *I Can't Get Over It: A Handbook for Trauma Survivors.* 2nd Ed. CA:New Harbinger Press.

overwhelming increase in the following (just to name a few):

- Lowered self-esteem

- Hopelessness

- Helplessness

- Rage

- Depression

- Emotional numbing to the point of separating from their body (depersonalization)

- Deep disappointment

- Disgust with themselves

- A desire to retaliate

Don't worry! Temporarily nurturing yourself in ways that were comforting to you as a child is only a season. In fact, you might choose to modify a few and use them long after PTSD has disappeared from your life! Remember, when it comes to healing from PTSD, *normal is what works.*

WARNING! DO NOT HEAL!

Remember when we said that no journey can be undertaken safely without counting the cost of making the trip? Part of counting the cost is figuring out potential obstacles so you can avoid them. We said that if you were taking a solo backpacking trip into the wilderness, you would give some thought to how long you'd be gone, if you could take time off from work, and how your absence would impact your family. One thing you wouldn't want to forget? Making sure your mode of transportation is in tip-top shape—that means you! No annoying leg cramps! You'd also want to be sure you knew what to do to avoid emergencies and obstacles. No washed out bridges! So, let's finish up counting the cost of healing and show you danger signs to watch out for.

Occasionally, the healing journey itself can trigger a healing crisis. By immersing yourself in an environment totally focused on PTSD education and healing, you may experience occasional increases in symptoms, trigger flashbacks and/or just push too hard, too fast. A healing crisis means there are very specific instances when participating in healing activities should be avoided.

Planning for a healing crisis is the best way to feel in control, if your symptoms flare up. Here are a few warning signs that indicate that it's time to put the brakes on any healing activities, temporarily:

- Feeling there's no hope

- Racing heart

- Unable to focus; spaced out

- Intrusive thoughts, visions or memories

Mild symptoms are expected over the course of the PTSD healing journey; however, extreme symptoms require the assistance of a mental health professional. Seek immediate professional help if you experience any of the following:

- Hyperventilation, uncontrollable shaking, or irregular heartbeat

- Self-mutilation or the desire to self-mutilate

- Emotional pain, anxiety or anger so intense you fear you are going to die

- Self-destructive behavior (e.g., alcohol or drug abuse, self-induced vomiting, over-working)

- Suicidal or homicidal thoughts

Severe shaking, losing touch with reality, or suicidal thoughts sometimes occur just before major breakthroughs in the healing process. These symptoms can be frightening, leaving you feeling exhausted for days. Do not navigate them alone.

Annmarie's Story

There were times during my healing journey when I would literally forget to breathe. Thank God I had a friend who would get on the phone with me to coach me, just like a midwife! It's only now, years later, that I understand why I'd hold my breath. It makes sense, really: Trapped in that remote cabin with a sexual predator stalking my every move, I knew I would never be able to escape and survive the Canadian wilderness. I also knew I would never have the strength to overpower an adult man triple my size. Even if I did, where would I run to? How would I get home? The only option left was to play dead. In my child-like brain, I hoped that if he found me asleep, he would leave me alone. I would lie very still, listening for his every move. My breath roared in my ears, so I stifled it in order to hear him coming.

Thinking Things Through . . . Symptoms

It can be difficult to sort out what symptoms belong to PTSD reactions and what symptoms are completely unrelated to the trauma. To make matters worse, if your mind runs away with you, every symptom can feel like a terminal illness. Anxiety associated with PTSD feels a lot like a heart attack. Sometimes, people even experience seizures or strokes because of unresolved stress. When the mind can't find a healthy pathway for resolving trauma, stress, or strong emotions, it will use the body as an "early warning device" to get your attention that something needs to be taken care of.

Take the time to get a physical and routine blood work analysis from your regular physician. Then, make a list of your most annoying symptoms, and one by one, address each one with an expert. Be sure to share your suspicions about PTSD being involved and ask them to rule out other possibilities. If you discover you're wrestling with something unrelated to PTSD, great! You can easily do whatever your doctor says is necessary to correct the problem. If your doctor is having trouble finding a source for your discomfort, you might be dealing with a legitimate PTSD symptom. When you're ready to begin the journey toward healing your mind, you'll find the relief you're looking for.

It is imperative to monitor your reactions to the healing process. This requires re-directing your tendency for hyper-vigilance away from your external environment and toward your body's internal environment, such as its physical responses and emotional climate. Later, you'll learn how to use an InnerAction Journal as a place to record what is going on with your body. Recording your internal environment is important, because these reactions need to be monitored in partnership with a qualified mental health professional.

Do not continue reading books, researching information on the Internet, or participating in any other healing activity if you are experiencing any of the following in this checklist[5]. Seek immediate professional help:

- Hyperventilation, uncontrollable shaking, or irregular heartbeat

- Feelings that you are losing touch with reality, even temporarily (e.g., hallucinations or extreme flashbacks of the event)

- Feeling disoriented, "spaced out," unreal, or as if you might be losing control

- Extreme nausea, diarrhea, hemorrhaging, or other physical problems, including intense, new, or unexplainable pains or an increase in symptoms of a preexisting medical problem (e.g., blood sugar problems if you are diabetic)

- Self-mutilation or the desire to self-mutilate

- Self-destructive behavior such as alcohol or drug abuse, self-induced vomiting, over working or overspending

- Suicidal or homicidal thoughts

- Memory problems

- Emotional pain, anxiety or anger so intense that you fear you are going to die

---

5 Resource: Matsakis, A. (1996). *I Can't Get Over It: A Handbook for Trauma Survivors.* 2nd Ed. CA: New Harbinger Press.

Reading recovery books, hearing the stories of other survivors or otherwise participating in the healing process can cause strong emotional and physical reactions. This does not mean that you are unable to heal, unwilling to heal or that you are a "failure."

Mild feelings of anxiety, fear or despair are entirely expected throughout the healing process, but extreme reactions, such as the ones listed above, require professional attention as soon as possible. If you are unable to contact a mental health professional and are truly frightened, go to the emergency room of a local hospital. Meanwhile, do the following:

- Stop reading, researching, or doing whatever healing work you are engaged in

- Focus on something else

- Touch a physical object

- Talk to someone right away

- Avoid isolating yourself

- Do not take alcohol, drugs or other mood-altering substances

- Express your anger or emotion in a safe way (e.g., talk to a friend, punch a pillow, tear up a telephone directory)

- Do something pleasurable and relaxing (e.g., take a hot bath, go for a long walk, listen to favorite music, cuddle with your pet)

Obviously, these things are easier said than done when you are in the throes of a healing crisis. It would be wise to develop an emergency plan during the times when you are feeling your best. In the section titled *Three Action Steps*, you'll make an Emergency Plan of Action. It's an emergency plan that includes contact information for your Healing Partner (something you'll learn about in the chapter *Season of Renewal*) and mental health professional, as well as direct, step-by-step instructions for what to do to calm your symptoms down. Creating an EPA in advance of a healing crisis will go a long way toward making your healing journey less strenuous and painful.

EMBRACING A LIFESTYLE CHANGE

PTSD is classified as an anxiety disorder (though I don't like the term "disorder"), which means that much of your everyday life is ramping up your adrenaline to the extent that you're having panic attacks, difficulty sleeping, or sensory overload (called hypervigilance or hyperarousal). Your mental, emotional, and physical system is taxed! By adding additional demands on an already overtaxed system, you run the risk of having that system break down, and we don't want that!

Weighing the Evidence . . . Hypervigilance

Whether you call it hyperarousal, hyperalertness, or hypervigilance, this symptom is unique to the PTSD diagnosis and is a consequence of chemicals produced in the brain. When a person thinks scary thoughts (for a scenario real or imagined), trauma-generated emotions result. Fear, anxiety, anger, and overwhelming grief are all emotions that charge up the body in preparation to fight, flee, or freeze. This charge electrifies the body, placing it in a state of overdrive; the heart rate and blood pressure skyrockets, muscles become rock solid, blood sugar goes through the roof, pupils dilate (making the eyes sensitive to light), and hearing becomes uncomfortably acute. Since traumatic memories are often intrusive (meaning that they pop into the mind unexpectedly and frequently), is it any wonder that PTSD survivors have trouble sleeping?

However, you must integrate new activities and demands into your everyday schedule in order to heal. Like recovering from a broken leg, you wouldn't just ignore the fact that it's broken and go on with your daily routine. In fact, much like wrestling with PTSD symptoms, it would be impossible! Instead, you would find a way to work in the time necessary for doctors appointments, physical therapy, and rest, as well as get a few friends to help you out with things you can't manage until you recover.

The best way to balance working in healing activities without overloading your already delicate system is to embrace a lifestyle shift—at least temporarily. Your lifestyle needs to shift toward a holistic, supportive routine in order to expedite healing. It's not just your brain or your emotions or your body crying out for healing—it's all of them! We are complex, multi-level, multi-faceted human beings with all of our systems interconnected. When one part of the system is struggling, the rest of the system is impacted as well, so it makes sense to support all of the systems at the same time. That way, you won't experience the frustration of "chasing" your symptoms as they morph from one unexplained symptom to the next, never feeling as if you're getting anywhere.

Annmarie's Story

Walking into a naturopathic physician's office was my last resort. For three years, I had a horrible skin condition that migrated to various parts of my body, and I was scared to death it would show up on my face next. First, my left breast acquired a red spot that was hot to the touch. That red "spot" grew to the size of a dessert plate, welted up more than half an inch, turned purple, cracked, bled and itched like crazy! Next, it showed up on my shins, and I started to develop unexplained staph infections on my toes, wounds that refused to heal.

While dealing with the external symptoms, I had my fair share of internal issues going on as well. I had been diagnosed with Crohn's Disease, even after a clear pathology of my intestinal tract, and was taking a regimen of fifteen pills a day. Although I was only in my early thirties, I stopped having my menstrual period, and my gynecologist recommended a hysterectomy, since my uterus was falling out of my vagina anyway. I stopped trying to find solutions for my chronic migraine headaches, jaw pain, and distorted vision and hearing. No one could seem to help me. I was tired of feeling awful and tired of being poked, prodded, and tested.

A friend at church suggested I see her naturopath. The thought of going over the dossier of crap I had on my body with yet one more physician, and offering another futile explanation that I was also struggling with Post Traumatic Stress was enough to send me over the edge. But I did it. Thankfully, the doctor was kind and believed in educating me about my body. He was thorough, asked questions, and had me fill out forms that described my environment at home and work, who else I lived with, the kind of diet I had, and so much more (four hours worth!). He really saved my physical life and helped change my unhealthy ways of thinking about my body and what it needed. To my relief, I discovered I had a food allergy, which was the cause of a large majority of my most uncomfortable symptoms. Through eliminating allergens and supporting my mental/emotional system with high-quality supplements, I found immediate relief. After taking care of everything I was doing to get in my own way, hindering the process of healing, I was left with true, honest-to-goodness PTSD symptoms. Finally, I had flushed out the enemy and was ready to declare war!

Choosing to live a well-balanced life full of healthy organic foods, fun physical exercise and supportive relationships is something we could all benefit from. The only difference between you and someone else who needs to change toward a more holistic lifestyle is that healing completely from PTSD requires it. For you, it might be a matter of life or death. Choose life! You might be surprised at how much you enjoy your new lifestyle, never to return to the poor eating, non-exercising and codependent habits of the past. How could that not be a good thing?

A healthy lifestyle shift might look something like this:

- Weaning off of added sugar, caffeine and alcohol

- Making room for ten minutes a day to move your body

- Joining a yoga, tai chi or karate class once in a while

- Investing time into learning how to quiet your thoughts and breathing

- Choosing one day that is PTSD free—no discussion, reading or practicing healing techniques

CONCEPT #3: WORK YOUR STRENGTHS

The horror of what happened is over. You have endured the trauma. Although you may still bear the pain, you're a survivor simply because you continue living. Found within the very being of survivors is strength, dignity, resilience, and entitlement of respect. On the other hand, victims are seen as passive, helpless, and deserving of pity. You are no longer a victim. You are a survivor.

You can unlock the secret, take your power back, shed the guilt and self-blame of the experience, and learn, finally, to be angry at what was done to you—instead of at yourself.

—Sue Blume, author of *Secret Survivors*.

Society and traditional Western therapy sees each after-effect as a problem to be eradicated or, at the very least, politely managed. But that's not who you are; you are a survivor. Together, we must help ourselves and society to view each after-effect as a survival tactic, not a conscious decision to be sick or difficult to live with. Deep within every survivor is a mysterious power to go on. Often that strength goes relatively unnoticed. At other times, it is attributed to having had a good support system, the responsibility of children to take care of, or the benefit of any number of religious faiths. But make no mistake! That strength comes from within *you*, and no matter what label you put on it, that strength is only called forth by your own conscious decision. So give yourself the respect, dignity and credit you deserve. You're still here. You're a survivor.

Annmarie's Story

My therapist said something to me on the very first day I met her. She said, "Annmarie, I want to know what kept you from going out in those woods and killing yourself when you were ten. Together, we'll discover the strength within you that kept you from doing that, and we'll use that same strength to get you out of this mess."

More than a little shocked by the validation I felt about having suicidal thoughts, I held on to the word that resonated deeper with me: strength. That was language I could understand. I had owned a successful life coaching business for several years and had helped hundreds of people discover the strengths lying dormant within them. This was the light at the end of the tunnel, a small, flickering ray of hope I could latch on to. I could do this.

If you will be still, you will notice something far below any of the symptoms you are feeling. It may be fleeting at times and off in the distance, but it is always there, burning like a small flame. Your biggest revelation of healing comes when you stop calling that strength something else, and take ownership of it. That strength was created within you for a purpose. It is a part of who you are, and you will use it to heal.

On a practical note: along the pathway of your life, you've likely left clues that point to habits, abilities or creative talents that could be a key to unlocking any unconscious resistance to healing. Did you used to play an instrument? Dig it out again! Were you once praised for your ability to draw, paint or make pottery? Clean off those tools in the back of your closet! Was there a time when you would bust out in song or jump up and dance? Do it again! The important part of discovering your strengths is to be intentional. Set aside small amounts of time to explore these "clues," and keep trying until you find a few that help to shift your thinking or emotions.

Welcome to being a survivor! Healing and wholeness are possible for those who believe in the power and strength they've drawn upon to survive. Call it what you'd like, but know it is always there to help you reclaim yourself.

> When she faces her past and reclaims herself, she will
> not just have survived; she will have triumphed.
>
> — E. Sue Blume

THREE KEY ACTION STEPS

THE FIRST STEP: A HEALING COMMITMENT

WHAT IS A SUCCESS STORY?

People don't usually heal willingly. Change or healing only occurs when the pain of who we are becomes greater than the pain of becoming who we need to be. What it means to successfully overcome PTSD is different for every survivor. Want to know what you or your loved one can expect to achieve?

Trauma experts (such as Aphrodite Matsakis, PhD) suggest that successful healing from PTSD is neither a mental state of positive thinking and positive behavior, nor a reduction or temporary elimination of symptoms. Rather, progress toward healing is measured by the amount of growth toward these six goals:

- Do you panic less at your PTSD symptoms? Are you able to recognize a PTSD symptom more quickly than in the past?

- Are you able to comfort or soothe yourself in non-destructive ways when you are suffering from a PTSD symptom?

- Are you increasingly able to cope with or manage your PTSD symptoms and the strong emotions that accompany remembering or being triggered without harming yourself or others?

- Are you growing in self-respect? Are you increasingly willing to take care of yourself physically and emotionally?

- Are your relationships non-destructive? Are you increasingly able to speak up in relationships or otherwise negotiate in relationships with friends, co-workers, and intimates?

- Are you increasingly able to derive some meaning from the trauma, or your life?

"The decision to heal is a powerful, life-affirming choice," remark Ellen Bass and Laura Davis, authors of *The Courage to Heal*. To experience healing moments from a nurturing family, caring friends or a satisfying career is very different from making a decision to heal. Bass and Davis go on to say, "Deciding to heal, making your own growth and recovery a priority, sets in motion a healing force that will bring to your life a richness and depth you never dreamed possible."

Annmarie's Story

Going down for the second time at thirty-four years old convinced me I would live with the burden of PTSD for the rest of my life. Nervous breakdowns are harder to take as you get older. The desire to control everything in your life is remarkably strong, and PTSD rips control away from you. It's not a pleasant feeling, succumbing to the idea that you probably have a mental illness that will slowly drag you off into the darkness of your mind, never to return. I wept at the thought of my loved ones visiting the shell of my body sitting listlessly in a mental ward somewhere; I truly believed that's where I was headed.

When I started therapy, I hadn't yet begun implementing other recovery activities, so it was the pure trust in a mental health professional's opinion that I wasn't crazy yet that motivated me. I didn't believe in healing. My thought at the time was that I'd learn how to live with my disorder so I could be a productive person. That idea in itself was depressing. Later, I changed my mind. As I involved more professionals to help, and engaged in off-the-couch activities that tested my new awareness and coping skills, I started hoping for an elimination of my physical symptoms. Soon, I didn't have any more physical symptoms. I had to set my sights on something else. Could I retrain my brain to think differently about the past? That's all I had left to do. I decided to give it everything I had.

You or someone you know is struggling with PTSD right now, when they could be experiencing:

- Reduced frequency of symptoms

- Reduced fear of the symptoms

- Reduced fear of insanity

- Redirecting anger and grief in positive directions

- Change from being a victim to being a survivor

- Change from rigidity to flexibility and spontaneity

- Increased appreciation of life

- A sense of humor

- A profound empathy for those who suffer

Decide today what healing looks like for you.

Making Sense of . . . Successful Healing

If you had no monetary limitations and every resource was available, what measure of healing would be a relief for you? Answer this, and you're one step away from the most remarkable journey of your life—something no one else can do for you. Healing PTSD is a gift that you give to yourself.

Have the answer?

Write down what healing looks like in your own life. Then, make a commitment to yourself right now.

Promise yourself that you'll not get in your own way, that you won't be the abuser, the wounder, the stigmatizer to yourself. Agree that you'll make a plan to heal and that you'll engage the plan when the time is right. For now, your promise is between you and me. I'll do my best to give you things to work on, if you'll do your part. Deal?

THE SECOND STEP: TAKING ACTION

PTSD symptoms often leave a person feeling stuck, paralyzed, or unable to advocate for their best interests, but taking small actions each day will move you closer to being free from them. Most importantly, begin your PTSD healing journey only when you feel ready for it, and continue along your path once you've started, but only as you feel able to do so. A skill you'll need to embrace is taking each day one single moment at a time. Today, you might feel like taking on a big challenge, such as confronting your conscious memories surrounding the trauma. Tomorrow, you may not feel like getting out of bed. If you suddenly feel out of sorts after a peaceful morning of clarity, be willing to cancel an appointment or two (unless it's your therapist), knock off early from work, or take a thirty-minute nap. Adjust your actions to meet the needs of your mind, emotions and body on a moment-by-moment basis.

Weighing the Evidence . . . Knowledge Is Power

Research. The very word brings to mind long hours writing a paper for school or scientists in lab coats. However, research is an important tool for advocacy. An advocate is someone who publicly supports a particular cause. In advocacy, research means learning all you can about a problem, so you can see all the possibilities for a solution. *PTSD Self Help* is teaching you how to advocate for yourself, or in other words, to publicly support your own healing. But what happens when you've read all the PTSD material, studied all the PTSD books, taken all the assessments and still don't know what to expect or how to move toward healing?

This is where experience plays a role. Sometimes, you can know a thing with your head, but not see the evidence of what you know in your life. There's no truth like a self-learned truth. Take what you've learned by gleaning information, then give it some legs and try walking it out in your life. Don't be afraid to see if what you learned in the books or on the therapist's couch is true for you. Remember, trauma came into your life by virtue of an experience; therefore, experience is what will undo it. If you're never leaving the couch, the bed, or what you feel comfortable doing, how will you ever have a new experience?

THE THIRD STEP: CHANGING YOUR MIND

Beliefs. What are they? When you think about it, beliefs are nothing more than stories we tell ourselves about the world around us. Beliefs are emotionally charged meaning we've attached to whatever we take in through our senses; beliefs are the reason for the flood of chemicals our brain produces to get us to take action. Beliefs not only create the life you're living—they can also keep you from healing. Hyrum Smith, creator of the Franklin day planner, explains this through the metaphor of the "Belief Window," as described in his book, *The 10 Natural Laws of Successful Time and Life Management.* Here's what he has to say:

We all have a belief window. You can't see your belief window because it's invisible, but we all have one. It is figuratively attached to your head and hangs in front of your face. Every time you move, that window goes with you. You look at the world through it, and what you see is filtered back to you through it. The tricky thing about a belief window is that you have placed perceptions on it which you believe are absolutely true, whether they reflect reality or not. Because you believe them, you unquestioningly act upon them. One of the most important things we can do is make sure our belief window is as clear as possible and truly reflects beliefs that will move us closer to our values and priorities. To do this we must take an honest look at our behavior. In doing so, you will achieve the critical first step in freeing yourself from erroneous self ideas and self talk that may be impeding your progress toward living out your values and priorities.

Using a concept like the Belief Window can help you understand how your brain and your thoughts collaborate to bring about emotions which, when combined with choices, propel you into behaviors that are communicated through your body. By briefly examining a few of these aspects, you'll begin unraveling the mystery surrounding many PTSD triggers and symptoms.

How You've Helped Create the Life You're Living

Let's use the Belief Window for a moment to examine our way of viewing the world around us. For just a moment, put away PTSD and all it entails so we can take a glimpse into the operation manual for your brain. Before we begin, consider your use of electricity. Do you understand how electricity works, where it comes from, or how it's generated? I sure don't! Even so, I use it every day and enjoy its benefits. Let's think about how we use our brain and ability to create thoughts in the same way. We may not grasp all the details, but we absolutely reap the benefits. Like electricity, using our brain can either help or hinder us, depending on our knowledge of how to use it. You wouldn't stick a fork in a light socket, would you?

Find a comfortable sitting position, take a few deep breaths, and look around you. What do you see? Let your eyes rest on something, anything. Maybe you're looking at your coffee cup. Think about it for a minute. Why do you call it a cup? Does it only ever hold coffee? Can you remember the first time you called it a coffee cup? Who told you it was called a coffee cup? The answers to these questions (and more!) show you how we attach meaning to things. When we hang on with all our might to the meaning, we miss the moment for miracles to happen.

Now, back to our Belief Window and showing you how your brain works. As Smith suggests, we each have a Belief Window. It hangs from an imaginary hook mounted on your forehead. I have one, too. So does your mother, your father, the barista at the corner coffee shop—everyone has a Belief Window, whether they know it exists or understand how it works, or not. We all view each other and the world around us through this window.

Have you ever tried to look through a window at night with the lights on around you? Or how about looking through a window that's so covered with dirt and grime, you can't see anything beyond? What do you see? Give it a try, if you must, but I'll tell you what you'll see: only a reflection of yourself looking back at you. When it comes to the Belief Window, we all have dirt, grime, cracks, smudges, even bird poop on our window. We also have parts of our window we manage to keep clear, clean and sometimes, thick as a magnifying glass. Some of these things we have placed on our window ourselves. Different things were placed there by others. Often, when things are placed on our window when we're very young, or through an extreme experience (like trauma), it can seem as if we never had a choice, both in what was placed on our window to begin with or in how those things would effect our view of the world beyond. On the other hand, now that you know you have a Belief Window, maybe you'd like to clean it up.

As you can imagine, interacting with anyone seems like an impossible task, especially when you consider that you're trying to communicate what you see—not only through your own Belief Window, but also through someone else's! You see the world through yours, they see the world through theirs, and you are both trying to find some sort of belief that sounds the same to each of you in order to communicate clearly. How frustrating! We've placed great meaning upon the beliefs we knowingly or unknowingly allow to remain on our Belief Window. But since we're trying to get to the bottom of why life seems like such a struggle, it makes sense to examine what's on our window. The things that hinder our view through the Belief Window are called limiting beliefs. Let's take a look at a few:

DO YOU HAVE LIMITING BELIEFS?

Limiting beliefs (negative) about self:

- I do not deserve positive attention from others.

- I should never burden others with my problems or fears.

- I am uncreative, nonproductive, ineffective, and untalented.

- I am worthless.

- I am powerless to solve my problems.

- I have so many problems, I might as well give up right now.

- I am so dumb about things, I can never solve anything as complex as this.

- I am the ugliest, most unattractive, unappealing slob in the world.

Limiting beliefs (negative) about others:

- No one cares about anyone else.

- All men (or women) are dishonest and are never to be trusted.

- Successful relationships are a trick; you have no control over how they turn out.

- People are out to get whatever they can from you; you always end up being used.

- People are so opinionated; they are never willing to listen to another's point of view.

- All people are out for number one; you need to know you'll always be number two, no matter what.

- It's not who you are—it's what you do that makes you attractive to another person.

- What counts in life are others' opinions of you.

- There is a need to be on guard in dealing with others to ensure that you don't get hurt.

Limiting beliefs on other topics:

- There is only one way of doing things.

- Work is the punishment man must endure for being human.

- A family that plays (prays) together always stays together.

- There are always two choices: right or wrong; black or white; win or lose; pass or fail; grow or stagnate.

- Admitting to a mistake or to failure is a sign of weakness.

- The showing of any kind of emotion is wrong, a sign of weakness, and not allowable.

- Asking for help from someone else is a way of admitting your weakness; it denies the belief that only you can solve your problems.

How can we recognize limiting beliefs?

Limiting beliefs can be present if we are caught up in a vicious cycle of addressing our problems: Repeatedly experiencing "catch-22" scenarios where every move we make to resolve a problem results in more or greater problems. Limiting beliefs show up if we:

- Have been suffering silently (or not so silently) with a problem for a long time, yet have not taken steps to get help to address the problem.

- Have decided on a creative problem-solving solution, yet find ourselves incapable of implementing it.

- Have chosen a problem-solving course of action and find that we are unhappy with it (while avoiding alternatives).

- Are afraid of pursuing a certain course of action because of the guilt we will feel if we do it.

- Are constantly obsessed with a problem yet take no steps to resolve it.

- Are immobilized in the face of our problems feeling that the only way to deal with problems is to avoid them, deny them, procrastinate about them, ignore them, run away from them, turn our back on them.

- Can argue both sides of our problem, becoming unable to make a decision, resulting in ultimate confusion.

By now, you're probably getting a good idea about how PTSD might fit into the concept of the Belief Window. Don't think about PTSD as a layer of grime over your window; rather, think of it as an opaque shade, rolled down covering your window entirely. Your own beliefs are still there behind the shade, but PTSD keeps you from viewing them with clarity. You know they're there, because you can see them in your every-day choices and behaviors—it's just that PTSD seems to be dominating everything you thought you knew about your world.

Why not roll up the shade? Better yet, once the shade is gone, why not open the window entirely? By identifying your beliefs, exploring new ones, or gaining new perspective on old ones, you can one day find yourself opening up that window and breathing in the fresh, clean air of freedom.

WHAT ARE THE BENEFITS OF DISOWNING OUR LIMITING BELIEFS?

By disowning our limiting beliefs we are able to:

- Unblock our emotions about ourselves and our problems.

- Become productive, realistic problem-solvers.

- Gain greater credibility with ourselves and others.

- Gain clarity, purpose, and intention in addressing our current problems.

- Reduce the fear of guilt or of hurting others in solving problems.

- Identify the barriers and obstacles that must first be hurdled before our problems can be resolved.

- Come to greater honesty about ourselves and our problems.

- Put our problem into a realistic perspective as to its importance, magnitude, and probability of being solved.

- Separate our feelings from the content of the problem.

- Live richer, more authentic lives.

- View our lives in a healthier perspective, with greater meaning and direction.

- Gain our sense of humor in the presence of our problems and in their resolution.

- Recognize our self-worth and goodness, and separate it from our errors and mistakes.

- Forgive ourselves and others for mistakes made.

- Treat ourselves and others with kindness, tenderness, and understanding during times of great stress.

- Gain a sense of purpose and order in our lives as we solve problems.

- Feel productive as we labor through the muck and mire of our problems.

- Respect our rights and the rights of others as we solve problems.

- Clarify our feelings about the behavior of others without self-censorship or fear of rejection.

- Gain a "win-win" solution to problems, which involves ourselves with others. It opens us up to be able to find a compromise.

In *Season of Hope*, we've taken a hard look at the most important part of beginning to walk away from the debilitating effects of PTSD forever: making a plan to do it! Remember, putting any *PTSD Self Help* suggestions into action is your choice . . . when you're ready. Healing is always on your terms and in your timing. However, it doesn't cost anything to plan! Let's review the bare bones of what *Season of Hope* has taught us about making a commitment to healing:

- Write down your vision of healing

- Count the cost

- Embrace the three core concepts:

1. *I am normal.*

2. *I will do what works.*

3. *I already have everything I need.*

- Discover the ego

- Consider the Belief Window

Whether you're hitting the ground running or are just thinking about whether or not to deal with your PTSD symptoms sometime in the future, understand that you don't have to absorb or do all of these things at once. Think about each suggestion. Make a schedule for yourself that includes time for developing a healing plan. Then, do what you can!

SEASON OF HOPE—PART II

PACKING FOR THE JOURNEY
TOOLS FOR YOUR BACKPACK

Now that you understand what you need to do in order to commit to the healing process, let's shift our focus toward actually packing for the journey by stocking up your Backpack. Your Backpack is the backbone of the *PTSD Self Help* healing plan. It's what you'll use to get the most out of your healing journey and collaborations with your Healing Team, which you'll begin recruiting in the *Season of Renewal*. It's the key to not only expediting your healing process, but also walking away from the effects of PTSD forever. You'll learn how to make time to invest in healing, create a Backpack filled with tools designed to help you develop new ways of immediately coping with PTSD, and grow your way toward healing from PTSD permanently.

Developing your Backpack will challenge you to set yourself up for success by equipping you for your healing journey. There are five things we'll do to fill up your Backpack; we will explore each of these in depth, but by way of introduction, these five things are listed below:

InnerAction Journal—A place to record information about your progress, symptoms, and Healing Team suggestions that will become an invaluable asset for discovering how to predict flashbacks and unravel the mysterious way your mind is dealing with the original trauma.

Enlightenment—Systematic instruction on what you don't already understand about PTSD, symptoms, or recovery methods. It is systematic only in the sense that you plan daily study activities and topics.

Emergency Plan of Action (EPA)—A list of instructions, activities and contacts for use by you and your family during a healing crisis.

HomeWork—Activities you do at home in collaboration with your Healing Team that, although it doesn't really feel like work at all, is an important part of the healing journey.

Toy Box—A collection of comfort items with which to reward yourself for hard work, to dig into when you need a break, or to use in conjunction with your EPA.

Once you decide to start traveling your PTSD healing path with these five tools and your commitment firmly in your back pocket, you'll find you're able to overcome potential obstacles to your recovery more quickly. Are you ready to get packing for the journey? Let's load up your Backpack!

TOOLS FOR YOUR BACKPACK - THE INNERACTION JOURNAL

The key to pulling all of your *PTSD Self Help* healing efforts together is the InnerAction Journal. Its name gives you a clue about how to use it. Your InnerAction Journal is a scrapbook of sorts, entirely dedicated to what's going on inside you. It is also a record-keeping tool where you make a note of the interactions you have with each member of your Healing Team. Designed as a place to record information about your progress, the InnerAction Journal is best described as a scientific observation of your symptoms and the results of implementing Healing Team suggestions. To a lesser degree, it's also a place to record your Healing Team's instructions, as well as your personal thoughts.

Thinking Things Through . . . Healing as a Release From Fear

Post Traumatic Stress is deeply rooted in fear, regardless of its form— so wouldn't healing ultimately be the elimination of that fear in all its forms? Freedom from the grip of PTSD means being able to enjoy life without worrying about bumping into some trigger or another, only to have to recover for days (or even weeks) from the aftereffects. The belief in having to dig up the past in order to make sense of the present is a common one; however, it's wrong. What a breath of fresh air! No need to investigate your unconscious past. Know why? Because it's manifesting at this very moment as a thought, an emotion, a desire, a reaction. You unravel the mystery of the past on the level of the present. Can you be present in the here and now? Enough to observe without labeling or making right or wrong meaning out of what you see? Watch for behavior, reactions, moods, thoughts, emotions, fear and desire as they show up in the here and now. This is a crucial step in dissolving the power of the past and returning that power to where it belongs—with you in the present.

For example, several months into your healing journey, you've recruited each one of the members of your Healing Team and are following their suggestions. As a result, some of your physical symptoms have improved, but you seem to be having more trouble with flashbacks and/or nightmares. After participating in a yoga class, you take a few moments to record your observations:

- Room was too hot!

- Table Top position made me feel combative, angry.

- Corpse pose helped me relax; bring a blanket to cover up next time!

- I'm really tuning back in to how my body feels.

Later, you get your weekly adjustment from your chiropractor who uses a manual method to align your spine. Normally, when he asks you to cross your arms over your chest, then lays you backward, using his body weight to relieve subluxations in your spine, it doesn't bother you. This time, you notice something different. You write in your journal:

- I numbed out my body and disconnected mentally from what was happening.

- When I got to my car, I was sweating and my heart was racing.

A few days later with your mental health professional (MHP), you share your alarm at an increase of flashbacks and nightmares. You explain that at night, you wake up in a sweat with an intense fear of someone creeping down the hallway to your bedroom and a residual sense of having been violated sexually. You go on to explain that during the daytime, you've had two incidents where a movie-like scene from your past plays out before your eyes. You know it isn't really happening, but can't help feeling as if it is.

Looking back to uncover clues about possible triggers and what the beginning of a flashback feels like in your body is easy. Just take out your InnerAction Journal and review your notes with your MHP, sharing all that you recorded about the past week.

Making Sense of . . . The InnerAction Journal in Action

MHP: Let's take a look back over the past week. What did you do? How did you feel?

You: Wow. . . I never noticed it before, but looking at my notes, I see that when I do yoga and chiropractic in the same week, I start having trouble sleeping and have flashbacks.

MHP: Why do you think that is?

You: Maybe it's because some of the yoga poses make me feel vulnerable. And, oh! I just remembered! When I was being sexually abused, the room was muggy and stifling. Do you think the yoga room being so hot could have triggered a memory?

MHP: Did you have any memories surface?

You: Not right away, but I guess the flashbacks and nightmares are memories in a way. Jeez, I can see why I felt so awful after being at the chiropractor's office!

MHP: What do you want to do about these bad feelings?

You: I want them to go away! I enjoy yoga and haven't had any head-aches since seeing the chiropractor, so making the triggers behave isn't a solution for me. I think I'll try doing another physical activity during the week I have chiropractic and see if it helps.

MHP: Great idea! That might help your physical symptoms. Do you feel up to exploring the memories your mind and body are bringing to the surface? Maybe we can solve the mystery about why these activities are triggers for you, once and for all.

A diary with a twist is the best way to describe the InnerAction Journal. If you're familiar with journaling, a slight modification to your mindset is all you'll need to put this powerful tool to work. For those who've never kept a diary or developed the practice of putting your thoughts to paper, the InnerAction Journal will easily become your best friend. Recording daily events is the stuff of diaries. Your entries in the InnerAction Journal may begin with events, but will ultimately end up becoming a scrapbook-like representation of your own inward inventory to see how the events of a day affect you. Making the time to update your InnerAction Journal quickly becomes a comforting ritual of both recording your steps along the path of your PTSD healing journey and periodically looking back over the progress you've made.

Since the beginning of time, it seems people have discovered new things about themselves and their world through journaling. How? Over the centuries, both men and women have kept a record of their lives, whether in the form of drawings scratched into the sides of caves or stories repeated from one generation to the next. Journaling is an act of discovery. Establishing this private discipline will alleviate stress by giving you a place in which you can reveal yourself totally and provide a means for reflection. Not only will you be glad you took up journaling, but also you might even shorten the healing process by doing so.

How Do I Start?

A simple notebook will do. However, since you'll be investing a significant amount of time with your journal, why not make those special moments inspiring? You might consider a design that's leather-bound, hard-bound, whimsical, or just plain silly. Your local stationary store, office supply or bookstore will carry a wide variety to choose from. What's important is to pick a journal you enjoy looking at and that you can carry with you.

WILL AN ELECTRONIC VERSION WORK?

It can. It's entirely up to you to decide what method will best serve your new journaling ritual. Consider what ways the format you've chosen might limit you; then, choose a way of preserving the details of your healing journey that will allow you to fully express yourself.

Annmarie's Story

Writing has always come naturally to me, and journaling about my life and early years of exploring Christianity became an enjoyable ritual. When I decided to start my own PTSD healing journey, I chose a plain old, half-inch-thick, hard-bound journal that said something like "A life worth living is a life worth writing about on the cover. Ugh. Considering that most days I felt like crawling in a hole to die, the sentiment did little to inspire me to unravel the mystery surrounding my PTSD symptoms. I filled up all the lined pages within a few weeks. Now, I have a library of journals of varying sizes and designs that contain details from my life, including every step I took along the way toward healing PTSD. I want to save you from the same fate (unless you like that kind of variety and have space for an entire library - then go for it!). Ultimately, I settled on an 8 1/2 x 11, hard-bound sketch book. The pristine blank pages of the sketch book (no lines!) unlocked a creative part of me I didn't know existed. When I couldn't find the words to express emotions, describe symptoms or communicate a state of mind, pictures were how I did it. Granted, I'm no artist, and stick people graced many of my initial pictures, but once in my therapist's office, the drawings brought me back to how I was feeling, what I was thinking, and details about memories that came up in my mind. It was a very useful tool!

You'll find it helpful to begin each entry with the date. You can be sure there will be times when you'll return to your entries and read about this time in your life. Don't feel pressured to write every single day, or be limited to writing only one page. Honor those days when you feel like writing a lot or not at all. Use a pen or pencil; either way, choose one that has a look and feel you really like. Most people find it helpful to designate a specific time of day and/or a specific location to spend with their InnerAction Journal in order to establish a habit and get the most out of using it. The time of day is not the important part; consistently making entries is.

What do you have to lose? Placing yourself in the position of an objective observer can create the distance you need to uncover clues about how PTSD is intertwined with your thinking and behavior. Also, while you're journaling, you may find it enjoyable or meaningful to illustrate your pages with keepsakes such as drawings, pictures, notes or cards from friends, pressed flowers, fortunes from fortune cookies, important quotations, cartoons or any other tangible souvenirs. These items can encourage you and remind you that you are more than just your PTSD symptoms. Be creative in your journal, and allow it to reflect and reveal the full spectrum of who you are.

Thinking Things Through . . . Ranking the InnerAction Journal Risk Factor

Feeling a little apprehensive about writing down sometimes painful details? Anyone who had a brother or sister prying into their privacy by picking the lock on their diary might feel this way. Try this. Answer each of the following statements as being true or false, then go back over the statements. On a scale from one to five—one being "No foreseeable risk" and five being "It freaks me out just thinking about it"—rank your risk factor:

- If I write it down, it makes it real.

- Being honest about my feelings, even if I never share them, is scary.

- I'm afraid of what might come up.

- I don't trust others in my household to respect my privacy.

- If I get emotional, don't think I can stop crying, being angry, etc.

Now, take a break from your efforts. When you have a few moments to yourself, take the position of The Observer and write down the details of how and why you feel the way you do about each statement. Then, review your notes by asking:

- Is there any truth to this?

- What are the facts?

- Does this resemble the way I've felt at other times in my life?

Hopefully, this will ease your concern and help to reframe the use of your InnerAction Journal as an important aspect of taking care of yourself.

It doesn't matter if your writing is legible or if you've got the spelling and grammar right. All that matters is that you seek to understand how your past is creating your future, and that you're ready to try using the InnerAction Journal to collect evidence you find along the path of your days. Know that by putting pen to paper, you'll be engaging both your right-brain and left-brain skills while bringing a clearer understanding of who you are in relation to the trauma you've experienced.

Making Sense of . . . The InnerAction Journal and Creativity

Are you at a loss for words to describe how an event impacted your day? Take a piece of paper and fold it in half. Fold it in half again, making two lines that cross in the middle and four "squares" when you open it up. Start in the upper left square of the paper and draw a representation of what happened just before you felt strong feelings or PTSD symptoms. In the next square, draw how you wanted to react to the event. In the third square, draw how you actually reacted. In the last square, draw how the event ended for you. If you feel up to it, jot down a few notes on the back about what you've drawn to help you remember the incident more clearly later.

Do you have a favorite beverage (coffee, tea, cocoa), a scented candle or cozy blanket you can enjoy *only* when journaling? Designating special items to use only while engaged in journaling can make the act of journaling very compelling. You just can't wait to unload the day's observations from your brain and relish a really good latte!

Do you prefer to get up early and write in the quiet of the morning? Or would emptying your mind just before bed be more helpful? Do you wake up in the middle of the night and find it hard to go back to sleep? Is there a slow time during the middle of the day you can claim as your own?

Do you have a favorite chair, window seat, public park or private backyard space that can afford you the privacy and focus to journal your thoughts?

Did you know journaling at times when you can't sleep might reveal what's keeping you awake at night? You'd be awake anyway, so why not take advantage of your mind's attempt at resolving a past issue and record your physical symptoms (if any) or inspired thoughts? As you're able to comprehend how triggers show up during stressful events and enter fully into practicing the skills you'll learn in *PTSD Self Help*, you cannot help but be changed! Your InnerAction Journal is the place to start.

WHAT DO I WRITE ABOUT?

You've chosen a perfect journal that is attractive and feels good in your hands, a pen with a weight to it and ink that flows easily onto the paper, and a time and place that inspires you. Now you're ready to sit down and write. As I mentioned earlier, the InnerAction Journal is a place to record information about your progress, symptoms, and Healing Team suggestions that will become an invaluable asset for discovering how to not only predict flashbacks, but also unravel the mysterious way your mind is dealing with the original trauma. With that in mind, you'll become a kind of detective looking for clues, or a scientist recording the results of each day in an effort to unlock the mystery behind what's driving your PTSD symptoms.

Begin your journaling time by taking a few moments to relax. Try breathing deeply and grounding yourself in the space you've chosen. If you are a spiritual person, give a few moments to prayer, meditation or asking for guidance. If distracting thoughts keep taking you off course, keep a separate note pad nearby to jot down enough to jog your memory, so you can deal with them later. If your distractions come in the form of others (pets included), try to communicate how important this time is to your overall ability to get well. If all else fails, lock them in another room (your pets, not others). Commit yourself to six weeks of trying each of the methods for journaling. Each method I'll introduce has its own style and feel. You'll discover your own method and rhythm that feels comfortable.

Journaling about your specific life experience can be a direct link to understanding more clearly how PTSD is showing up in the details of your day. Discovering *how* it shows up is the first step toward eliminating it altogether. Soon, you'll be writing narratives, jotting down notes, sketching or doodling, and making lists surrounding these things:

- The events of everyday life

- Responses to reading PTSD material

- Dreams, nightmares, flashbacks and daydreams

- Visualization exercises or meditation

- Conversations and dialogues with your Healing Team members

- Hopes for the future

EVERYDAY LIFE EVENTS

Journaling about the things that go on in your everyday world doesn't mean keeping a list of your appointments, who you talked to or what you did each day. Rather, journaling everyday life events is about recording how those experiences have affected your spirit in a way that stands out from the mundane aspects of your day. It is a way to explore the hidden rooms of your heart where you've stored up meaning and attachments. It is also a way to open up and examine your reactions to the world, as well as how PTSD is at work in all aspects of your life. Try using these questions to get you started:

- How am I feeling about myself (at work, in relationships, as a parent, as a survivor) today?

- Where today did I specifically see or feel the presence of PTSD working in my life?

- What attitudes or actions were blocking my ability to be myself?

- In what ways was I able to bring an awareness of the effect of PTSD to the various parts of my life?

- Were there specific events today that helped me understand who I am apart from PTSD?

- Is there a conversation or event I feel the need to look at more closely?

- Do I have unresolved feelings about what someone said or did today?

- Did I spend part of my day continuing a conversation with someone in my mind, thinking about what I could have said or done differently?

- Was there a time today when I felt a strong emotion? Why might this emotion have surfaced? What was happening at the time and how did I feel about it?

- Are there things I'd like to say (questions, expressions of gratitude, explanations) to someone (co-worker, spouse, child, God) in response to this day?

If you're having trouble engaging the events of your day, or if the day's events just don't seem to fit, try completing any of the following thoughts:

- My life is . . .

- I am . . .

- I feel the most vulnerable when . . .

- My need to protect myself, unplug from the world, or split off from my body shows up when . . .

VISUALIZATION EXERCISES, PRAYER AND MEDITATION

Sometimes when we place ourselves in a very relaxed state, our own inner wisdom is able to rise to the surface. How you choose to approach relaxation can be as varied as spending time in prayer, taking a meditative walk, or practicing breathing exercises. Remember what Denis Waitley had to say: If you go there in the mind, you'll go there in the body. This is never more true than when we visualize or mentally rehearse. Why not take this opportunity to begin creating a safe, relaxing place within yourself that you can carry with you? Whatever method you choose, keep your InnerAction Journal close by and record any insights, *ah-ha!* moments or inspired thoughts that came to you during your practice. You might want to keep a separate piece of paper designated for "to do" items that interrupt your ability to fully relax. By jotting "to do" items down as they come to you, it frees up your mind to think about something else!

Annmarie's Story

Since I was a kid, I've had a vivid imagination. It's served me well in business by helping me see the end result of my endeavors in perfect clarity. My imagination was one of the strengths that saved me from succumbing to PTSD. The first time I saw a psychiatrist, he walked me through a visualization exercise to help me relax. He asked me to picture a place where I felt safe. Right away, I pictured a mountain meadow that resembled the meadows I had explored growing up near Mt. Rainier. He asked me to picture the trees. That was easy - I was from Washington State. Douglas Fir and Cedar are everywhere! We went on for an hour constructing details about my special place. By the time I was finished, I had an interesting, symbolic representation of where I was at in my healing journey.

Many of the things I chose to have in what I called my prayer place stayed with me from that first encounter until I was ready to fully commit to the healing process many years later. That's when I actively started adding things to my prayer place that gave me comfort - things like fine, warm brown sand that felt like brown sugar under my feet, an old wooden bridge stretched over a softly babbling brook, worn smooth by my many visits, and a grand rose garden with blooms that changed color each time I visited.

What I didn't expect were the things that showed up on their own, meaning that I didn't consciously create them there - things like a large, black horse; big, comfy chairs with sheer fabric hanging from above, billowing in soft breezes; and, most surprisingly, a man who seemed vaguely familiar, waiting there for me: It was Jesus.

As I entered deeper into the healing process, I began bringing my concerns and fears to this place and sharing them with my new "friends." Also, I began to be very aware of several child-like parts of myself that had a fair amount to say during my journaling time. It would have been easy for me to dismiss these things as make-believe, evidence that I was indeed going crazy. But I was desperate! I wasn't getting the help I needed from my church, my friends, or even my family. I decided that it couldn't hurt to allow that creative part of myself to resurface. Besides, maybe thinking about these things in a new and entirely different way was the key. I suspended my inner critic and withheld judgement about what was coming to me from that deepest part of myself.

One of these inner children refused to speak, instead choosing to act out unexpectedly during my days at work or when I was trying to sleep. In my mind's eye, I could see her. She was about ten years old, the same age I was when I was sexually abused, and she was causing me trouble. At my wits end, I decided to try taking her along with me to my prayer place. She loved the meadow, the water, the bridge and most of all, Jesus - so much so that once I took her there, she stayed and didn't bother me any more.

READING PTSD MATERIAL

The InnerAction Journal is a quest for a breakthrough in how you view your own stories surrounding the original traumatic event and how the resulting PTSD is impacting your world. Search for other people's stories that either reinforce your desire to heal or open up a new perspective you hadn't considered before. In reading about PTSD or any of the myriad ways it comes into a person's life, allow portions of the text to intrude into your life, to speak to you, to confront you. If you don't take time to absorb elements of text that stand out to you, you'll miss out on the gift of having it speak to you about your own experience.

One way to do this is to integrate the tool of Enlightenment with your InnerAction Journal on a level that will begin your shift toward healing. The tool, Enlightenment (which you'll learn about in the next section) is a systematic education focusing on aspects of Post Traumatic Stress that you currently have a low level of knowledge about. Begin by reading a paragraph or two of text and then journal in response to what you've read. This method helps pull you from informative reading for the sake of knowledge toward a transformational interaction with your spirit. Remember, the goal is not to read a certain amount of material or to analyze the methods described in or the meaning of the text; the goal is to understand the text as it intimately relates to you today, in the here and now.

FLASHBACKS, NIGHTMARES AND DAYDREAMS

You'll definitely want to use your InnerAction Journal to record the activities of your subconscious mind. It is when you're most relaxed that your mind often goes to work. During times of sleep or deep relaxation, such as therapeutic massage or meditation, your mind is relieved from the daily barrage of decision making and stressing out about your symptoms. Taking advantage of this opportunity, your mind swirls the past, present and future together with a healthy dose of creativity to form mental images that represent something you're trying to work out. Recording the details of these images to the best of your ability and how they made you feel can reveal the mysteries hiding behind many triggers. Another method is to record the image in detail; then, insert yourself as each of the characters and central figures.

Annmarie's Story

Every morning, I would wake up at three, walk to a window and look out as if I expected to witness something. Usually, I could get a glass of water and go back to bed. Sometimes going back to bed was impossible. In either case, I got in the habit of journaling. When my son was little, he would come into my room and gently wake me if he wasn't feeling well or had trouble sleeping. I used this idea to connect with my own inner child, assuming that she was waking up in the middle of the night for a reason. Just like any child who wakes in the night, they want to be comforted and helped in returning to the safety of their sleep. So I began to ask the child within, "Why are you up? What's wrong?" Here's one of my journal entries:

April 2, 2005

I am looking out the window. My body is tired but my mind is awake and listening. I'm afraid, sitting here in the dark - of SPIDERS. It makes my heart pound & I can't breathe.

The walls in my place are melting away as I sit here at my desk, looking at the fireplace. Things that are familiar to me are disappearing and the main room in the cabin is creeping into my mind.

Ooooh, I don't like this. Should I run upstairs to Mike? (child's voice) Run, run!! Heartburn! Oh! No more goat cheese pizza & talk about Secret Survivors before bedtime! I'm soooo thirsty.

There was a fireplace & a hide-a-bed there in close to the same positions as mine are now. How could that happen here?! This is my place!

Maybe if I go to Mike it will all go away. Waaaaahhh, I don't want to :(

I'm afraid if I go to Mike he might think I trust him. He might think I'm all better. If he thinks I trust him & that I'm all better then he'll want more from me - work & sex.

I have to have a BM. I HATE THIS!!!

The shadows on the wall from the candle I've lit look like monsters! Are they moving? (child's voice) Run, run!! I can't stay here! I can't breathe. My stomach hurts.

Oh, yeah, Mike will really like this (going to him) - sarcastic. He'll think he's tough stuff (?)

What is that phrase? Tough stuff? I don't use that. Why does it make my heart feel icy and my chest tight? That phrase scares me when I hear it in my head.

OK ARE YOU DONE!? I want to be done... bed-one.

Bed, hot, dark, pain inside, bright light, suffocating, hiding, go away, I want to go away, tired, burning eyes, endless, endless, when will it be done... bed-one?

(adult, rational voice) It's ok, it's ok. Your body is just remembering, don't hate it (your body).

I want to come out of my skin. I don't want anyone to touch me. Although, I know if someone holds me I will eventually break down or fall asleep.

Oh, boy. This is good. But it sure hurts. I feel like I want to cry but I can't.

I don't want to go to him (Mike)! But I have to . . . I want this to end somehow.

Haunting, sad melodies are running through my head & tears are coming. I'm getting cold now.

It's 4 a.m.

It's interesting to note that writing the words "be done" actually caused the flashback I was experiencing to shift. When my mind rearranged the letters in a symbolic way from "be done" to "bed-one," it opened me up to the deepest, most painful aspect of one traumatic experience.

Another big plus in using your InnerAction Journal is the benefit of grounding yourself in the here and now during a flashback. While experiencing a flashback, you have your journal and pen in your hand as a reminder that you are safe, that what you are seeing, hearing, smelling or tasting is not actually taking place—even though it may feel as if it is. Press through the flashback by diligently recording the details of the space you are in, the flashback details and how they manifest, your physical responses, what you're thinking, and what your inner voice is saying. Afterward, you'll likely need to rest. Close your journal. Take some time to recover. You've safely preserved the flashback in the pages of your InnerAction Journal for later analysis with your mental health professional or other member of your Healing Team.

CONVERSATIONS
Your InnerAction Journal is a one-stop depository for suggestions,

assignments, prescriptions or epiphanies passed on to you from members of your Healing Team. You've recruited competent professionals and trusted allies as members of your Healing Team. Your InnerAction Journal is the place to jot down nuggets of wisdom they pass your way, suggestions of books to read, dietary changes to make, exercises to try or observations they make. Capturing these things in one location gives you a better chance of actually implementing the suggestions or acting upon the advice given, since you can go back after the encounter is over to review your thoughts about an appointment.

HOPES FOR THE FUTURE

Set aside time to use your InnerAction Journal in a more traditional way by writing about your desires for future healing. What will your life look like? How will it be different? What are you willing to let go of to achieve the healing you envision? Write about these things and anything else you hope for.

Now that we've explored all the ways to use your InnerAction Journal, this is a great place to tell you about the next tool in your Backpack: Enlightenment.

TOOLS FOR YOUR BACKPACK - ENLIGHTENMENT

As I've mentioned, *PTSD Self Help* won't take you on a gut-wrenching dissertation about how terrible PTSD symptoms can be or how destructive your negative coping methods are to your relationships and to your life. You already know this, because you're living it! In *Season of Transformation: Let the Journey Begin!* you'll learn how the *PTSD Self Help* methods assist in healing specific aspects of these symptoms; however, if you're not familiar with PTSD vocabulary, like flashbacks, triggers, stigma, secondary wounding or disassociation, the Enlightenment tool is a unique way to approach an independent study of PTSD.

Planning time for study and keeping a healing perspective are the keys to making Enlightenment work; therefore, this tool is defined as systematic instruction on what you don't already understand about PTSD, symptoms, or recovery methods. The only thing that makes Enlightenment systematic is that you are intentional about planning daily or weekly study activities and topics. Consider gathering more information about PTSD topics like:

- Symptoms (flashbacks, triggers, disassociation, sleep disorders)

- Treatment methods such as Eye Movement Desensitization and Reprocessing (EMDR), Cognitive Behavioral Therapy, The Tapping Solution, Psychotherapy, Neurofeedback

- Medication

- How the brain processes emotion and memories

- The fight/flight/freeze response

- Statistics

SURVIVOR STORIES

Stories of others' PTSD struggles and victories mean the most to us when we feel the stories are a part of us. When we are able to fully enter into another person's experience, we deeply grasp the courage, strength and determination required to reclaim a healthy quality of life. Books, blogs and discussion groups on the Internet are full of other people's examples of what it's like to live with PTSD. Some stories have a happy ending. Some do not. Some stories are helpful in validating our own story about trauma and others are just plain disturbing. Use caution when exposing yourself to others' traumatic experiences. Since your mind doesn't know the difference between experiencing trauma or a rehearsal of a traumatic experience, such as reading vivid details, it's possible that exposing yourself to others stories could trigger adverse symptoms. If you must read about other peoples' experiences, try to choose stories with a positive focus on healing instead of painful stories that wallow around in the past. As you begin to comprehend that walking away from PTSD is possible, you'll find the light at the end of a very long tunnel; when you find hope, you cannot help but be changed by it—but you have to be looking in the right place.

ONLINE CAUTIONS

PTSD is rapidly becoming the new money-making venture of the twenty-first century. For this reason, it is wise to understand the source of your information. The Internet is an interactive community open to people all over the world. Not everyone has advice that fits every survivor's experience, or worse, sometimes people aren't who they seem to be. Some general guidelines:

- Look for trusted sources

- Shrug off extreme views or suggestions

- Beware of anyone asking you for money

- If it sounds too easy to be true, it probably is

The Internet is a wonderful tool for helping you start your PTSD healing journey—just be sure to use it wisely by reading the bios of blog authors, asking for verification of their information sources, and sticking to mainstream healthcare sites when looking for advice about medication. For more information, check out the *PTSD Self Help* website to download the Federal Trade Commission's free PDF guidebook, *Who Cares: Sources of Information About Online Health Care Advice.*

How Do I Get The Most Out of Enlightenment?

Support and Therapy Groups

A unique way to find positive information and healing stories is to participate in a group. Instead of reading text, live interaction with other survivors provides you with ideas, perspectives and experiences you have yet to discover. Another plus is the helpful stories and experiences you can bring to a group. Sharing your struggles and *ah-ha!* moments in a helpful and positive way with others just like yourself can help you feel better about your journey and stay the course should obstacles rise up. You'll have all those people in your group counting on you to get through the difficult times, so when you share how you did it, they can be successful too. Look for a group that's focused on forward motion toward healing, however. Sometimes groups can be about sharing pain, too. Be sure about the group's culture by talking with the facilitator or sponsoring agency.

RESOURCES FROM YOUR MENTAL HEALTH PROFESSIONAL

Once you've recruited a PTSD-informed, strengths-based mental health professional (MHP)(something you'll learn about in *Season of Renewal: Recruiting Your Healing Team*), don't hesitate to use them as a resource for credible information. A valuable philosophy held by the very best trauma experts is the idea of giving clients something to do in between office visits. Ask your MHP to recommend books, websites or activities that you can incorporate into your Enlightenment schedule. That way, you'll be sure to add a little bit to your understanding on a consistent basis and avoid overwhelming yourself.

SCHEDULING TIME FOR ENLIGHTENMENT

The symptoms of PTSD can be unpredictable, making it difficult to manage everyday life. You already have plenty to juggle just trying to hold down a job, keeping your relationships from falling apart, and managing a household, so adding time to educate yourself could seem like an easy thing to ignore. Don't make that mistake! In order to defuse the power PTSD has over your life, you must first acknowledge the negative impact it's having; the only way to do that is to understand how it operates. You've heard the saying, "Knowledge is power," and in this case it couldn't be more true. Once you have a cursory understanding of the many facets of PTSD, you'll be more able to distinguish actual symptoms from those related to other issues.

Annmarie's Story

After my first nervous breakdown at age twenty-five, I became a ravenous consumer of information. During the early '90s, there wasn't a lot of information available about how to overcome PTSD. Much of it was hidden in books about child sexual abuse, recovering as an adult child of an alcoholic (ACOA) or some other major life issue. The commercialization of the Internet - what we know as the World Wide Web - wasn't a reality until 1996, so reliable information about PTSD and its aftereffects was unreachable. So, I read, studied and experienced everything I could find that was even remotely related.

My experience with support groups was limited to my attendance at Al-Anon and AA meetings (in support of my second husband) and engaging in chat room discussions about recovering from molestation. Both experiences left a lot to be desired. It frightened me to realize there were so many people living miserable lives and not finding the help they were crying out for. Would that be my fate, too? Always searching for a solution and never finding an answer? Some participants seemed to have found some amount of balance for their lives, but there was no joy, no authentic happiness. Oftentimes, they couldn't articulate exactly how they'd found their way to the level of healing they had attained. I always felt awful after engaging in one of these groups. Not once did I ever leave feeling hopeful or encouraged. In frustration, I retreated from that dead end.

During my interview of potential therapists, I made it clear that I didn't want to be sitting around doing nothing in between office visits. I had taken time off from my life to accomplish whatever measure of healing was out there for me, and I had every intention of milking it for every-thing it was worth. The therapist I ended up recruiting was refreshed to work with someone who was willing to work so hard (although I suspect she figured it was a symptom of my control issues - and she was right!). I kept her on her toes finding new resources I could absorb. Some things I read, I agreed with. Some I didn't. By then, I had learned to "chew the meat and spit out the bones," so to speak. It was also where I learned that normal is what works.

On the *PTSD Self Help* website, you can watch a short video of me teaching you about priority management. Priority management is different from time management. Instead of driving yourself nutty trying to cram a million "to do" items into a single day, priority management helps you decide what's really important and when to do it. You may never have given yourself the permission to do what *you* want or need over the wants and needs of others. But guess what? As my grandmother used to say, "You won't get any golden eggs if you don't take care of the goose." Did you get that? You, and anyone else in your life that you care about, won't get any—zero, zilch—of what you give out, golden or not, if you're unable to function. If you have people you care about, the most loving thing you can do is to give them the very best version of *you* that you can be. And that, my friend, takes time and intention.

Making Sense of . . . Enlightenment

Start planning Enlightenment and other healing activities, including appointments with your Healing Team members, by writing down a short list of six to eight areas of your life that are the most important to you. This is your non-negotiable priority list. Your list might look like this:

- Healing

- Children

- Exercise

- Eating right

- Marriage

- Spirituality

- Career

Next, take out a calendar, day planner or whatever you use to keep track of appointments. Look at your schedule for the upcoming week. How many of your appointments fit into one or more of the non-negotiable categories on your list? Now, take out your "to do" list or quickly make one. You know, the list of stuff like taking the dog to the vet, going grocery shopping, and painting the house—all the little things you never seem to find time to get to that's cluttering up your mind. How many of the things on your "to do" list are things someone else can do? You might need to let go of perfectionist ideas about getting them done in order to free up your time. Assign them to others by putting a line through them, then writing their name next to the task. Are there things that fit into one of your non-negotiable categories? These are things only you can do, since they're aspects of *your* priorities. Keep them on the list.

Now you're ready to get busy. If you have a personal mission statement, say it quietly to yourself as a reminder of what you're all about in this world. Look again at your schedule for the next week. Place into your schedule any appointments you have that qualify as a non-negotiable. Next, review your "to do" list for those tasks that qualify as a non-negotiable and are things only you can do. Place them in your schedule with plenty of wiggle room—extra time to regroup, a drive across town, or taking care of emergencies that might pop up. Finally, place the items that you've assigned to others in a neat list off to the side; then, in your calendar, schedule reminders to yourself to check up on them. This keeps you delegating instead of dumping and makes sure you keep your relationships intact.

Appointments are likely already set "in stone" so to speak, with a few exceptions. Maybe you realize meeting with that friend who never has anything positive to say isn't as important as you once thought. In fact, maybe it's contributing to how awful you feel. Cancel it and be honest with your friend. Try saying something like:

"You know I've been struggling, so I'm making a few changes to try and help myself heal. I need some extra time to make a few appointments. Would you mind if we didn't have coffee this week?"

At some point, you're going to have to come clean with your friend about how his/her behavior impacts you and what their role could be in helping you heal from PTSD, but save that for later, after you've read *Season of Renewal: Recruiting Your Healing Team.*

Tools for Your Backpack - An Emergency Plan of Action (EPA)

Extreme symptoms often come just before a major breakthrough in healing. They do not mean that you are a failure, are unwilling to heal, or can't overcome your PTSD. Be kind to yourself! Move forward on the healing journey at a pace your body and mind can maintain.

Healing from PTSD isn't a sprint—it's a marathon. Set yourself up for success! When you're feeling your best, make a plan for how you'll handle emergencies. Whether you are civilian or military, these suggestions are helpful in developing an Emergency Plan of Action:

- Download the PTSD Coach Mobile App (free) from the Department of Veterans Affairs' National Center for PTSD at www.ptsd. va.gov

- Print a copy of *Having a Healing Crisis? Do Not Heal!* from the *PTSD Self Help* website or review *Warning! Do Not Heal!* in the section *Concept #2 - Normal is What Works* found at the beginning of this book.

- Create a contact list in order of who to call first:

  1. Your mental health professional's emergency contact number

  2. Your Healing Partner (depending upon your agreement)

  3. Spouse

  4. Other close family members or friends who've agreed in advance to help you through a healing crisis

  5. Suicide prevention hotline

- Create a list of comfort activities that help you feel safe

- Remind yourself to use your InnerAction Journal

- Don't forget to engage in emergency breathing

- Post your EPA in a prominent place

- Give your Healing Partner and Spouse/significant other a copy of your EPA

Making Sense of . . . Emergency Breathing

Did you know something as simple as changing how you breathe can derail a panic attack? People who are physically active (such as casual joggers, marathon runners, weight lifters, Zumba fanatics, Pilates enthusiasts, or yoga practitioners) understand the need to control the breath to get the most out of a workout. What most people don't realize is that we've unlearned how to breathe properly for everyday health. Our chaotic lifestyles have brought so much stress to ordinary living that our body can't help but respond to the increase in adrenaline, which means most people only use the top one-third of their lungs to not only take in oxygen, but also regulate CO_2 in our bloodstream. Add the pressures of dealing with PTSD symptoms to the extra burdens we've taken on in Western culture, and you've got a recipe for disease. Here's how to stop panic attacks in their tracks by engaging the Emergency Breathing technique:

1. Begin by letting your Healing Partner, Spouse/Significant other know you're having a hard time and that you need to activate Emergency Breathing.

2. In your safe space (internal or external), sit up straight and allow your shoulders to fall away from your ears. Take off your shoes. Place your hand on the lower part of your abdomen and take three slow, deep breaths, breathing in through your nose and out through your mouth. Can you feel your hand rise as you inhale, fall as you exhale?

3. Press your feet in to the floor. Remind yourself that you're safe and secure in the present moment, that what has already past cannot harm you.

   • Breathe in, enough to move your hand on your abdomen; then hold the breath for a count of three. Honor any feelings that arise by being patient and present with them. As if comforting a friend, allow yourself to be okay with these feelings.

   • Release the breath slowly, say to yourself, *I'm right where I need to be* and release the feelings from your body, allowing them to flow back into the universe.

   • Breathe in . . . Hold 1-2-3 . . . breathe out . . . saying to yourself, *I'm experiencing exactly what I need to heal* and releasing the feelings.

   • Breathe in . . . hold . . . and release. *I'm right where I need to be.*

   • Breathe in . . . hold . . . and release. *I'm experiencing exactly what I need to heal.*

4. Continue breathing deeply and reciting the affirmations until you feel you've let go of the feeling for the day.

5. Return to breathing normally and sit in stillness. When you're ready, wiggle your fingers and toes, returning to the sensation of being centered in your body before opening your eyes.

6. Record your experience in your InnerAction Journal.

7. Rest and recover.

8. Check in with your Healing Partner, Spouse/Significant other to let them know you're okay and that you've completed your exercise. Share your experience with them when you're ready and only after an adequate amount of rest and recovery.

Weighing the Evidence . . . Relearning How to Breathe

Did you know CO_2 is just as important to our health and wellness as oxygen? A proper level of CO_2 is needed for your cells to maintain a necessary level of acidity in order to function properly. That's why people who are having a panic attack or migraine headaches are sometimes able to find relief by breathing into a paper bag. The bag increases the CO_2 levels taken in on the breath. It's also why some yoga and meditation practices encourage a brief pause, where one holds their breath, between the inhale and exhale. Pay attention to any animal or even yourself under stress. You'll notice quick, shallow breathing from the top of the lungs is building the body's circulatory system up for a big dump of adrenaline in preparation for fight or flight mode. Introducing more CO_2 into your bloodstream will fool your body and your brain into believing you're ready to take a nap instead. You'll learn more about proper breathing in *Season of Transformation: Let the Journey Begin!* What's the cost of not getting enough oxygen and CO_2?

- Muscle fatigue

- Tiredness / lethargy

- Skin problems

- Spaced-out feelings

- Panic attacks

- Insomnia

- Organ damage

TOOLS FOR YOUR BACKPACK - HOMEWORK

The idea of HomeWork is that it's a tool you'll use to supplement suggestions, activities and recommendations given to you by key members of your Healing Team, such as your Mental Health Professional. Heck, even this book could be considered HomeWork. Maybe you even picked it up because your therapist, doctor or good friend recommended it. If you did, then you already understand and are enjoying the benefit of the *PTSD Self Help* concept of HomeWork!

WHAT IS HOMEWORK?

There's nothing worse than feeling victimized by your PTSD symptoms, let alone the originating traumatic experience! Add to that feeling the sense that doctors are examining you like a bug under a microscope, poking around in your head, giving advice, then sending you home to figure it out. That experience can add to the burden of feeling acted upon. We don't want that!

It's important to feel in charge of how much you do and when. Once you realize the damage PTSD is doing to your relationships, your career, your family and your health, taking the bull by the horns to facilitate your own healing journey will be an easy decision. Your first action steps toward healing will be the ones that secure your ultimate victory over "being acted upon" and allow you to take control in a healthy way. Remember our cross country backpacking analogy? We said that taking a trip across the country safely requires making sure you are in tip-top shape, but first you have to get yourself out of bed. In other words, turning to face a problem is the first action step toward solving it. Action steps . . . that's where HomeWork comes in!

In *Season of Transformation: Let the Journey Begin!* you'll be introduced to HomeWork activities that can help you clean up your Belief Window and complement the hard work you'll be doing with your Healing Team. The beginning of your PTSD healing journey is a good time to get real about who you've become and why. Think about it: you were minding your own business, living as a certain kind of person with unique skills, quirks, and ways of being yourself . . . and then trauma happened. It rocked your boat and turned your world upside down. But the upheaval didn't stop after the trauma was done—your world continued to spin out of control. Sure, you had days that were okay, even happy. But something was lurking behind you. You began to see it in your behaviors and you could hear it in your thoughts.

Eventually you broke, maybe more than once. However long you've lived with PTSD in your life, you spent that time figuring out how to deal, how to cope, how to survive. You picked up little habits, ways of thinking and perspectives on the world around you that are driven by the fear the original trauma left behind. You're tired of living in fear that PTSD will raise its ugly head to do more damage—*worse* damage. Now you're ready to do something about it. HomeWork activities can help reveal limiting beliefs, incredible strengths and deep cellular memories.

Although HomeWork weaves its way throughout your PTSD healing journey, often overlapping work you're doing with multiple members of your Healing Team, it serves a very specific purpose. By putting what you hear in the professionals' office into practice, you get the opportunity to experience the results yourself, then record those results for later examination with your Healing Team. This process puts *you* in the driver's seat of reclaiming your life.

TOOLS FOR YOUR BACKPACK - TOY BOX

Putting this tool together is fun! A Toy Box is a collection of comfort items you'll turn to when rewarding yourself for the hard work of collaborating with a Healing Team member or to use in an emergency, such as when you're surprised by a powerful trigger. Your Toy Box doesn't have to literally be a box; it can be a drawer, a shelf in the closet, an oversized basket or any other container you find pleasing where you can store all of your comfort supplies. At first, when putting your Toy Box together, you may think that wrapping up in a soft, fluffy blanket might be indulgent. Trust me—after a day of unanticipated surprises, curling up with that blanket in a warm pocket of sunshine can be just the thing to bring you back to yourself.

Your "toys" can include anything. The only qualifier is that the toy must bring you a sense of immediate pleasure. Below is a list of "toys" you can glean from and add your own special items to. Take your time developing your Toy Box, adding new items as you stumble across things that hearken back to simpler times and bring you a feeling of escape.

Toys For Your Toy Box

- Playdough

- Crayons, colored pencils or markers

- Sidewalk chalk

- Soft, fluffy blanket and/or pillow

- Stuffed animal

- Yo-yo

- Juggling balls or bean bags

- Big pieces of butcher paper

- A children's book, such as *The Blue Day Book: A Lesson in Cheering Yourself Up,* by Bradley Trevor Greive

In the next chapter, you'll move forward from contemplating the PTSD healing journey and making a concrete plan for what you'll do to heal, toward recruiting important individuals who can help you along. A few of these people are professionals, and a few are everyday folks.

SEASON OF RENEWAL

RECRUITING YOUR HEALING TEAM:
IT TAKES A COMMUNITY
—AND ONE DAY, A NATION

One of the big, red flags of danger associated with PTSD is the tendency toward isolation. Most survivors don't isolate intentionally. It is a slow, mostly accidental result of feeling overloaded by stimulus in your environment. That becomes a problem when the stimulus is your spouse, children or coworkers. Not choosing to actively heal from PTSD? One day you might wake up divorced, disconnected from your children and unemployed, or worse—contemplating suicide.

Don't fall into these denial traps!

I just need . . .

- a little time alone

- to bury myself in work, kids, etc.

- some space to get my shit together

- to take a break

Not one person has successfully healed from the debilitating aftereffects of trauma on their own. It takes the care and compassion of others, as well as care and compassion toward yourself to overcome PTSD. Historically, PTSD recovery meant a one-size-fits-all approach achieved through multiple sessions of talk therapy, sometimes combined with group therapy and/or medication. Unfortunately, that method took years of dedication and wasn't successful in helping survivors rise to a thriving quality of life. Now, it is understood that successful recovery from PTSD requires a holistic approach that addresses the entire individual, not just their mental state. Start by putting together a Healing Team, and you'll be making a positive step toward walking away from PTSD for good!

How A Healing Team Works

When I coach survivors who are healing from PTSD, one thing I hear often is, "I feel like such a burden. Sometimes, I wonder if it would just be better if I . . ." When their family members, spouses or significant others find the courage to share their deepest fears concerning their loved one struggling with PTSD, they say things like:

- *I have no idea what to do or how to help.*

- *I'm exhausted trying to be the only person there for her/him!*

- *We've been dealing with this on our own and it's not getting better.*

- *Sometimes I wonder if I'm doing more harm than good.*

- *How did I end up being the enemy?*

- *I'm starting to have issues of my own and don't want to abandon my loved one.*

The entire *PTSD Self Help* method will go a very long way toward alleviating many of these concerns, but creating a Healing Team is probably the most effective element in ensuring that fear and frustration doesn't take root. In this section, you'll learn what role each member plays in the bigger picture of the team and how each member can defer to other members of the team. The result? No one team member feels they are carrying the entire burden of helping. Better yet, each team member will know exactly what they can do to help and what not to do to keep from making things worse. Below are seven individuals crucial to helping you overcome the debilitating effects of PTSD. Don't start a healing journey without:

Yourself – Your commitment to seeing the healing process through to the end and communicating your expertise on all things *you* puts you in the number one position on your Healing Team. You are the most important member of your own Healing Team. After all, you've been living your life with PTSD for a long time. That makes you an expert! No one knows *you* better than you. So, healing from PTSD begins with your commitment and determination to never let it sneak up on you or steamroll your life again. If you haven't already made a commitment to do whatever it takes to reclaim a life worth living, go back and read *Season of Hope - Part I: Planning - Three Key Action Steps.*

Mental Health Professional – We're not talking about just any mental health professional. You'll want to locate someone skilled in not only working with PTSD survivors, but also helping survivors integrate the healing process into their lifestyle.

Spouse / Significant Other – If you are involved in an intimate relationship, that individual's participation is imperative. The healing journey takes many unexpected twists and turns that only your spouse or significant other can help you navigate.

Healing Partner – This person is someone you trust to be a Jack or Jill of all trades, so to speak. They are your go-to, multi-purpose support person with a high level of dedication to your healing commitment. Sorry, spouses/significant others are excluded from this place on the team.

Naturopathic Physician – Often, survivors dislike taking medication of any kind. Enlisting a naturopath to your Healing Team will help you feel better about supporting the needs of your mind and body through the use of nutrition and natural supplements.

Chiropractic Doctor – When your body cries out in an effort to get your attention to the healing needs of your mind, you need a professional who can open the communication line between your brain and the rest of your body, so it can do what it does naturally—heal. Don't miss out on adding this important member to your team!

Massage Therapist – Often PTSD manifests in chronic holding patterns found in the muscle tissue, called body armor. One surefire method of unlocking cellular memory, chronic tension and fear responses is massage. No fluff-n-buff here! Only a PTSD-informed therapist will do.

WHAT ABOUT MY REGULAR DOCTOR?

If you've lived with the aftereffects of trauma for very long, you've likely exhausted the efforts of your primary care physician in finding explanations for symptoms such as:

- Digestive discomfort

- Headaches

- Dizziness

- Insomnia

- Fatigue

- Jaw/tooth pain

- Unexplained weight gain/loss

However, don't forget to include him or her on your healing journey! Let your regular physician know about the team you're building. Ask them not only to work with you, but also to work with the advice you glean from other professionals. Most doctors are interested in learning more about treating PTSD symptoms and will welcome your openness.

The primary key to making your Healing Team a successful part of the overall healing journey is communication. Share what you're trying out, what works best for you, and the knowledge you've gained with all the members of your team! It's important for all Healing Team members to know if you're trying medication, supplements or the do-it-yourself healing activities recommended here in *PTSD Self Help*. If they know what's going on in all areas of your life, they can better assist you if bumps in the road occur.

RECRUITING A MENTAL HEALTH PROFESSIONAL

People burdened with Post Traumatic Stress are no longer satisfied with simply surviving. They long to thrive! That means old therapy methods focused on exorcising a disorder need some revamping. As I've already mentioned, successful recovery from PTSD requires a holistic approach that addresses the entire individual, not just their mental state; however, next to yourself, the second most important member of your Healing Team is a PTSD-informed, strengths-based mental health profession (MHP).

Hiring an MHP who acknowledges the strengths a survivor uses to not only endure the original trauma, but also to continue living an every-day life is paramount. However, making sure they also understand the myriad of ways PTSD wreaks emotional and behavioral havoc upon the lives of survivors is just as important. These two elements—strengths used to survive and symptom manifestation—must be present in an MHP's understanding and professional experience in order to expedite a complete healing process. Hire the right professional, and as you abandon old, unhealthy ways of coping with PTSD symptoms, you'll easily overcome the common feelings of vulnerability every survivor experiences as new, healthy coping behaviors set in.

Remember, you're hiring one of the most important members of your team, so you have the right to shop around. Unfortunately, passivity and low self-esteem brought on by years of struggling with PTSD's effects could keep you from making the best choice. When you finally reach the point where you're desperate for the help of a mental health professional, you're probably not in the best frame of mind to do the research required to make an informed choice. Hopefully, *PTSD Self Help* found its way into your hands long before desperation overtook you, and you're reading this as a proactive step in developing a healing plan. If not, and you find yourself in the midst of a healing crisis, help is found by relying on your Healing Team. Here's an example of how two key members' roles play out using the *PTSD Self Help* method:

A Healing Partner can assist by researching mental health professionals in your local area. Once you, your Healing Partner, and your Significant

Other discuss together the qualifications and relevant experience of likely candidates, a top five list is formed. Your Significant Other can then call to make inquiries about each candidate's qualifications and set interview appointments. When the day of your interview appointment comes, it's entirely up to you. You are the only person who can choose this integral member of your team, so plan to not only interview only one candidate in a day, but also rest and recover from each appointment.

MENTAL HEALTH PROFESSIONALS - WHO ARE THEY? WHAT DO THEY DO?

Even with the help of others in locating a likely MHP candidate, a multitude of options are available. Which professional will provide you with the care you need to see the PTSD healing journey through to the end? There's nothing worse than having to switch to another therapist at what could be a crucial turning point in your healing process. Having to tell your story over and over again in an effort to get both medical and mental health professionals on the same page becomes exhausting, shifting the focus toward a rehashing of the trauma instead of moving you forward toward a resolution of the past and the inevitable healing that waits for you in the future.

There are six types of licensed mental health professionals practicing in every state across America. Each state provides their own licensure (and varying titles) for a professional to practice. However, mental health professionals, regardless of their title, are regulated by both federal and state laws which protect clients and define the scope of a professional's practice.

Also, every state requires a mental health professional to obtain a master's degree or doctorate degree in counseling/psychology or related field, demonstrate supervised clinical experience and pass a state licensing exam. Additionally, if they are a member of a professional organization or have additional certifications, they must adhere to that organization's or certifying body's code of ethics. Certifications and professional memberships are voluntary; however, since state licensure requires on-going continuing education and verification of credentials, most professionals will align with a prominent organization.

When interviewing a mental health professional, ask them for a copy of their credentials, then verify with each organization that the professional's status is up to date. You can check out the National Board for Certified Counselors to verify the credentials of a counselor in your state, the American Board of Psychiatry (to not only verify credentials but also to locate a psychiatrist in your state) or the American Board of Professional Psychology (to do the same for a psychologist).

Next, you'll learn about six common titles for an MHP, along with definitions of what they do, to help you in your search for a therapist who:

- Understands how trauma affects your behavior, relationships and physical health

- Seeks to discover and educate you about the strengths and natural abilities you've used to survive

- Assigns healing tasks for you to do outside of scheduled appointments

- Is willing to collaborate with you and other professionals on your Healing Team toward a holistic approach in healing PTSD and its symptoms

- Has the resources at hand to move you through the healing journey from beginning to end

PSYCHIATRIST (PHD, PSYD)

Psychiatrists have a license to practice medicine and can order diagnostic laboratory tests, prescribe medications, provide psychotherapy, evaluate and treat psychological and interpersonal problems, and give continuing care for psychiatric problems. Psychiatrists are also prepared to intervene with individuals and families who are experiencing a crisis or dealing with great stress. Psychiatrists may also act as consultants to primary care physicians, or to non-physicians such as psychologists, social workers and nurses.

PSYCHOLOGIST (LP)

Psychologists are trained in the use of techniques based on experiential relationship building, dialogue, communication and behavior change. Psychologists employ these methods in conjunction with psychological testing to aid in diagnosis and treatment to alleviate mental distress as opposed to the medical model used by psychiatrists. Psychologists generally do not prescribe medication, but they do rely upon therapies such as behavioral, cognitive, humanistic, existential, psychodynamic, and systematic approaches. The American Psychological Association recognizes training for psychologists as being either "applied" or "research" oriented. You'll want to find a psychologist who is a "practitioner," a clinical psychologist or counseling psychologist as opposed to a clinical researcher, scientist or teacher.

LICENSED PROFESSIONAL COUNSELOR (LPC)

Generally, counselors are permitted to screen a client's level of mental impairment using the DSM-5 and may guide a client in adjusting to life situations, developing new skills and making desired changes. Each state defines the scope of practice for an LPC. For example, Washington State requires that an LPC not be the sole provider for a client with a global assessment of functioning score of sixty or less. Search Google for the requirements in your state by using the search terms "scope of practice for a Licensed Professional Counselor in" and include the abbreviation for your state.

LICENSED MENTAL HEALTH COUNSELOR (LMHC)

A mental health counselor typically combines traditional psychotherapy with a practical, problem-solving approach for change and problem resolution. An LMHC can provide assessment, diagnosis, treatment planning, brief and solution-focused therapy, crisis management, as well as alcoholism and substance abuse treatment. Most states' licensure requirements are equivalent to those for social workers and marriage/family therapists; however, each state defines an LMHC's limitations of practice. Search Google for the requirements in your state by using the search terms "scope of practice for a Licensed Mental Health Counselor in" and include the abbreviation for your state.

LICENSED MARRIAGE AND FAMILY THERAPIST (LMFT, MFT)

Marriage and family therapists are permitted to practice some form of evaluation, assessment or identification of varying mental health conditions, as well as apply counseling techniques as they relate to individuals, couples, families or groups involving interpersonal relationships. Your state defines exactly what an LMFT can and cannot do. Search Google for the requirements in your state by using the search terms "scope of practice for a Licensed Marriage and Family Therapist in" and include the abbreviation for your state.

Social Worker (MSW, CSW, LSW, LCSW, DCSW, LMSW)

Social workers, often the first to diagnose and treat people with emotional and behavioral disturbances, can be found practicing at community mental health centers, hospitals, substance use treatment and recovery programs, schools, primary health care centers, child welfare agencies, aging services, employee assistance programs, and private practice settings. Social workers focus on the mental, emotional and behavioral well-being of individuals, couples, families and groups by centering on a holistic approach to therapy with an emphasis on the client's relationship with his/her environment.

Social workers generally can provide clinical intervention with individuals, families and groups, should be knowledgable about community services and make appropriate referrals, be accessible during emergency and non-emergency situations, maintain access to professional supervision and/or consultation, and maintain cultural competency.

Once again, social workers are regulated by each individual state. Search Google for the requirements in your state by using the search terms "scope of practice for a Clinical Social Worker in . . . " and include the abbreviation for your state.

Don't see a string of letters that match what your potential therapist claims as credentials? *Psychology Today's* website has more information on line about credentials that are not listed.

Basics To Remember

Here are a few tips from author E. Sue Blume of *Secret Survivors* for adding a PTSD informed, strengths-based professional to your team:

- Choose an adult-onset or childhood trauma specialist (If you need to use therapist run services at a public clinic, choose family service agencies rather than mental health clinics.)

- Choose a therapist that respects your decision to screen him/her and is willing to answer your questions

- Choose someone who is "strengths focused" and will honor what you did to survive

- Choose a therapist who will recommend reading and emotional work outside of your visits

- Choose, most of all, a therapist you can talk to (Do you feel accepted and listened to? Is power shared?)

You can find helpful bios and contact information for therapists in your local area online through *Psychology Today*'s therapist finder. It's vital that you select a therapist that's a good match for meeting your needs, so be sure to interview each one before making a commitment.

INTERVIEW QUESTIONS AND CONSIDERATIONS

Here are two revealing questions to ask a potential therapist: "When is sexual abuse/incest/molestation the fault of the child?" and "When is PTSD the fault of the survivor?" (Ask it plainly, just like that). Any answer other than, "NEVER!" should send you out the door. Additional information you'll want to consider, including specific questions to ask, has been compiled from the books *I Can't Get Over It!* and *The Courage to Heal*. These questions are relevant to recruiting a therapist, as well as investigating therapeutic PTSD recovery program qualifications.

- Do they view the trauma as real and important, separate from any pre-existing psychological or current social, family or personal issues?

- Do they see you as a survivor capable of being healed (not as a willing participant in the trauma)?

- Will they educate you about PTSD, secondary wounding, specific factors in your category of trauma that may affect you, and the healing process?

- Can they either teach you coping skills (such as, assertiveness, stress management, relaxation techniques, anger management) or make appropriate referrals to you to receive such help?

- Do they use medication when appropriate, and pair it with behavior-management techniques?

- Will they offer a balanced examination of your present and your past with the goal of understanding what occurred and your feelings about those events?

- Will they avoid sex-role stereotyping, racism and blame-the-victim attitudes when guiding you through the healing process?

PRACTICAL CONSIDERATIONS

- What are the fees?

- Is there a sliding scale?

- How are payments made?

- What happens if you miss an appointment?

- Are there any openings for a new client?

- Are the available time slots workable for your schedule?

- Does the therapist seem warm and supportive?

- Is he or she respectful toward you?

- Do you feel as if you could talk with this person about your feelings surrounding the trauma?

- What is your gut feeling about the therapist?

MORE QUESTIONS TO ASK

- How long have you been in practice?

- Are you a member of any professional organizations?

- How many trauma survivors have you seen in therapy?

- What is your background in the area of trauma?

- What, in your view, does the healing process look like for a victim of trauma?

- What experience have you had in treating people suffering from depression/eating disorders/alcoholism? (Gear your questions toward your own struggles.)

- How much and what kind of training have you had in these areas?

- What approaches would you take toward healing depression/eating disorders/alcoholism?

- What techniques do you use when working with survivors?

- Are you willing to work with and consult other professionals, such as a nutritionist, naturopath, psychiatrist or other physician?

- What would you do if I became suicidal?

- What is your view on self help or group therapy? Would you support my decision to participate in either of these?

- Do you also conduct family therapy? Can you recommend a PTSD-qualified professional who does?

- How do you communicate with your clients outside of appointments? Do you accept phone calls or email? To your office only or also at home? Is there a charge for time spent on phone calls/email?

Healing from PTSD is an ongoing education. You learn more than you thought you could about yourself, the healthcare system, relationships and psychology, so don't be shy about asking your therapist questions that are important to you—not only in the beginning, but also throughout your healing journey.

Getting Your Spouse on the Team

If you're without a special someone in your life when you discover you're ready to commit to healing from PTSD, you have a lot to be thankful for! You're facing a wonderful opportunity to relinquish troublesome behaviors, ways of thinking and emotional baggage, and in effect, creating a clean slate for welcoming that special someone into your life in the future.

For couples who suddenly find themselves facing the PTSD healing process well into their relationship, this is a once-in-a-lifetime opportunity to create an unbreakable relationship! It is likely your coupledom is no stranger to garden variety difficulties. However, finding one half of your partnership reduced to emotional jello with no end in sight can be daunting. Welcome to the in-sickness-and-in-health wedding disclaimer (just keepin' it real, here). Seize the chance to experience the rich and rewarding benefits of conquering a seemingly insurmountable foe together!

As you now know, it wasn't always understood that successful recovery from PTSD requires a holistic approach that addresses the entire individual, not just their mental state. Since we are relational beings, it is wise to include our most trusted relationships in the process. It's easy to isolate yourself when daily survival is at the top of your list. However, healing from PTSD cannot be done alone. As a survivor, there are specific things you need to do in order to enter the PTSD healing journey as a responsible spouse or significant other. They are:

Shift
Your PTSD struggle has shifted. This isn't just about you anymore. In order to heal from PTSD successfully *and* retain a healthy partnership with your loved one, you and your spouse/significant other must wrap your minds around a new concept; being allies working toward a common goal. You'll either become invincible allies or terrible foes. It all starts here, with your thought life.

Ask
It is probably no mystery to your spouse/significant other that you haven't been acting like yourself. However, it is important to respect your relationship enough to ask for your loved one's help, instead of

just assuming it will be there. Your partner will have their own set of issues to ponder and decisions to make as a result of your commitment to the PTSD healing process, so it's only fair to give them a choice in the matter. Ask them to partner with you and your Healing Team of professionals in overcoming this challenge to your relationship. Then, promise to resource each other with helpful information and insight as you work through healing PTSD together (be sure to check out the *PTSD Self Help* website for Support for Spouses).

BE TRANSPARENT

Remember, you didn't create the difficulties you're both facing. The trauma was something that happened *to* you, so try to overcome the fear of communicating openly with your spouse about how you're feeling throughout the healing process. Doing so frankly and respectfully, although difficult at times, reinforces one of the cornerstones in your relationship: trust.

BELIEVE

Choose to believe in change and love. The good news is, being in a love relationship during the healing process means your relationship is growing. It is not stagnant or dying, even if at times the process becomes difficult. Your relationship will never be the same again, because *you* won't be the same; you and your relationship will be better. Choose to focus on the deeper character qualities that you fell in love with, and see your partner not as a victim of your inability to cope, but as a courageous person willing to do whatever it takes to help your relationship be healthy.

CHOOSING A HEALING PARTNER

One key member of your Healing Team is a Healing Partner. Similar to a "sponsor" in the well-known twelve-step program Alcoholics Anonymous, a Healing Parter agrees to be a point of accountability and source for practical assistance. For example, a Healing Partner might agree to meet with you once a week to hear about what you've learned from your research time and/or other members of your Healing Team. Knowing that you have a set appointment to update someone on your progress will keep you focused on moving forward, when it might be tempting to isolate or take a break as a form of denial or avoidance.

Another way a Healing Partner can be effective is by being a source of help. On occasion, the PTSD healing process can become a heavy burden. Survivors sometimes wonder if it would just be easier to live with the pain. Trust me—it's not! More than that, it's dangerous. Your healing partner could agree to help you in practical ways like:

- Researching potential Healing Team professionals in your area

- Making appointments

- Cooking a meal or two

- Helping out around the house

- Driving you around or running errands

- Reading resource material along with you

- Taking your mind off of healing once in awhile

You'll want to avoid asking your Healing Partner to do things that would be more appropriate for your spouse to attend to (decide with your spouse what those things are). Also, things that are a consistent part of creating a schedule and environment for healing might be more appropriate if assigned to other people, like hiring a house cleaner or baby sitter.

Your Healing Partner's role is to serve you—and yes, by cleaning house or watching the kids, they are in a roundabout way helping you. However, when implemented properly, a Healing Partner can shave years off of the healing journey. Aren't you ready to put PTSD behind you forever, *now?*

Properly utilizing a Healing Partner means:

They provide direct assistance to you on a personal level. Think of it like having a personal assistant who can pick up the loose ends for you, in a sense, acting on your behalf.

You trust them. As you may have gathered, choosing a Healing Partner requires a certain level of trust, since you will be sharing your entire healing journey with them. Choose wisely.

They are one member of a team. To rely entirely on one person to help you through the healing process is a recipe for a long and arduous journey. A Healing Partner is only effective when they know they are a part of an entire of team of people, including some outstanding professionals, who are on board to help as well.

Here are some ideas from *The Courage to Heal* about people you might consider recruiting for the Healing Partner role on your PTSD Healing Team:

- Another survivor

- A member of a support group

- A nurturing friend

- A compassionate family member

- A sibling who was also abused

Once you've chosen someone, it's important to respectfully ask them to participate in your healing journey. Do so clearly, outlining your expectations. Be transparent about your limitations. Make it clear that although they might be a great friend or close family member, you are asking them to take on a different role for an unknown amount of time.

Be prepared. They may not agree to partner with you. Don't take this personally! Often, when people react strongly or distance themselves upon hearing about your PTSD struggle, they are doing so out of their own pain and unresolved past. Your decision to heal from PTSD might remind them about how much they've neglected their own need to heal.

If you encounter resistance, thank the person for hearing your request. Assure them that you still feel the same about them and your relationship. Let them know that because you are entering into an intensive healing journey, you might be out of touch for awhile and that your absence/silence is nothing personal; then move on to asking the next person you have in mind. Need a little extra help? Check out *PTSD Self Help.com* for scripts you can use to gather your thoughts about asking for help.

Finding a Naturopathic Physician

Many survivors struggle with taking medication. The reluctance to take medication, from aspirin to cold medicine to anti-depression/anxiety meds, stems from the fear of losing control. Not only does a survivor's original trauma have roots in making a person feel victimized, but also the steamroller effect of physical and emotional PTSD symptoms make a person feel out of control—another form of victimization. Child abuse, rape, natural disaster, or wartime battles are all events that act upon us, usually without warning, deeply imbedding the sense of the event as having been beyond your control.

One way to overcome this fear, as it relates to helping support your mind and body's attempts to heal, is to employ the services of a naturopathic physician. These special doctors combine modern science with the wisdom of nature to focus on holistic, proactive prevention. They also are dedicated to complete diagnosis and treatment of physical ailments.

Naturopaths ascribe to the belief that the human body has a built-in ability to restore and maintain good health. They help identify and remove barriers to good health by helping you create a healing internal and external environment. Also called NDs, they are trained to utilize prescription drugs, although most emphasize the use of natural healing agents.

Consider carefully the use of prescription medication, since chemicals will affect your body; side effects can be troublesome and many long term effects are unknown. Why take the chance? You're already committed to becoming the best version of you that you can be. Why not extend that idea to every part of your life?

What PTSD symptoms can a Naturopath help you with? Here are just a few:

• Digestive distress

- Anxiety

- Sleep challenges

- Lack of energy

- Fogginess of mind

Naturopaths are great for helping you figure out how you might be sabotaging yourself though nutritional and lifestyle choices. Additionally, if you have chronic issues unrelated to PTSD, such as allergies, PMS, or inflammation, a naturopath can help address the distraction they bring to your focus on healing PTSD. My motto is "Do everything you can to address your symptoms by changing your lifestyle and getting advice from well-qualified professionals; then, you can be sure that whatever is still bugging you is likely related to the original trauma."

Ready to find a naturopath who can help you unravel the mystery about your PTSD symptoms? You'll want someone who:

- You feel comfortable being honest with

- Will take time to address your concerns

- Can and will educate you about how your body works

- Takes all aspects of your life into consideration

- Understands physical manifestations of PTSD symptoms

Check your medical insurance. Most major providers cover some form of naturopathic medicine, usually only requiring you to pay a co-payment for face-to-face meetings with the doctor, but making you pay for any supplements out of pocket. Considering the cost of prescription medication, giving supplements a try is worth the savings. To learn more about what a naturopathic physician can do for you and to find one in your local area, the American Association of Naturopathic Physicians is a great place to start!

Choosing A Chiropractor

Have you ever cut your finger only to find it healed itself after a few days? That's your amazing body at work keeping you healthy! And guess what? Your body can do the same thing to heal your mind. This is how it works: Your brain sends "healing" signals down your spine to the rest of your body telling the cells in your body to be healthy. If your spine is pinched in certain areas, the signal to heal can't get through. Going to a chiropractor can help keep your spine straight, so the signal to heal can get through fast.

Spinal adjustments performed by a chiropractor correct misalignments in the bones of the spine. These misalignments, called subluxations, can create pressure on and irritation of spinal nerves, resulting in an interruption of nerve energy and a myriad of symptoms throughout your body. According to Dr. John Duppenthaler at Maritime Chiropractic, in Gig Harbor, Washington, "New studies are telling us that it doesn't require misalignments to create an interruption of nerve functioning. A spine with limited motion or a locked structure can create nerve interference, too."

Symptoms like numbness, soreness, weakness or localized pain (including headaches) could be signs of subluxation. By receiving adjustments, you can restore your body to its natural state of health. For PTSD survivors, this means clearing the pathways your mind uses to heal itself. Two things that can cause subluxation are physical traumas and emotional stress. Dr. Duppenthaler says, "We've seen people in our office who have experienced extreme emotional stress, and their spine resembles the spine of someone who has suffered physical trauma. "

Since the primary muscles in your back hold and anchor your spinal bones in their proper position, chronic tension in these important muscles can pull your spine out of alignment or simply create nerve interference. PTSD survivors struggle on a daily basis with the emotional burden of existing in their environment which causes body armoring—a cycle of tension resembling a locked muscle structure.

Making Sense of . . . Chiropractic Benefits

Are you a little squeamish about trying a chiropractor? Give your body the benefit of chiropractic principles by trying a few of the doctor's after-care prescriptions:

BRIDGE
Position:
On back with knees bent and arms at side.

MOVEMENT:
Tighten the abdominal muscles and slightly squeeze the buttocks. Then, tilt the pelvis into a "neutral" position and raise pelvis off the floor. Hold this position for a count of ___ seconds*, then return to the starting position.

Want a challenge? Once in the bridge position as described above, raise one leg bringing the foot approximately 6 inches off the floor. Hold this position for a count of ___ seconds,* then return the foot to the floor. Repeat this movement with the opposite leg.

DEAD BUG
Position:
On back with knees bent and arms at side.

MOVEMENT:
First, tighten the abdominal muscles and slightly squeeze the buttocks in order to press the small of the lower back into the floor, and tilt the pelvis into a "neutral" position. Now, slowly extend one arm above the head and return it back down to the side. Next, perform the same movement with the opposite arm. Perform a total of ___ repetitions.*

Want a challenge? Add the legs! First, tighten the abdominal muscles and slightly squeeze the buttocks in order to press the small of the lower back into the floor and tilt the pelvis into a "neutral" position. Now, slowly lift one foot approximately six inches off the floor, hold it for a count of ___ seconds,* then return it back to the floor. Next, perform the same movement with the opposite leg. Perform a total of

___ repetitions.★

CAT/COW
Position:
Hands and knees on floor in Table Top position.

MOVEMENT
Slowly arch the back upwards and tuck the chin by flexing the head forward and tightening the abdominal muscles—the "cat" position. Hold this position for a count of ___ seconds.★ Then, lift the head upwards and extend the lower back so that the abdominal section hangs downward (Cow position). Hold each position for a count of ___ seconds.★

TABLE TOP STRETCH
Position:
Hands and knees on floor.

MOVEMENT:
In the "on all fours" position, tighten the abdominal muscles and flatten the back to maintain a "neutral spine" position. Next, slowly extend one arm in front of the body, hold for a count of ___ seconds,★ then return to the starting position. Repeat this movement with the opposite arm. Perform a total of ___ repetitions.★

Want a challenge? In the "on all fours" position, tighten the abdominal muscles and flatten the back to maintain a "neutral spine" position. Next, slowly extend one arm in front of the body while simultaneously extending the opposite side leg backwards, hold for a count of ___ seconds,★ then return to the starting position. Repeat this movement with the opposite arm and leg. Perform a total of ___ repetitions.★

IMPORTANT: If this or any other stretch/exercise causes pain, tingling, numbness or other abnormality discontinue and contact your chiropractic or regular physician's office immediately. Attempting to perform these exercises/stretches without regard to proper instructions or pain, tingling, numbness or other abnormality could result in serious injury or a worsening of existing conditions.

* Begin any exercise routine slowly by performing one to three repetitions or holding a position for 30 seconds; then build up to more repetitions and time as you feel comfortable. Don't forget to talk to your doctor about starting a new exercise program. It's important to make sure you're physically able to exercise safely.

For this reason alone, if you are a PTSD survivor, you would benefit from investigating the possibility of chiropractic care, especially if your traumatic event also included a physical assault or other trauma to the body. "I want people to understand that their normal state of being is one of great vitality, and my goal is to simply remove the interference, to restore motion and fluidity to the spine," remarks Dr. Duppenthaler. "Seeing a chiropractor regularly can break the tension cycle." You'll find most chiropractors feel the same, which is why you want a great one on your PTSD Healing Team! It is my opinion that no chiropractor should make an adjustment without first examining X-rays of your spine, so during your search, you should determine whether or not a chiropractor uses X-rays. Also, inquire about what kind of techniques a chiropractor uses to adjust the spine. Some chiropractors use their hands in a low-force method of manipulating the spine, while others use much deeper methods or even instruments to achieve the best results for your condition. You should ask how long the sessions last and how often you will require this chiropractic treatment program. At this time, you should determine if a practitioner uses other chiropractic techniques such as nutritional counseling, rehabilitation and strength training. One important thing to learn is if it's the chiropractor's policy to refer you to other practitioners if the chiropractic treatment program is not as effective as it could be.

Worried about the money? A lot of providers offer great deals for first-time visitors and convenient payment options. Most chiropractors will give you a free initial consultation. Best of all, they understand how chiropractic can help you feel better right away. When it comes to healing from PTSD, you can't put a price on your health!

A directory like the American Chiropractic Association or ChiropractorGuide.com is a great place to gather more information like this short list of suggestions from ChiropractorGuide.com:

METHODS

One great way to find the right chiropractor is through personal references. For instance, obtaining chiropractor recommendations from a medical doctor is an excellent start. Also, references from co-workers and friends can be helpful. If these individuals recommend the same chiropractor, you may have an example of an effective practitioner.

MEETING YOUR NEEDS

That said, it is important that a chiropractor meets your unique needs exactly. For example, it is an excellent idea to find out exactly what educational and practical experience a chiropractor has in aiding your specific health issue. At this time, it is also a good idea to determine where the chiropractor went to school and exactly how long the chiropractor has been actively practicing.

ACCREDITATION AND REPUTATION

You should also ensure that any prospective chiropractor is accredited by the Council on Chiropractic Education. Furthermore, it is a good idea to determine whether or not the chiropractor in question has received any disciplinary actions against him or her. To obtain this information, simply check with each state's Chiropractic Board of Examiners – this information is often available on their respective websites. If you have health insurance, you can also ask your insurance company if the chiropractors have had any complaints in the past. Additionally, to be cautious, you should ask a chiropractor for references from both former and current patients.

X-RAY USE

As mentioned earlier, it is my opinion that no chiropractor should make an adjustment without first examining X-rays of your spine. You should determine whether or not a chiropractor uses X-rays. Some chiropractors take X-rays as a standard procedure while other chiropractors only take X-rays in certain situations. In the cases of bone disease such as arthritis, trauma injuries, long-standing pain that is unresponsive to treatment, and in the elderly, X-rays should definitely be taken. When these x-rays are taken you should ensure that there is a correlation between your pain and the X-ray. If a chiropractor states that you should have treatment in a particular area, and yet you feel no pain in this area, it's advisable to obtain a second opinion from another chiropractor.

Practical Details

You should also determine some basic practical information about a potential chiropractor's practice. If you can't make daytime appointments, choose a chiropractor that offers nighttime hours. You should determine if your health insurance covers all or some of the treatment with a certain chiropractor. In cases where insurance is denied, determine beforehand if your chiropractor will then offer you these services at a discount. If health insurance coverage is not an option for you, determine whether or not you can afford a particular chiropractor's services, and if these rates are comparable to other chiropractors in your area. At this time, it may be a good idea to find out if a chiropractor also offers discounts for volume and/or immediate cash payments.

Likeability Factor

Last but not least, you should feel "at ease" and communicate well with your chiropractor. You should determine whether or not the chiropractor listens to you and offers explanations in a manner that is complete and respectful. While this characteristic is not a tangible one, patients do tend to heal better when there is effective communication between patients and caregivers.

Overall, it may take some effort to determine if a particular chiropractor is the right fit for you, but in the end, you will surely be glad that you took the time to go through this highly effective screening process.

Ready to find yourself a great chiropractor? To find a provider near you and ask about a consultation, be sure to head on over to ChiropractorGuide.com and get more expert advice! You can also find a link to ChiropractorGuide.com on the *PTSD Self Help* website.

Choosing a Massage Therapist

It's easy to find a compassionate, skilled massage therapist that will recognize the needs of your body. However, it might be more difficult to find one that understands PTSD's emotional triggers. PTSD survivors report a remarkable decrease or total elimination of the following symptoms when massage and acupressure is used in conjunction with PTSD-informed psychotherapy:

- Depression

- Anxiety

- Headaches

- Insomnia

- Chronic muscle tension

- Fogginess of mind

- Disconnectedness

Seeing my massage therapist every two weeks increased by body's ability to cope with the mental challenges of healing from PTSD. Doing the mental work of remembering what I could, then experiencing the feelings connected to those memories was an essential part of grieving what I lost as a ten-year-old girl.

As a result, the muscles in my neck, shoulders and lower back were groaning with residual toxins left behind, thanks to my brain's cascade of powerful chemicals. Usually, after having a deep tissue/acupressure/reflexology treatment, awarenesses and understanding that I just couldn't reach from my psychologist's couch would descend on my mind over the next several days. PTSD would still be a reality for me if it weren't for my massage therapist's help. My body would have hindered my emotional healing.

Authors Michael Gach and Beth Henning explain in their book *Acupressure for Emotional Healing* that tension and pain accumulate at certain points within the body and, ". . . as a point is held, muscular tension yields to finger pressure, enabling the fibers of the muscle to elongate and relax, blood to flow freely, and toxins to be released and eliminated."

As a PTSD survivor, here are some things you'll want to communicate to a massage therapist before you get on the massage table:

- Your level of comfort with being touched

- Your level of comfort with not being able to see the therapist at all times

- How much clothing you're willing to take off

- Your need to be told exactly what is going to happen and why

- Ask the therapist to help you practice breathing and visualization during the massage

As you begin to tune back in to your body through the therapies suggested by your PTSD Healing Team, you'll discover other needs your body is trying to tell you about. Listen! It could mean the difference between seeing relief within weeks instead of months or years. Then, consider trying one of these forms of massage defined by the folks at MassageTherapy.com:

ACUPRESSURE
Also called trigger point therapy, utilizes steady, firm pressure applied by the fingers to press key points on the surface of the skin to release your body's natural pain-relieving chemicals called endorphins.

DEEP TISSUE
Similar to acupressure, this therapy can accomplish the same results as acupressure by applying pressure to an entire set of muscles to affect the sub-layer of musculature and fascia. This technique requires advanced training and a thorough understanding of anatomy and physiology. The muscles must be relaxed before deep-tissue massage, otherwise tight surface muscles prevent the practitioner from reaching deeper musculature, resulting in bruising of your skin.

SWEDISH
A vigorous system of treatment designed to energize the body by stimulating circulation. Therapists use a combination of kneading, rolling, vibrational, percussive, and tapping movements, with the application of oil to reduce friction on the skin. The many benefits of Swedish massage may include generalized relaxation, dissolution of scar tissue adhesions, and improved circulation, which may speed healing and reduce swelling from injury.

LOMILOMI

Similar to Swedish massage in many aspects, this system of massage utilizes very large, broad movements. Two-handed, forearm, and elbow application of strokes, which cover a broad area, is characteristic of lomilomi. Also, this system uses prayer and the acknowledgment of the existence of a higher power as an integral part of the technique. Lomilomi–Hawaiian for *rub rub*–is known as ". . . the loving touch–a connection between heart, hand, and soul with the source of all life."[6]

REFLEXOLOGY

Based on an ancient Chinese therapy, reflexology involves manipulation of specific reflex areas in the foot, hands, and ears that correspond to other parts of the body. Sometimes referred to as zone therapy, this bodywork involves application of pressure to these reflex zones to stimulate body organs and relieve areas of congestion. It is especially useful in stress-related illness and emotional disorders. Reflexology is also convenient in cases where an area of the body is traumatized or diseased to the extent that direct manipulation is not appropriate.

All *licensed* massage therapists are governed by your state (some states don't require licensure) and must adhere to strict regulations, such as proper draping techniques. This means the therapist keeps your body completely covered with a blanket/sheet, with the exception of the part of the body they are working on. For this reason alone, survivors who are shy about stripping off all their clothing can breathe a sigh of relief. Ready to find a Massage Therapist to add to your Healing Team? Connect with the Associated Bodywork & Massage Professionals' public education website, www.MassageTherapy.com—a great online resource to learn more about massage and to find a massage therapist near you.

---

6 http://www.huna.org/html/lomilomi.html

RECRUITING A NATION TO CARE

Every time you turn around, it seems that PTSD is in the news. Unfortunately, the media is the first line of information and education for much of the free world (they don't call it television programming for nothing); consequently, American society-at-large knows only what the media reveals to them about PTSD and its effects. First, let me say that the media doesn't reflect accurate portrayals of PTSD for the same reason veterans are reluctant to be diagnosed with it—to do so might be a career-ender. Consider the billions of dollars being spent out of just a few media moguls' pockets to influence the American public, and you'll understand why media messages all boil down to politics.

The world's largest media conglomerates find their home here in the United States. At the top of the 2010 Fortune 500 list is The Walt Disney Company, followed by News Corp., Time Warner, and Viacom. What are the motivations and intentions of these top four who control the media airwaves? A cursory look at the political alignment of media influencers might reveal a lot about what subjects they support. If they're in any way interested in staying clear of rocking the Department of Defense's boat, they'll also stay clear of the controversy surrounding the devastating impact of PTSD on American soldiers.

However, we, as a nation and as individuals, have a fair share of responsibility for our views about PTSD and those who suffer from it. In a culture addicted to reality television, drama, tragedy and suffering sell. As a result, a few Hollywood creations can be found that somewhat accurately depict various aspects of PTSD symptomology. Ilona Meagher, author of *Moving a Nation to Care: Post Traumatic Stress Disorder and America's Returning Troops* offers an excellent resource list[7] of Vietnam-era films, documentaries, feature films and independent shorts on her blog *PTSD Combat.*

On the flip side, the 2010 feature film *Shutter Island* inspired some hearty online discussion about the need for Hollywood's ethical commitment to appropriately depicting PTSD. There are a number of other films that depict the more tragic aspects of PTSD; however, one of the best depictions I've seen to date was featured on the television series NCIS. By best, I mean an authentic, accurate account of the PTSD struggle from the perspective of multiple survivors choosing to cope with their trauma individually in very different ways. You may want to watch *NCIS: Shell Shock* (Part I & II) Season 10, Episode 6 which aired November 2012.

In many respects, these films have done a lot for increasing the public's awareness of combat-related PTSD. Still, the mainstream film industry falls short of identifying other PTSD survivors and accurately educating audiences, thus leaving enough room for misinformation, fear and the resulting stigma associated with a PTSD diagnosis.

Stories of soldiers succumbing to the debilitating effects of PTSD and the U.S. Department of Veterans Affairs' inability to meet diagnosed veterans' needs have painted a deplorable picture of suffering for veterans. Regrettably, news coverage and mainstream films have remained silent about Americans who have struggled with PTSD long before Iraq or Vietnam—namely women.

Although the media frenzy surrounding our recent war in Iraq and Afghanistan has brought PTSD back to the forefront, film or news reports neglect to capture the reality of actually recovering from it. Consequently, negligence of that sort keeps people wrestling with PTSD symptoms instead of getting the help they need.

---

7 http://ptsdcombat.blogspot.ca/2006/03/at-movies-film-and-ptsd.html

THE ORIGINS OF PTSD STIGMA AND RAPE CULTURE

Even a cursory review of the history surrounding the development of Post Traumatic Stress Disorder as a diagnosis reveals at least one deep social stigma. Consequently, those struggling with PTSD symptoms also struggle with trying to get the help they need because of the subtle, social humiliation attached to the diagnosis. It is past time to not only confront the origins of stereotypes surrounding PTSD, but also put a human face on the reality of PTSD stigmatization.

The general public's access to accurate and helpful information about PTSD is improving . . . somewhat. However, unless they go looking for it, their education and understanding of what to look for and how to get help for themselves or someone they love is severely lacking, as expressed in this Tacoma, Washington mother's comment:

> As for my thoughts on PTSD, I don't want to be named. Like many people, my thoughts are a mishmash of half information. I know that PTSD for a soldier is different than for a childhood rape victim, but that's about it.[8]

This woman is the mother of a childhood rape victim who is now an adult. At the time of the rape, social ignorance and stigma kept her from getting the help her daughter needed.

The earliest recorded incidents of what we now call PTSD were identified by the English surgeon John Eric Erichsen (1866, 1886). When male soldiers began exhibiting "cowardice" during battle, Erichsen ". . . warned against confusing symptoms with those of hysteria, a condition that he, and most of his contemporaries, claimed only occurred in women," according to *Handbook of PTSD: Science and Practice*. The social message was clear: men don't get hysteria, and those that do are exhibiting feminine qualities.

Although we now know that PTSD can affect both men and women,

---

8 From an interview I conducted for the article Healing PTSD: Support for Partners, Spouses and Family found at http://www.examiner.com/article/healing-ptsd-support-for-partners-spouses-and-family

we also know that they are not affected in like proportions. General population studies consistently find that women are approximately twice as likely as males to meet criteria for PTSD at some point in their lives. Interestingly, research shows that men are more likely to experience at least one trauma in their lifetime, but women are more likely to experience a trauma with a high probability of developing PTSD.[9]

These findings strengthen the social message that to have PTSD is to identify with feminine qualities; translated in the context of a world still dominated by male leadership, PTSD equals weakness. The findings also implore an obvious question and an underlying disturbing one: Why do women develop PTSD more often than men? and is PTSD being discounted in the public policy arena because its victims are

1. simply women; or

2. men who are viewed as having a feminine quality of acquiring PTSD?

At Joint Base Lewis-McChord in Washington State, military psychologists acknowledge the difficulty in getting soldiers to receive treatment for PTSD, as revealed in an August 7, 2010, news report from KIRO 7 news.[10] Whether from fear of losing their job status, ignorance about PTSD symptoms, or shame at being diagnosed, soldiers often refuse to seek help when they most need it. It is clear that an examination of what drives fear, ignorance and shame associated with a PTSD diagnosis is in order. Moreover, we need a coordinated effort to educate and enlighten society about the reality of living with PTSD, debunk the myths, reveal the criticisms, and examine social policies surrounding the diagnosis.

So, why do women develop PTSD more often than men?

For millennia, women have been viewed as the weaker part of the human equation. Worse, for a substantial period of time, women (and children) have been viewed openly in some cultures and secretly

9 Friedman, Matthew J., Keane, Terence M., & Resick, Patricia A. (Eds.). (2007). Handbook of PTSD: Science and Practice. New York: Guilford Press.

10 http://www.kirotv.com/news/news/army-working-on-virtual-computer-program-to-treat-/nK36n/

in others as property, chattel or commodities. When people are de-humanized, reduced to "things," they become as disposable as your last Starbucks coffee cup.

Regardless of gender, important characteristics that substantiate a PTSD diagnosis are:

- Severity of injury

- Relationship to assailants

- Chronicity

However, statistics show that following crimes that meet those crite-ria, women, not men, consistently developed PTSD. As revealed in *The Handbook of PTSD* ". . . one perspective on PTSD posits that women's greater risk (for PTSD) can be explained by their experience of more severe traumas . . . such as molestation, physical attack, being threatened with a weapon, and childhood physical abuse. No gender differences emerged on rates of PTSD following natural disaster, accidents, and wit-nessing the injury and/or death of another."

Did you know that additional studies surrounding PTSD and its symp-toms have identified that the cultural roles we have assigned to women put them at greater risk for PTSD? According to the authors of *Gender Issues in PTSD*[11]:

> . . . certain social roles function as gender-specific risks for PTSD. For example, women in the roles of mothers and wives were particularly at risk for poorer outcomes. Additionally, being married was a risk factor for poorer outcome among women, but not men.

Social roles aren't the only risk factor. Considering the relational nature of women, it appears their desire for relationship makes them targets for traumatic incidents. Making matters worse, how society treats women after those incidents could actually be contributing to PTSD.

---

11 Friedman, Matthew J., Keane, Terence M., & Resick, Patricia A. (Eds.). (2007). Handbook of PTSD: Science and Practice. New York: Guilford Press.

Women are also more often victims of interpersonal violent crimes associated with negative or stigmatizing social responses, such as rape. Negative social responses experienced by female crime victims may partly explain women's elevated rates of PTSD symptoms . . . however, PTSD symptoms [also] appear to be more prevalent among female patients [because] . . . women [are at] greater risk for these "betrayal" types of chronic, interpersonal violence perpetrated by intimates, such as child sexual abuse or intimate partner violence. (*Gender Issues in PTSD*)

Dare we go a step further to suggest that the majority of violence inflicted upon women is perpetrated by men? The Washington State Department of Health has these statistics to share:

- Approximately one of every six adult women in Washington has been a victim of one or more completed forcible rapes during their lifetime.

- One in five Washington women[12] reports being injured by domestic violence sometime in her lifetime.

- At least thirty percent of all female homicide victims in Washington State[13] are killed by a current or former intimate partner.

- Between 1997 and 2001, more than half of the people murdered in domestic violence-related homicides were women killed by their current or former husbands or boyfriends.

- An estimated ten to twenty percent of emergency department visits by women with intimate partners are a result of domestic violence.

And that's just in my home state. What about where you live? In fact, worldwide statistics consistently show that those who are victimized happen to be women. Violence against women is a war that has been

---

12 http://academicdepartments.musc.edu/ncvc/grants/50_states_reports/washington.pdf
13 http://www.wscadv.org/resourcesPublications.cfm?aId=CAB98E1B-C298-58F6-0553B0606651FABD

raging for centuries, leaving women to suffer with the aftereffects of social stigma and PTSD. These statistics would seem to suggest that women have a weakened ability to process traumatic events. Actually, they reveal society's endorsement of a rape culture. What is a rape culture? According to the authors of *Transforming A Rape Culture*, it is beliefs that encourage male sexual aggression and support violence against women.

OVERCOMING A RAPE CULTURE: BE A CHANGE AGENT

Do you know a woman? Of course you do. We all have a mom, grandma, friend or co-worker who is a woman. Some people are blessed enough to also have a sister, aunt or daughter. What you don't know about the women in your life is that nearly all of them bear a closely held burden.

The organization Darkness to Light[14] reports that for every four women you know, one of them has experienced some form of childhood sexual abuse—and was brave enough to tell someone. Potentially, two of those four women have had age inappropriate sexual contact and never told anyone. There would be no statistics at all if women remained as silent as they had until the early eighties. Let's honor and bring hope to those who have yet to find the courage to speak out by not turning away from the reality of childhood sexual abuse and its aftereffects. Here's something else you don't know about the women survivors in your life: most are still suffering from the aftereffects of their childhood sexual abuse, and they don't know it. The aftereffects such as anxiety, depression, being overweight, or having a "disconnected" feeling can be debilitating and can occur over a lifetime, culminating into the diagnosis known as Post Traumatic Stress Disorder.

And, if you didn't know this, you should! You can help! Begin a transformation revolution for women in your home state. Pass this book along to women you know. Commit to becoming informed about Post Traumatic Stress Disorder. Seek out media messages loaded with wisdom, resources and restoration for women survivors and the people who love them. The women in your life will be transformed and love

---

14 http://www.d2l.org/site/c.4dICIJOkGcISE/b.6035035/k.8258/Prevent_Child_Sexual_Abuse.htm#.UmnL4GTwJQM

you for it. If we ever hope to transform our tendency as a rape culture, we must be willing to courageously look at the foundational beliefs we hold about women and children.

OVERCOMING A RAPE CULTURE: MALE VICTIMS OF DOMESTIC VIOLENCE

Think it doesn't happen? You'd be wrong. Like the recent revelations about child sexual abuse perpetrated against boys within the Catholic church, people are surprised to hear about this cause for PTSD in the male population. Not many statistical studies have been done to track male victims of female perpetrated intimate partner violence. This is unfortunate, because statistical studies are what generate funding for prevention and treatment. In the interest of overcoming social stigma, let's examine this by starting with what we know about PTSD.

Studies say that for men, there is a high level of risk for developing PTSD associated with:

- Combat

- Childhood neglect

- Childhood abuse

- Being molested

Interestingly, the common traumatic events leading to PTSD for women are:

- Being threatened with a weapon

- Being physically attacked

- Childhood neglect

- Childhood physical abuse

- Sexual molestation

Hmmm . . . I don't know about you, but the word *combat* and the phrases *threatened with a weapon* or *physically attacked* describe similar traumatic incidents to me. Military veterans would agree that combat includes being threatened with a weapon and being physically attacked. Moreover, men and women who have been terrorized in their own home with guns or physical abuse would agree that life seemed like a war zone. The difference in terminology apparently lies in whether you're talking about men or women—and possibly, the label used to describe the circumstances surrounding the traumatic incident. Now let's look at what the American Bar Association's Commission on Domestic Violence has to say about male victims of Intimate Partner Violence. Here are some fast facts:

- 835,000 men are physically assaulted by an intimate partner annually in the United States.

- In the year 2000, 440 men were killed by an intimate partner. In recent years, an intimate partner killed approximately four percent of male murder victims.

- Between 1998 and 2002, almost 3.5 million violent crimes were committed against family members; forty-nine percent of these were crimes against spouses.

- 370,990 men are stalked annually in the United States; thirty percent of those male victims are stalked by an intimate partner.

What do you think? Putting these two perspectives together, male or female, if you were threatened with a weapon, physically attacked or overpowered by someone you've shared intimate relations with, would it leave a deep emotional wound? If you are a woman, the numeric language of science speaks a resounding "Yes!" and a much quieter "We don't know," if you happen to be a male victim of Intimate Partner Violence. Although there are documented links between Intimate Partner Violence and PTSD, unfortunately, the numbers only represent incidents occurring to women.

PTSD STIGMA: WHAT DOES IT LOOK LIKE?

Each time stigmatization occurs in the life of a survivor, the door to suicide is opened. If you're feeling suicidal (or know someone with PTSD who does), either stigmatization has occurred, or someone has inflicted pain through the carelessness of their words. Understanding subtle discrimination and stigmatization can be the first step toward releasing yourself from the impact of these deadly triggers. So, let's take a look, shall we? Closely tied to secondary wounding, stigmatization occurs because of:

Ignorance: People who have never been hurt sometimes have difficulty understanding and being patient with people who have. Then, there are some people who are just not strong enough to accept the negative, ugly and painful side of life. Surprisingly, survivors who have chosen to reject or bottle up their own trauma will snub or ridicule other survivors to block out their own need for healing and to keep their system of denial intact.

There are few courses in violence prevention offered to medical, legal or mental health professionals—and *none* are offered in our elementary, secondary or higher education system. Where such training exists, it is rare to find sufficient levels of funding to devote adequate training hours to the subject of violence prevention.

Burnout: Many helping professions come with the inherent risk of emotional depletion. Moreover, people who enter into those professions often do so because of their own personal experiences. Consequently, it's entirely possible that helping professionals such as police, rescue workers, doctors, and emergency room staff are themselves suffering from PTSD.

A "Just" World Philosophy: The basic assumption that people get what they deserve is a common philosophy. Therefore, people who suffer trauma are somehow to blame or seen as being inherently weak or ineffectual. Arising out of the human need to have control over one's own life, a "just world" philosophy combats the fear of life's uncertainty by believing that, if you are "sufficiently careful, intelligent, moral, or competent, you can avoid misfortune."

Annmarie's Story

I heard the most hurtful things from the people I expected compassion from. My grandfather said, "Well, just be thankful you didn't have any brothers." A pastor at my church said, "I really think it's just hormones. If you'd take better care of yourself, you wouldn't be causing such a mess in your marriage." My husband said, "You're spending an awful lot of time with your best friend. Are you sleeping with her?" A Christian marriage counselor said, "I don't know anything about PTSD, but you need to stop expecting so much from your husband. He and I really want to help you with your problem." Every time I heard those things, I thought, My God, I'm already struggling to help myself. That's why I'm talking to them. If they can't help me, there's no hope, and I can't live like this.

Making Sense of . . . Secondary Wounding

People are the most important part of healing from PTSD; however, they can also do more harm than good. The devastating effects of ignorance and insensitivity can take many forms resulting in what are called secondary wounding experiences. Many PTSD survivors report that secondary wounding is often more painful and devastating than the original traumatic event. Survivors with PTSD already struggle on a daily basis with numerous challenges to their self-esteem. Secondary wounding intensifies these challenges and their resulting emotional, physical and psychological symptoms. Survivors respond to secondary wounding by going through an overwhelming increase in the following (just to name a few):

- Lowered self-esteem

- Hopelessness

- Helplessness

- Rage

- Depression

- Emotional numbing to the point of separating from their body (depersonalization)

- Deep disappointment

- Disgust with themselves

- A desire to retaliate

What does secondary wounding look like? Secondary wounding can be committed by anyone to whom the survivor turns to for assistance or reveals their PTSD struggle to, such as:

- People close to the survivor (friends, family, spouse, or children)

- Institutions (religious, legal, medical, or assistance related)

- Caregivers (mental health professionals, doctors, parents, healing partner, or teachers)

Secondary wounding occurs by responding negatively to the survivor's account of the trauma, the magnitude of its aftereffects, the meaning to the survivor, or its impact on the survivor's life in one of the following ways:

- Disbelief – doubting or distrusting

- Denial – refusing to believe

- Discounting – dismissing or minimizing through comparisons or outright statements

- Blaming the survivor – on some level, suspecting the survivor deserved it

- Stigmatization – judging the survivor negatively for normal reactions to the trauma or long-term symptoms

- Denial of assistance (discrimination) – withholding necessary, expected services based on a personal or procedural judgment of the survivor's need or lack of entitlement

---

Cultural influence: "Our country is so bountiful and so full of opportunities that anyone who wants the good life can have it; all they have to do is pull themselves up by their own bootstraps." This is hard to do when someone steals your boots.

Generalization: Being labeled as a victim is very difficult to overcome. Once you are socially labeled as a victim, there is a tendency for others to view most of your emotions and behavior from that perspective. Being "emotionally scarred for life" doesn't leave any room for the possibility of healing.

Cruelty: All stigmatization feels cruel. Nevertheless, there are people who intentionally use a survivor's trauma as a weapon to control, manipulate or otherwise inflict abuse. The reality is that these people will find any reason to be cruel. Your trauma just happens to be easy for them to use.

PTSD STIGMA: WHAT DOES IT SOUND LIKE?

Examples of the devastating effects of PTSD ignorance and insensitivity have taken many forms in the news media recently. You see it in shock-value stories about survivor suicides and violent crimes with subtle side notes ("It was reported that he had PTSD"). Unfortunately, these examples result in and perpetuate the stigmatization of PTSD survivors, making them people to be feared, distrusted, or shunned as unproductive members of society. Individuals, institutions, caregivers, people close to the survivor, and even other survivors may be contributing to the social stigma of a PTSD diagnosis—and not know it.

Without a doubt, PTSD healing cannot be accomplished without the help of caring, compassionate people. Although most have good intentions at heart, those same people can also unintentionally do more harm than good. There are really only four possibilities for inadvertently contributing to PTSD stigmatization:

- Responding negatively to the survivor's account of the traumatic incident itself or partial memories of it

- Responding negatively to the survivor's account of the magnitude of the trauma's aftereffects

- Responding negatively to the survivor's account of the meaning of the trauma or the healing journey to the survivor

- Responding negatively to the survivor's account of the impact of the trauma or the healing journey on the survivor's life now

We could all speculate about whether or not we've had thoughts or made statements that cross the boundaries listed above. Maybe you know someone attempting to heal from PTSD (and working hard to do so, I might add). Perhaps you are that person, and feel confused by messages received from people who supposedly love you or are in a position to help. So, just to be sure we're clear about what PTSD stigmatization sounds like in everyday language, let's look at these actual statements made to survivors:

Disbelief – doubting or distrusting
Which sounds like:
You're exaggerating.
I can't believe it!
Are you kidding? That's impossible.
Tell me the real truth.

Denial – refusing to believe
Which sounds like:
It must be your imagination.
You've been watching too much TV.
That could never happen.
There must be some other explanation.
He/she would never hurt you!

Discounting – dismissing or minimizing through comparisons or outright statements
Which sounds like:
It happened so long ago. It's over now.
How could this have affected you that much?
Just get over it!
Come on now, it wasn't that bad. Why, I went through. . .

Blaming the survivor – on some level, suspecting the survivor deserved it
Which sounds like:

I guess that's what you get.
You're doing this to yourself.
You've always been sensitive.
I told you, you shouldn't have. . .
You signed up for the job and its consequences.

Judgment – forming a negative opinion about the survivor for normal reactions to and ways of coping with the trauma, long-term symptoms or the healing path they choose (notice this list is longer)
Which sounds like:
You're just doing this for (attention, money, sympathy).
Wow, you've got some real mental problems, don't you?
Are you gay?
You must not be (praying, repenting, confessing, believing) enough, or you would be healed.
Wow, I wish I had all the time in the world to get massages, go to yoga and hang out with my best friend.
Oh, you've always had to learn the hard way.
You just hate men/women!
You know you're not being a (biblical wife, Proverbs 31 woman, good wife or submitting to your husband) if you withhold sex from him.

Denial of assistance – withholding necessary, expected services or support based on a personal or procedural judgment of the survivor's need or lack of entitlement
Which sounds like:
Let's wait and see if you get better.
Well, can you prove it happened?
There are other people who really need assistance.
I'm sorry. You just haven't demonstrated an urgent need.
If you're crazy, I'm outta here! I didn't sign up for that!
You aren't (praying, reading your Bible, casting out demons, getting to church/temple/synagogue) enough.

You can be sure you are participating in PTSD stigma if you respond in one of the above ways. Whether you're at work or with your family, if you respond directly to a survivor or comment about PTSD to others in this manner, you'll become an accomplice. It might be surprising for you to realize that if you're allowing yourself to be treated in this manner or actually buy in to this derogatory perspective, you're participating in PTSD stigma, too. Remember, it doesn't take a spoken word for stigmatization to occur. If you've thought it (about yourself or others), it's already happened.

All stigmatization, regardless of where it comes from or why, feels cruel to a survivor. Sometimes, it is enough to push them over the edge, cause them to give up and take their own life. For this reason, it is difficult for survivors to determine if stigmatization or secondary wounding occurs from other people's desire to cause pain and inflict abuse, or whether it arises from one of the other known causes of stigma we've already discussed. As you can imagine, for someone who has already suffered so much, it's not surprising survivors have a hard time overcoming trust issues and have a tendency to isolate themselves.

If you are a PTSD survivor, for the most part, strangers who don't know your situation may unintentionally say something cruel. However, so can people who love you most. As difficult as it is, you must break free of the isolation associated with PTSD and secure the help of other people. It's just plain impossible to heal from PTSD without the care and assistance of others. To be sure you're making good choices about who you allow on your Healing Team and who you spend your time with during the healing process, keep the above points in mind.

SEASON OF TRANSFORMATION

LET THE JOURNEY BEGIN!

BRINGING IT ALL TOGETHER

PTSD Self Help presents the concepts, the method and the resources that will put you on the fast track towards leaving PTSD behind forever. It is not necessary to do all of the exercises or implement all of the suggestions recommended in this book. Instead, after recruiting your Healing Team, approach it as an à la carte type program. As you feel more empowered, take on a few more exercises or exercises at a higher level of difficulty.

Begin with *Season of Hope: Plan & Pack* which will change your mind about how you think about PTSD and its involvement in your life. Decide that you'll make a commitment to yourself to walk away from PTSD forever. Then choose not to let anyone, anything, or any story you have created about the healing process—or even yourself—stand in the way of getting what you deserve: an exceptional, extraordinary quality of life.

Next, in *Season of Renewal: Recruiting Your Healing Team*, begin designing a supportive, professional group of folks dedicated to helping you get relief fast and reaching your successful healing goals. Interview, research and recruit one person for each role on the team. Don't leave anyone out! Each member of the team serves to bring you closer to your vision for living a life of wholeness. Leaving a team member off the team would be the same as buying a brand-new pair of hiking boots for your journey, but never putting them on; you're not going to get where you want to be very quickly.

Once your mindset and your Healing Team is in place, you can decide to start your healing journey. That's where we find ourselves now, in *Season of Transformation: Bringing It All Together!* During the process of learning about commitment and recruiting your Healing Team members, your healing was already set in motion. Taking the next step to make healing from PTSD a part of your life every day will come quite naturally.

As you participate in your healing journey, be sure to stay in communication with each of your Healing Team members, sharing information with each one of them in a collaborative way. When you experience a breakthrough working with horses, share that experience with your mental-health professional, your healing partner, and your spouse. You may even find that your massage therapist or your chiropractor has an affinity for horses. Share the experience with them too! They will be amazed by the revelations you've had!

On a more practical level, sharing information collaboratively with your Healing Team will open up additional healing experiences for you. For example, you may be struggling with a season of flashbacks. By sharing this information with your chiropractor, he or she can make additional spinal adjustments that may clear the pathways to help your brain heal more quickly. By sharing this information with your naturopath, he or she may be able to supplement your diet with herbs that can help your mind and body process the old traumatic information that's coming up in a new way. The easiest way to help your Healing Team understand the method that you're undertaking to achieve your healing, is to share this book with them. That way they'll understand exactly what their role is and how they can best work together with your other team members, even recommending and directing you towards those other team members when appropriate.

A WORD ABOUT MARRIAGE

Not every marriage has what it takes to survive the PTSD healing journey. Despite a commitment to one another and to the PTSD healing process, sometimes marriages don't make it. If a marriage fails, it can deliver a crushing blow that is difficult to overcome, and can stall the healing process indefinitely. Worse, it can be the final blow that causes an already overtaxed survivor to take their life. Getting your spouse on board early in the healing journey is not just a nice suggestion—it will save you additional heartache and possibly save your life. If a spouse is unwilling or unable to be at least one hundred percent supportive in your healing efforts, it is best to know this upfront and discuss options you can both agree to should the healing journey become too difficult for your marriage to bear.

In doing this, you and your spouse will, in a sense, be creating an Emergency Plan of Action for your marriage. This way, you can stay on course in reclaiming your life while addressing the needs of your marriage. Furthermore, you'll have assurance that you've made clear-minded decisions about how you will proceed in times when your thinking might become more clouded and emotionally charged. The possibilities for protecting your marriage from disaster are endless but begin with authentic, timely communication; it is especially important to stay open-minded about alternatives that can help you get the healing done while giving your marriage every opportunity to withstand the storm.

It's no surprise that marriages built on a weak foundation can succumb to divorce when exposed to the grueling pressures of PTSD. What many survivors don't expect is for their spouse to refuse to "do whatever it takes" to help them get better—however, it does happen. Even well-meaning spouses can enter into the healing process with their loved one, only to discover part way in that this isn't at all what they signed up for.

The bottom line is this: Whatever weaknesses your marriage has will be magnified a hundredfold by the healing process. You can approach this several ways, depending on the level of healing crisis you're experiencing:

1. Wait to engage the healing process and focus first on strengthening your marriage.

2. Enter into the healing process without your spouse's involvement (your spouse can refuse involvement or you can refuse to allow their involvement. Either way, it's not recommended.)

3. Enter into the healing process together. Should things become un-

manageable, separate for a period of time with the agreement that you both will come back together to deal with your marriage issues at a time when you are stronger.

4. Enter into the healing process along with your spouse, with both parties doing their best, agreeing in advance to specific terms or a certain course of action should the process take the marriage off course.

I've tried all of these, with the exception of number four. In retrospect, I wish someone would have told me exactly how difficult it would be and how I could expect the healing process to impact my marriages. Yes, two—I've had two marriages succumb to the collateral damage of PTSD. I want your marriage to thrive! I want this healing journey to bring the two of you together more closely than you've ever been before! It *will* be the most difficult thing you've ever done, but if you both can move toward each other instead of away when difficulties arise, you will wake up one day with a nuke-proof marriage. And that, my friend, is a fantastic feeling! If the two of you can beat PTSD, there's nothing you can't do!

A WORD ABOUT MEDICATION

Many survivors struggle with taking medication. The reluctance to take medication, from aspirin to cold medicine to anti-depression/anxiety meds, stems from the fear of losing control. However, if PTSD symptoms are so distressing that they distract you from being able to do the mental/emotional work of healing, then medication (used in conjunction with cognitive restructuring techniques and the development of healthy coping skills) can be effective. As a matter of fact, medication alone will not get rid of flashbacks or the emotional feelings connected with the trauma. If a doctor wants to prescribe medication to treat PTSD, they should also be giving a psychotherapy referral. In truth, medications associated with treating PTSD should really only be prescribed by a psychiatrist. The most common medications prescribed are:

Selective Serotonin Reuptake Inhibitors (SSRIs): These are antidepressants that go by the names fluoxetine (Prozac), sertraline (Zoloft), and paroxetine (Paxil) and only reduce anxiety, depression, panic, aggression, impulsivity or suicidal thoughts.

Anti-Psychotics: These are used as alternatives to antidepressants and go by the names risperidone (Risperdal), olanzapine (Zyprexa), and que-tiapine (Seroquel). These minimize agitation, dissociation, hyervigilance, paranoia or brief breaks in being in touch with reality (psychotic breaks).

Mood Stabilizers: These chemicals reduce the sway of emotion experienced with PTSD and are called lamotrigine (Lamictal), tiagabine (Gabitril), and divalproex sodium (Depakote).

Physical Symptom Relief: These include drugs such as clonidine (Catapres), guaneficine (Tenex), and propranolol, as well as, benzodiazepines, commonly referred to as minor tranquilizers, sleeping tablets, or anti-anxiety medications. However, benzodiazepines are highly addictive and over the long term can increase PTSD symptoms.

NATURAL VS. CHEMICAL

Did you know your body has difficulty knowing what to do with chemicals or artificial ingredients? You are a natural, living organism. The things you take into your body need to be made up of the same stuff you are made up of in order for your body to be capable of assimilating it well and without side effects. Supplements prescribed by your naturopath are made from plants, minerals and other living substances, making it easy for your body to recognize.

However, easy doesn't mean fast. Just because your body can assimilate supplements easier doesn't mean you'll always see results quickly. Plant materials are gentle, working with the body's systems instead of bombarding them. For this reason, it takes a few days to load your system up with the supplement, then following a consistent regimen of maintaining acceptable levels to begin seeing the amazing effects.

Prescription medication can be helpful in abating PTSD symptoms in crisis mode. However, you should know that it can take up to eight weeks to see any results, you'll likely have to try several different medications and doses to find one that works and the side effects can be troublesome. In some cases, you get a trade-off effect where you get relief from one symptom only to have another crop up as a side effect from the medication. Nevertheless, if you are having trouble regulating suicidal thoughts or are acting out with behaviors that could be dangerous to yourself or others, prescription medication along with immediate, intensive psychotherapy may be needed until the crisis mode passes.

STUDY MEDICATION

By the time this book hits the virtual shelves, it's likely that science and medicine will have explored any number of new ways to treat PTSD symptoms. However, cutting edge medications are on the horizon, showing promising results. One organization is at the forefront of finding a unique cure for PTSD: The Multidisciplinary Association for Psychedelic Studies (MAPS), founded in 1986, is a research and educational organization dedicated to developing a therapeutic treatment for PTSD that includes the careful pairing of psychotherapy and prescription marijuana or psychedelics. Before you go all 1960s trippin', this is a serious effort to minimize recreational usage and help make marijuana and psychedelics into prescription medicines to be used as tools that are approached with reason and care.

Why psychedelics? Psychedelic medicine administered by a trained psychotherapist doesn't just help people manage their PTSD symptoms, it can show them a way out. Psychedelics have the unique ability to increase a person's range of positive emotions toward themselves and others, increases interpersonal trust without causing sensory distortions or inhibiting access to difficult emotions, and decreases activity in the part of the brain associated with fear and traumatic memories. MAPS explains that in a controlled psychotherapeutic setting, psychedelics can make it easier for people with chronic, treatment-resistant PTSD to confront their traumatic memories, often for the first time. Since the medication raises a patient's level of trust, it can have the added effect of increasing the effectiveness of psychotherapy sessions by strengthening the alliance between patient and therapist.

After traditional forms of treatment (such as CBT, PE, cognitive processing therapy, EMDR), more than a third of patients continue to struggle with symptoms several times a week, even after ten years. However, psychedelic medication only need be administered a few times; even a single session can have a profound effect. A recent MAPS clinical trial discovered that participants who had received just two sessions of psychedelic-assisted psychotherapy and had reported no symptoms immediately after continued to have no sign of symptoms four years later.

MAPS' research develops medicinal options and psychotherapist training that promote real solutions, so PTSD survivors can look their fears in the eye instead of running away. They've worked hard to gain a respected collaborative relationship with the Federal Drug Administration (FDA) and over 500 human subjects have participated in clinical studies without a single serious adverse event occurring as a result of the drug. MAPS states that psychedelics can help open a window between the extremes of fear and avoidance in survivors undergoing psychotherapy for PTSD, and hold it open long enough for them to step through.

Here's a look at the top two drugs being examined as a cure for PTSD:

MDMA-The Party Drug

Methylenedioxymethamphetamine (MDMA), in its pure form is not X, Ecstasy or the party drug, because it isn't mixed with the harmful additives found on the street. Pure MDMA is being tested as a tool to assist psychotherapy for the treatment of PTSD. Preliminary studies have shown that MDMA in conjunction with psychotherapy can help people overcome PTSD, and possibly other disorders as well. MDMA is known for increasing feelings of trust and compassion towards others, which are deficient in the mind and behaviors of survivors struggling with PTSD symptoms. For this reason, it could make for an ideal collaborative approach to medicinal support and psychotherapy for treating PTSD.

In MDMA-assisted psychotherapy, MDMA is only administered a few times, unlike most medications for mental illnesses which are often taken daily for years, and sometimes forever, causing severe side effects or relapses. Remember, MDMA is not the same as Ecstasy. Substances sold on the street under the name Ecstasy do often contain MDMA, but frequently also contain harmful contaminants used to "cut" the drug. In laboratory studies, pure MDMA—but not Ecstasy—has been proven sufficiently safe for human consumption when taken a limited number of times in moderate doses.

MEDICAL MARIJUANA

Researchers at New York University Langone Medical Center recently used brain imaging technology to discover a connection between the number of cannabinoid receptors in the brain and PTSD. Cannabinoid receptors, known as CB1 receptors, help regulate mood and anxiety. When a person uses cannabis, these CB1 receptors are switched on in the brain. Lead author of the study, Dr. Alexander Neumeister, director of the molecular imaging program in the departments of psychiatry and radiology at NYU School of Medicine, says patients often report that smoking marijuana works better for them than any other legal medication. Researchers knew that cannabis use not only energized the CB1 receptors, but also caused memory loss. Until now, memory loss was thought of as a downside to using cannabis, but since invasive traumatic memories are a core issue in the diagnosis of PTSD, maybe a little memory loss wouldn't be such a bad thing. This led researchers to believe that manipulating CB1 receptors in the brain may alleviate trauma symptoms.

Neumeister explains in an interview with Fox News that, "About eight years ago, the first animal study was published showing that everybody has endogenous cannabinoids, or endocannabinoids, in the brain – meaning this substance is in the brain of every person." Endocannabinoids act like a naturally-occurring cannabis, binding to CB1 receptors in the brain to help wipe out traumatic memories. In a way, it's another example of how our amazing brain attempts to protect us from trauma by producing a kind of natural medication. In Neumeister's recent study, people struggling with the effects of PTSD were found to have higher levels of CB1 receptors in the areas of their brain associated with fear and anxiety. However, they also produced lower levels of endocannabinoids. They discovered the brain actually increases its ability to harvest endocannabinoids by creating more CB1 receptors. Unfortunately, endocannabinoid production isn't able to increase to fulfill the demand throwing the brain's system for minimizing the effects of trauma out of whack.

"[The] animal studies have suggested that increasing cannabinoids in the brain helps them to forget painful events and form new memories, so they start to learn to digest what they went through and get over it. We thought this may be relevant to PTSD. [We] have developed a compound that is able to increase the concentration of endocanna-bioniods . . . It helps restore a normal balance of this chemical in the brains of those with PTSD." Neumeister said their PTSD medication would rely on promoting CB1 equilibrium and claims the compound is very safe and does not come with the added health problems caused by chronic marijuana use.[15]

It's imperative to remember that any medication should be combined with the skill of a qualified mental health professional to help overcome negative coping habits. Consider carefully the use of prescription or study medication, since chemicals will affect your body; the side effects can be troublesome and many long-term effects are unknown. If you would like more information about MAPS, their research and educa-tional programs, you can download a PDF brochure on the *PTSD Self Help* website.

Making Sense of . . . Practical Application Guides

Don't forget about the *Three Levels of Engagement!*

So far, you've been challenged to take specific action toward your healing in ways that took into consideration where you're at on the healing pathway, what healing season you're in, and any fatigue you may be experiencing. Much of these challenges have been internal and reflective for this very reason. However, in *Season of Transformation* you get serious about putting your boots to the path, so you'll find three levels of activity to choose from. This way, you can choose from easy to more challenging activities based on your daily energy levels, emotional strength, or financial resources. One day you might be *All In!* while the very next day *Be Gentle!* will be more appropriate. However you choose to engage is up to you—but be sure to choose something each and every day.

Be Gentle! suggestions are easy, low or no-cost activities developed as action steps which can be taken when uncertain or wrestling with a

---

15 http://www.foxnews.com/health/2013/05/14/marijuana-like-compound-could-lead-to-first-ever-medication-for-ptsd/#ixzz2ZS0AATqh

healing crisis.

I'm Open! suggestions are moderate activities for the person who is willing and able to take on a little more challenge.

All In! suggestions can (but not always) include intense activities designed for the person dedicated to completing the healing journey as quickly as possible, without limitations on cost, location, or time commitment.

SCHEDULING TIME

Let's start off your journey by creating a schedule that structures your time according to what's most important to you right now. Taking the extra time to do this will minimize any potential anxiety associated with committing to the healing process, new information you learn or working healthy activities into your schedule and it's easy! Just apply one or all of the following simple time management techniques I used while traveling my own path.

BE GENTLE!
Watch a video of me showing you an easy-to-remember demonstration about scheduling your time on the *PTSD Self Help* website. This brief five-minute video will show you why just letting life happen by accident isn't helpful in getting you what you want, and will teach you how to live life on purpose! As you watch, keep in mind that healing activities are some of the "big rocks" in the jar of your life. Important tasks are the "gravel" and stuff you feel pressured to do is the "sand." Schedule each of these elements in the proper order—rocks, gravel, then sand—and you'll be amazed at how quickly you'll be on your way toward healing!

I'M OPEN!
Keep the main thing the main thing, and try adding just one healing activity a week to see how it goes. Really commit to the experiment and vow to not let anything get in the way of planning or fulfilling this weekly activity. It needs to be what I call a non-negotiable. You deserve it anyway! It's about time you invested a few moments in yourself. Here's how to make it happen:

1. Pick one hour once a week to plan (I like Sunday evenings)

2. Review the upcoming week for *non-negotiable appointments and events

3. Choose one non-negotiable healing activity to do every day. You might want to try:

   • An exercise or task from the Home Work or Enlightenment section of your Backpack

   • A field trip or adventure from the Collaborative Healing Activities section of this chapter

   • Thirty minutes or an hour writing or drawing in your Inner-Action Journal

4. Plug your non-negotiable healing activity into a calendar, making sure to allow adequate time for travel, as well as sacred healing moments for rest and recovery.

5. This is where the rubber meets the road. Devise a way to remind yourself of your healing appointment. You can use the calendar function of your Smartphone, an old-fashioned paper calendar on the fridge or Post-it notes plastered everywhere you look. Just don't break your appointment with yourself! Then, be sure to follow through with what you planned to do.

If you managed to make this *I'm Open!* suggestion happen, congratulate yourself! Do a quick review and ask:

• Did I feel good about doing it?

• What did I like about the activity I chose?

• What would I do differently?

Getting positive results, even small ones, are the building blocks to restoring trust in yourself as the one you can count on to make healing a possibility in your life. If you had a good time, do the exercise again and choose a different activity. When you're ready, expand this method to include all the important parts of your life. You'll learn how by trying the next *All In!* suggestion.

ALL IN!
Try this ten-step method for scheduling your time. If you apply this method consistently each week for one month, you'll feel more in control of your life, find satisfaction in your relationships, and discover hope for achieving your goals—not only for healing from PTSD, but also for every other area of your life!

1. Pick one hour once a week to plan (I like Sunday evenings)

2. Review the upcoming week for *non-negotiable appointments and events

3. Choose one non-negotiable healing activity to do every day from the HomeWork or Enlightenment section of your Backpack

4. Plug your non-negotiables into a calendar making sure to allow adequate time for travel, as well as sacred healing moments for rest and recovery.

5. Plug thirty minutes to one hour every day into your calendar for recording information into your InnerAction journal, making sure to allow for a quiet, uninterrupted environment where you can be alone or with someone you trust.

6. List **important tasks, appointments or events you would like to engage in

7. Choose two or three important tasks, appointments or events

8. Plug your important tasks, appointments or events into the calendar making sure to allow adequate time for travel, as well as—you guessed it—rest and recovery activities.

9. List any event, activity, appointment or task that, because you haven't scheduled it in the calendar, you feel pressured to do.

10. Delegate all or portions of these remaining events, activities, appointments or tasks to others who love and care about you. Trust me—if you let them know how hard you're working to heal, they will be more than willing to help out. Don't abuse this: do your part, which is to heal.

non-negotiable means stuff you absolutely want to do, need to do, or can't get out of doing

**important means stuff that is necessary to the over-all smooth functioning of your life*

SACRED HEALING MOMENTS - PLANNING TIME FOR REST & RECOVERY

Careful planning can mean the difference between frustration and success when it comes to healing PTSD. Leave plenty of unplanned, unscheduled time to deal with unexpected consequences of the healing journey (e.g., flashbacks, triggers, increased anxiety, new or intensified symptoms). Generally, you'll want to plan time to not only engage in collaborative healing activities, but also recover from them. Healing takes a lot out of you and it's wise to plan for what you'll need to do to recharge, so you can get back to living and healing. Also, it's important to celebrate the successes, both big and small! Do so by reviewing the things that worked well, how you felt about them and the results they've brought you in your InnerAction Journal. This way, you can learn from missteps, discover activities that don't fit your particular style of traveling on the PTSD healing journey, and get on with what works!

As a general rule, plan as much time to rest and recover from the new discoveries you've made as it took you to engage in the healing activity (e.g., one hour of reading/research = one hour of rest and recovery). Here are some of the challenges I started planning for after learning the hard way:

RECOVERING FROM READING

Learning about the effects of PTSD can sometimes take its toll. You know the devastation PTSD has caused in your life. Why burden yourself or cause unnecessary pain by reliving the traumatic experiences of others? There will be time for that later. As you read books, blogs and articles, you can't help but reflect on how the new information applies to your own circumstance. That kind of reflection can be exhausting.

BE GENTLE!
When engaging in educational reading and research, try to stick to material that limits anecdotal stories (stories about other survivors' traumatic past) and presents objective information.

I'M OPEN!
Ask your Healing Partner, a trusted family member, or your spouse/significant other to read something for you, then give you the highlights. They can do this verbally by sharing what they feel to be the important aspects of the text, or by highlighting with a pen so you can skim the relevant information.

ALL IN!
Use the emotions your reading has stirred up as clues to uncovering details about your traumatic past or as opportunities to practice being The Observer. In either case, you'll want to have your InnerAction Journal and a pen in hand, so you can record the ego's thoughts, legitimate ideas from that wise part of yourself, memories that bubble to the surface, as well as physical symptoms that flare up, fears you wish you could (and will eventually) confront, and/or questions you may come up with for your Healing Team members.

RECOVERING FROM TRIGGERS

Triggers are everywhere—period. Trying to live a life avoiding triggers or making the people in your world "stop" triggering you is impossible. Occasionally, you might want to try planning for triggers. For example, attending family events, going on outings (whether you come into contact with people or not), approaching the season/anniversary of the original trauma or being intimate (sexually or not) are all prime opportunities to expect to be triggered. Try one of these suggestions in advance of being triggered:

BE GENTLE!

Alter your daily schedule to accommodate for the preparation, engagement and recovery time required to participate.

I'M OPEN!

You decide what the terms of your engagement in these activities will be. For example:

- How long will you participate?

- What are you willing to do?

- What won't you do?

ALL IN!

Try it all. Be intentional about your engagement in activities that you suspect will hold triggers for you. This is where scheduling your time comes in handy. In advance, when you recognize the possibility of everyday interactions that could include coming into contact with people outside of your support system, engaging in an activity that requires you to become vulnerable and/or sensory aspects that resemble those of the original traumatic event, follow these three suggestions:

1. Alter your daily schedule to accommodate for the preparation, engagement and recovery time required to participate.

2. You decide what the terms of your engagement in these activities will be. For example:

   - How long will you participate?

   - What are you willing to do?

   - What won't you do?

3. Use the emotions, thoughts, legitimate ideas, memories and/or physical symptoms that will likely reveal themselves as opportunities for a do-over, what I call an overlay. You discover clues about the past, limiting beliefs or new attempts by the ego to take you off course. You'll also have opportunities to practice any number of the

exercises you've learned so far. Why not use the moment to gain the skill of being The Observer, grounding techniques, Emergency Breathing or trying new rest and recovery activities? As always, you'll want to have your InnerAction Journal and a pen in hand, so you can record questions you may have later for your Healing Team members.

RECOVERING FROM REVELATIONS

Having an *ah-ha!* moment can pack a punch. The healing journey is all at once exhilarating, crushing, empowering, disarming—and it is certainly never easy. When engaged in journaling, sharing new awarenesses and trying new, outside-of-the-box activities, you'll gain amazing clarity about how you've coped with the original trauma. Sometimes, but not always, these revelations can temporarily level you emotionally.

BE GENTLE!
Reward yourself for gaining the awareness regardless of the impact the revelation has on you. You're no longer allowing PTSD to run you: you're facing it head-on and that is to be congratulated! Rewarding even the smallest of achievements during this process will create a snowball effect of momentum moving you closer to wholeness and healing. Try taking yourself out for coffee, dinner or a walk in the park.

I'M OPEN!
The guilt factor is rarely anticipated in the PTSD healing equation, but you can be sure it'll show up in some measure. Guilt feelings are the preservers of time by inducing fears of retaliation or abandonment, and thus ensure that the future will be like the past. You can accept the eternity of now in exchange. Think about it. It's always now. See? There it went, into the past. It's now again. Ooops—there it goes again! And . . . it's now once more. It'll be this way forever—always now. When you choose to make this exchange, you will simultaneously be exchanging guilt for joy, viciousness for love and pain for peace. Let's practice being in the present moment by way of review without labeling or judging our thoughts or the environment around us. Check out the practical application guide titled *Making Sense of . . . Observing Your Thoughts* (Appendix A). This time, have your InnerAction Journal close by and record the guilt-ridden statements that arise. Be sure to take the position of The Observer and ask yourself these questions:

- Do I notice any patterns, common themes or repetitive subject matter?

- Who do the statements sound like they're coming from? You? Someone in your past?

- Are any of the statements dealing with things that have already happened that can't be undone?

- How many of the statements are about things that haven't happened yet? What could you do to create a guilt free outcome for yourself?

ALL IN!

Surrendering to the grief process is one of the most difficult coping skills for survivors to embrace. The difficulty stems from fear—mostly, the fear that once the floodgates of emotion are opened, the pain and sorrow will be overwhelming enough to destroy them and/or never stop. This is an illusion. As you travel on your path, you'll realize how tragic the impact of trauma has been. You'll feel sorry for the relationships you've lost, the time wasted being stuck in life, and the way you've taught other people how to treat you. The past is over. It cannot be regained, and now you're here, finally dealing with the mess. These thoughts and feelings are a wonderful chance to pry open that Belief Window and see what the world looks like on the other side. Give meditation a try by adding a little twist on the Emergency Breathing exercise:

1. Begin by letting your Healing Partner, Spouse/Significant other or your MHP know that you're going to try actively processing difficult emotions and what you'll need from them to help you during and afterward.

2. In your safe space, sit up straight or lay flat on your back, allow your shoulders to fall away from your ears. Place your hand on the lower part of your abdomen and take three slow, deep breaths, breathing in through your nose and out through your mouth. Can you feel your hand rise as you inhale, fall as you exhale?

3. Take a moment to recall when you felt fearful, anxious or as if you were avoiding something today. Encourage the feelings you had

earlier to return (or allow the feelings you're having in the present moment to wash over you).

4. Press your feet in to the floor or become aware of the floor supporting the weight of your body. Remind yourself that you're safe and secure in the present moment and that what has already past cannot harm you.

- Keep breathing deeply, enough to move your hand on your abdomen. When you breathe in, invite the feelings to fill you. Honor your feelings. Be patient and present with them. As if comforting a friend, allow yourself to be okay with these feelings.

- When you release the breath, say to yourself, *I'm right where I need to be* and release the feeling to flow back into the universe.

- Breathe in . . . a feeling fills you. Breath out . . . saying to yourself, *I'm experiencing exactly what I need to heal* and releasing the feeling.

- Breathe in . . . and release. *I'm right where I need to be.*

- Allow your feelings and any responses your body may have to deepen, honoring them.

- Breathe in . . . and release. *I'm experiencing exactly what I need to heal.*

5. Continue breathing deeply and reciting the affirmations as you now let go of the feeling for the day.

6. As the feeling begins to dissolve and loose its energy, sit in stillness while continuing the cycle of breath and allow yourself to experience any wisdom that comes to you.

7. Sit in stillness as you return to breathing normally and when you're ready, wiggle your fingers and toes, returning to the sensation of your body before opening your eyes.

8. Record your experience in your InnerAction Journal.

9. Rest and recover.

10.Check in with your Healing Partner, Spouse/Significant other or your MHP to let them know you're okay and that you've completed your exercise. Share your experience with them when you're ready and only after an adequate amount of rest and recovery.

Recovering from Flashbacks

Flashbacks are a major symptom that can be difficult to navigate. However, flashbacks are also opportunities to achieve huge advancements in the healing process when they are viewed as overlays. Often there are clear warning signs that a flashback is imminent. We just aren't paying attention, so we are caught unprepared and feel steamrolled by the experience.

Be Gentle!

Be diligent to record your physical, emotional and mental state in your InnerAction journal. It's best to do this during a flashback, but if you're unable to do so, at least record what you can as soon as possible afterward. Upon review, this record will provide invaluable information on how to predict flashbacks. Better yet, it will lead you to an eventual shift in perspective toward the concept of overlays. Remember to be kind to yourself in the hours and days following a flashback by lightening your everyday schedule. Also, immediately follow both planned activities that you suspect may be difficult, and unplanned opportunities that just showed up out of nowhere, with restful recovery moments like these:

- Adequate amounts of down-time where no expectations are placed upon you

- A quiet place where you can be alone or with someone you trust

- Using the PTSD Coach application on your Smartphone

- An activity inspired by the Toy Box you created in *Season of Renewal*

I'M OPEN!

Choose to view flashbacks as an opportunity for a "do over," what I call an overlay. Flashbacks are reminders that are eerily similar to the original traumatic event. They begin by creeping into one or more of our five senses—touch, smell, sight, sound or taste. Then, before you know it, it can seem as if the whole world has joined together to create a circumstance that looks remarkably like your traumatic past. Flashbacks can seem like unbelievable coincidences and feel as if the universe is out to get you, unless you choose to look at them differently.

An overlay is a healthy, healing term for referring to flashbacks. After awhile, you'll get so good at anticipating triggers, you'll start to recognize activities, circumstances or interactions in advance that could hold the potential for not only triggers, but also the escalation of a trigger to the point of a flashback. What you've done is begin to build a new pathway for your brain to process the toxic emotions connected to the trauma.

Making Sense of . . . Overlays

Remember overhead projectors? In the days before WIFI, HDMI and streaming video, classroom teachers used light boxes with a mirror assembly that projected images (usually the teacher's handwriting) from a thin, plastic sheet, called a transparency, onto a screen. The beauty of transparencies was that you could layer them, showing each of the dynamic systems of the body, for instance, (skeletal, musculature, circulatory, etc.) until you layered the last transparency, which would magically show you everything going on under the skin at once. Guess what? This overlaying process happens during healing, too, but you have to be looking for it.

What's easy is noticing that triggers present an opportunity to embrace an overlay: remembering that opportunity before emotions and chemical responses cloud your vision requires a bit more practice. But guess what? You're already more than half way there! Aren't you well into the swing of knowing when and maybe even how you've been triggered? All that's needed to turn triggers into triumphs is a minor adjustment to your Belief Window. Here's an example:

During my healing journey I was put in touch with my Great Aunt, the woman who (at the time) was married to the pedophile from my childhood. Since my mother had died years before, our family was small and not many people knew about the abuse I'd suffered, it was important to me to have a relationship with my aunt. She had information about my past, like who I was before abuse entered into my life and my mother's relationship with me as an infant, that was important to me. Before long, she invited me to come for a visit.

When I felt ready to make the long flight from Seattle to South Carolina, I started making plans. As I thought about what I would need to do to feel safe so far away from home, I recalled my aunt's tendency to keep every thing, a pack rat of sorts. I remembered how much her new husband's physical appearance reminded me of the pedophile. Plus, she wanted the three of us to spend a weekend at their lakeside cabin. That's when I began to feel fearful about making the trip. But there was something else I was sensing; the possibility that *this time* things could be different. After all, I was a thirty-something adult (not a ten year old child), her husband was a completely different person and a mother-like figure who was a member of my immediate family would be with me. I had the BIG ah-ha! moment. Was this life's way of bringing about circumstances remarkably similar to one of my traumas for the purpose of doing things differently? I wanted so badly to heal my pain and leave the past behind. I had to find out.

Hooray! With careful planning and clear communication, I got the 'do-over' I needed. There were plenty of triggers during that trip, but I saw my way through them all. The most important moment was near the end of my stay, when I woke up early at the cabin one morning. Worn down by the trip and my triggers, I woke up in full flash back mode. I was ten years old, trapped in that cabin by the lake. Getting out of bed, I felt as if my feet were small, my eyes wide with fear, and I wanted to cry. I went straight to my aunt and sitting across from her, told her what was happening. She asked what she could do. "Hold me," I said. It may have been a bit overwhelming for her, but I bawled my eyes out! She was kind to me, the auntie I remembered from my childhood. After I had a chance to reflect and share the experience with my Healing Partner and my therapist upon my return home, I knew I had the skills needed to take on anything PTSD had to offer not only because it couldn't surprise me anymore, but also because I now saw triggers as a sign that life was trying to help me create a new, healthy memory to overwrite the old—an overlay.

If you think of this new insight not so much as an early warning system, but rather as a heads-up from your teacher that there's going to be a pop quiz, you'll start to feel excited for the opportunity to have overlays show up! That's right—all it takes is one time predicting the potential of a situation to cause a flashback (remember, we're calling them overlays); by allowing emotions and sensory symptoms to have time and space when they rise up (while using your tools to keep yourself feeling safe and in control), the result is that the Healing Crisis passes quickly. This leaves you with an amazing revelation about the past, along with feelings of confidence about having weathered this small storm, and guilt-free motivation to do whatever you need to rest and recover.

Never having those same triggers rise up again is the transformative effect of an overlay perspective. Flashbacks are going to happen, whether you want them to or not. Why not put them to good use and choose to believe in overlays instead? Choose to believe the whole universe is bending over backward to bring you the chance to do things differently, in a more healthy, wholehearted, healing way. You'll never feel like a victim of life again.

All In!
Review the above *I'm Open!* suggestion and the practical application guide titled *Making Sense of . . . Overlays*; then decide that this week when you set your schedule, you'll look for overlays. When you review the appointments and activities you've scheduled for the upcoming week, ask yourself these questions:

- Does it seem as if circumstances are showing up that could remind me of a traumatic event?

- What can I do to prepare, well in advance, for the possibility I might have a Healing Crisis?

- When I think back on that past trauma, what do I wish I could have done differently? What do I wish others would have done for me?

Now, set your intention to do what you can to put your ideas into action should an overlay present itself. Communicate clearly what your needs are (or will be) to others who may be involved or present during the upcoming activity or circumstance. Cut yourself a break—give yourself lots of emotional room to process whatever comes up, if anything. And definitely remember to bring your InnerAction Journal, so you can record the amazing miracle moment.

HOMEWORK

Remember—in order to heal from PTSD, you must integrate new activities and non-negotiables into your everyday schedule. We said it was like recovering from a broken leg. You wouldn't just ignore the fact that it's broken and go on with your daily routine. In fact, much like wrestling with PTSD symptoms, it would be impossible! Remember, you would find a way to work in the time necessary for doctors' appointments, physical therapy, and rest, as well as asking a few friends to help you out with things you can't manage until you recover.

HomeWork activities are designed to complement the work you're doing with your Healing Team by giving you the chance to practice what you've learned. HomeWork will also help you:

- rediscover who you were intended to be before trauma visited your life

- discover who you've become as a result of valiantly trying to survive

- ask yourself why you became that person

By using what you've gathered for your Backpack to participate in HomeWork activities, you'll be guided into deciding what you want to keep (the healthy, strong—and perhaps misdirected—parts) and what you want to let go (the self-defeating, co-dependent habits you picked up). So, let's assign some HomeWork with *you* in mind! Here are two

HomeWork assignments that will put you in touch with yourself:

SCAVENGER HUNT: A LOOK THROUGH
THE BELIEF WINDOW

In *Season of Hope: Plan & Pack* you were introduced to the concept of The Belief Window. As a reminder, you learned we all have a Belief Window and that you can't see your Belief Window because it's invisible. Everyone has a Belief Window that's figuratively attached to their head and hangs in front of their face. Every time you move, that window goes with you. You look at the world through it, and what you see is filtered back to you through it. The tricky thing about a Belief Window is that you and others in your life have placed perceptions on it (like crazy little window clings) which you believe are absolutely true, whether they reflect reality or not. Because you believe them, they stay on your window, skewing your ability to see clearly. Unknowingly, you act upon them without question.

One of the most important things we can do is make sure our Belief Window is as clear as possible or truly reflects beliefs that will move us closer to our values and priorities, like healing from PTSD. To do this, we must take an honest look at our behavior. Our behavior will give us clues about what kind of perceptions we've placed on our window. By looking closely at your behavior, you will have achieved the critical first step in freeing yourself from erroneous self-ideas and self-talk that may be impeding your progress toward living out your values, priorities and healing. So, let's begin by looking at the window itself.

The function of the Belief Window is to act as a filter through which you view your world. Ultimately, your Belief Window causes you to make decisions and follow through on those decisions with behaviors that are based on perceived needs, unspoken rules, and beliefs. These four elements (behaviors, perceived needs, unspoken rules, and beliefs) are the panes of glass in your Belief Window. By identifying any one of these elements as an effect, you can accurately predict the cause and consequently, future behavior of any individual—including yourself. These elements may manifest negatively in fear, suspicion, and anger, or they may manifest positively in confidence, love, and faith. As you take a look through the Belief Window, step-by-step, you'll begin to identify strengths, as well as weaknesses. Not only that, but you'll begin to gradually clean your window, so that you can see the whole, healed, vibrant life that was intended for you.

This exercise is the first step toward cleaning your Belief Window. It's important to understand we are what we have experienced up until the present time. We have been shaped and molded by what life has thrown at us. While it may be difficult, we do have the power to chart our own course; we are not victims or puppets. This exercise will give you a better idea of how your thoughts and patterns were formed. Your future is yet to be written, and you are holding the pencil; don't let anyone else author your life story . . . it must be completed by you. Good luck, and remember—pencils have erasers!

DIRECTIONS

Schedule one hour when you can be alone and undisturbed. Have your InnerAction Journal and pen with you. Settle yourself in a comfortable place where you feel safe and peaceful. Include comfort items, such as a cup of tea, a scented candle or soft music. Comfort items, the paper and pen, along with being in an undisturbed safe place, will help you to remain present to today as you travel back in your memories to find clues along the pathway of your life. These clues will point to strengths (and weaknesses) you've probably forgotten about, yet depended on to get you through the seasons of your life (good and difficult). The answers to these questions are for your eyes only...unless you choose to share them. Here we go:

- Describe your relationship with your mother.

- Describe your relationship with your father.

- Did you have any brothers or sisters? If so, how many, and in what order did you fall?

- As a child, what was your favorite activity? What would you do for hours that would bring happiness and release?

- Describe the culture of the house you grew up in. Was it loving, tense, relaxed, etc?

- Describe the physical structure of the house you lived in. Describe your bedroom.

- Briefly describe your parents' political affiliations. Were they involved in social issues and causes? If so, which ones? Do you ever remember them going to vote when you were a child?

- Did either parent serve in the Armed Forces?

- Describe the faith element of your home as you grew up. Did you attend worship services as a family unit or alone?

- How did you do in grade school? What was your favorite subject?

- Did you attend college? If so, what was your major?

- Do you pay federal, state and local income taxes? How do you feel about paying?

- Do you receive government assistance in any form? How do you feel about receiving assistance?

- List your favorite relationships.

- List your most difficult or broken relationships.

- Identify a relationship that needs reconciliation.

- Have you ever experienced a traumatic event in your life? Did you get professional help? If so, when? Right after the event or how long after? Or have you made it on your own thus far?

- Describe what it means to be a friend.

- List your best friends. Whose list would you be on?

- In your opinion, what are your strengths?

- In your opinion, what are your weaknesses?

- If you could spend time with anyone that has lived throughout history, who would it be and what questions might you ask?

- In what ways have the answers you provided affected the way you view life? How has your view through The Belief Window been formed as a result of your life's experiences?

Reward yourself! Looking inward to re-discover ways you used to comfort yourself, creative outlets you had for processing your experience of the world around you and natural talents or abilities you've long forgotten is not an easy task. Often, an exploration for these healthy coping skills inadvertently brings with it uncomfortable realizations and/or memories. This is the time to put to use what you've learned about rest and recovery. Hopefully, you scheduled this exercise along with some added time to do just that—rest and recover. Take the time you need to process any emotions that have come up and to just let go of the exercise by bringing yourself back to a firm grounding in the here and now. Play with your children or pets. Go for a walk outside. Put on your favorite song and have a mini dance party!

PERSONAL HEALING STATEMENT

Most people wander through their lives making decisions based on what they think they should do, what they think is normal, and what they think is expected from them. I call this living life by accident. And that's usually what it turns out feeling like—just one accident or mistake after another. Major corporations understand the wisdom of having a clear agenda or reason for being in business. It couldn't hurt for each of us to do the same. In this case, our agenda is healing PTSD, and as you travel along this pathway, you'll hopefully gain insight into how you want to be in this world. Although many businesses have mission statements, few employees of those businesses are able to tell you what it is. Why? Because it's usually more than a statement. Their missions are long, boring documents that set up pie-in-the-sky values with no way of delivering on them. That's not where we're headed!

Laurie Beth Jones, author of *The Path*, developed an easy, straight forward process for creating your very own mission statement. She suggests considering the cost of not having a clear sense of direction in life. We see the cost in suicide, crime and unemployment rates. Just imagine a world where everyone knew why they were here and were busy about the business of fulfilling it. We wouldn't be getting in each other's way, trapped in unrewarding jobs that are really meant for someone else (and that they'd be satisfied doing, by the way!). And we'd certainly be kinder to each other with the understanding that each person is dedicated to a special purpose reserved just for them.

Webster's Dictionary defines a mission as an important assignment; a group of people taking part in such an assignment, a vocation or calling, and orders given by higher headquarters. What more important assignment could you have than healing PTSD and becoming the best version of *you* that you can be?

In her book, Jones drives this fact home: Every decision you make is moving you closer to or further away from who you want to be in life and what you want to achieve. Do you want to heal from PTSD? The kind of mission statement you'll create with *the PTSD Self Help* method is called a Personal Healing Statement and can act as a filter through which you pass all your decisions, including the ones that will bring you to the brink of walking away from PTSD forever. You can find the Create Your Personal Healing Statement PDF on the PTSD Self Help website.

GUIDELINES FOR USE

Print out copies of your healing statement and plaster them everywhere—on the fridge, on the bathroom mirror, in your car, on your desk at work. Set reminders in your phone so you'll read your statement periodically throughout the day, but especially review it upon waking, before you go to sleep and during any meditation.

For the next several weeks, ask yourself these questions about your healing statement:

- Does this sound like me (on a good day)?

- Could I be about this and only this?

- Could I fulfill this at home? At work? At school? At church?

- Do I feel excited about demonstrating this to myself? My children? My spouse/significant other? My co-workers? My friends? My family?

Keep your eyes open to other words that may be a better fit. You'll find juicy, motivating words on magazine covers, newspaper headlines, advertisements, in inspirational stories, quotes and music lyrics. Try any interesting words on for size, or even consider dropping one or more verbs or core values altogether.

When faced with a decision—big or small—ask yourself this question:

Will (whatever you might do, say or be) get me closer to or further away from (restate your mission)?

In this way, you'll be using your personal healing statement to direct your steps, and before you know it, you'll be making decisions that keep you on course automatically.

Each evening (or once a week during your scheduling time) invest a few moments to write down examples of how you fulfilled your mission from the past week. On days when you're not feeling your best, review these examples, and know that a new start begins with your very next decision.

Chomping at the bit to create your personal healing statement? Check out PTSDSelfHelp.com for more on how to get it done!

Staying The Course: Decision-making & Unplugging From Triggers

We make thousands of decisions each day, hour, moment, even every second. Most decisions are made without us knowing it has happened. Unfortunately, we're only aware of the impact of our decisions after they've been made. We see the result of the decisions we've made in our life. If you're someone who tries hard to make "good" decisions, you do the best you can to forecast the outcome by collecting as much information as possible before you make a decision. Disappointment sometimes follows anyway, because we just can't know all of the dynamics that play into our decision-making. For example, we all have the ability to choose. When your decision impacts another, they have the ability to choose their response. Sometimes, the response of others is not what we expect. We did our homework, thought through all the possibilities, and chose a course of action we thought would bring a certain kind of result; then the free will of another inserts itself into the equation, bringing either a more positive or a more negative result than we anticipated. Welcome to life! The human factor is a mysterious element that's just plain unpredictable . . . for the most part.

CAUSE & EFFECT

We all learned about cause and effect from our high school science class. The theory of causality is found in physics and philosophy. It states that for every effect there is an equal and opposite cause; however, every cause has a mysterious element that doesn't allow you to predict its effect with one-hundred percent accuracy. The Universal Law of cause and effect doesn't allow you to predict the future, because of another Universal Law—free will. One thing we do know for sure is that every cause does have an effect, and it's likely you're witnessing many of PTSD's effects in your life every day. So, if we know the cause is trauma, why are we surprised, ambushed by shame, or filled with guilt when PTSD results? I'll tell you why.

STORIES

Remember earlier when I talked to you about the Belief Window? We said that beliefs are nothing more than stories we tell ourselves about the world around us; that beliefs are emotionally charged *meaning* we've attached to whatever we take in through our senses; beliefs are the reason for the flood of chemicals our brain produces to get us to take action. We also learned that our amazing brain doesn't know the difference between what is real or imagined, past or future, harmful or safe. Our brain just does its job—collecting information, storing it, comparing new information with what's stored, and sending out orders to take action based on past outcomes. This is the key to understanding how our brain is getting in the way of healing.

The Law of Cause and Effect says we can't predict an effect by examining a cause, yet our brain attempts to do so and succeeds, miserably in the case of PTSD, unless we stop it. Unfortunately, many psychological methods ask a person to do what the Law of Cause & Effect says is impossible: examine the cause, so you can predictably understand the effect in the hope of changing it. But what about those people who can't remember the details of a traumatic incident? Are they lost forever to the effects of PTSD, unable to heal? Some might believe that's true, or worse, really want you to believe it.

Let's look at a real-life example: you're minding your own business, and your spouse loudly says to an empty room, "Where in the heck did my wallet go? I left it right here!" You're down the hall and hear this exclamation. That's when your mind goes to work rifling through the files of your historic past for similar statements, tone of voice, time of day, and environmental conditions. When it finds a circumstance that's even remotely similar, it quickly recalls the outcome of those previous circumstances, which in this example were possibly:

- Accusatory statements made by your older brother when you were growing up

- The precursor to a bout of the blame game played by you and your ex-spouse

- Guilty feelings felt by you because you're stretched thin by work, family and life demands

- Resentment for not getting the support and help you need around the house

Your brain decides that the outcome in this present moment will likely be the same, so in order to prove itself right, it sends out a chemical stream along old neural pathways that tells you to react the way you have in the past. Voilà! You have just successfully recreated the past in the present moment, which is great if you're creating what you want in your life; not so great if you're creating what you don't.

Once again, recall that the Law of Cause & Effect only allows us to identify a cause by examining effects. This is great news to people who want to heal from past traumatic events! It means you don't have to examine your past (cause) in order to understand what's happening in your present life (effects). Whether you realize it or not, or intend to or not, you're witnessing the past recreated in the present every day. In order to understand the suffering you're experiencing today, just look at what your brain is doing and at how you're reacting to it. You do this by becoming aware of your thoughts and noticing the emotions that arise and want to push you toward a certain behavior or action. This is what I call being The Observer.

This is also where stories come into play. Thoughts can become stories when you create an identity attached to them. We've all done it. A thought comes:

What's wrong with me? I've been forgetting things lately.

Our brain says, *Yes, that's right! You have been forgetting things. I'll make sure you forget some more.*

After awhile, our forgetfulness starts bugging us. We get on the Internet and research memory problems. Soon, we start creating a story:

Maybe I have a brain tumor. What if it's cancer? Or what if it's Alzheimer's?

Our brain, with the help of the ego, loves stories. It feeds on them. Next thing you know, you're seeing the doctor and *all* your little symptoms, from indigestion to headaches, must be related to the story you've been feeding your ego and its employee—your brain. Doing what the brain was created to do, it sends out chemicals that confirm the story. You know this is true by the effects you see in your body and your emotions. Next thing you know, you've created an identity that defines who you are in this world and dictates how you'll behave:

I'm sick. I can't do things like normal people. I won't be able to enjoy my life.

And it all started with a thought. Start today! Stop giving the ego any extra help! You can do this when you stop feeding it stories that are out of line with your goal of healing from PTSD. Say "You're fired!" to the ego. Step up and be the best boss you can be, and employ your wonderful brain to create a life worth living! So, how do we take control?

Thinking Things Through . . . The Power of Our Mind

Catherine Collaut, PhD is a master at helping people understand their limiting beliefs about how to leverage the power of their subconscious mind. What do you believe about the power of your mind? We've all heard the studies that say we don't use all that our mind is capable of. Some say we use anywhere from one to five percent of our mind in a conscious way, meaning we use it intentionally. So, let's estimate we use somewhere in the middle, like three percent. That leaves ninety-seven percent of our brain operating on automatic pilot via the subconscious. You don't have to think about digesting food, breathing, making your heart beat or a million other tasks and habits assigned to this part of your brain. Thank goodness! That would be exhausting!

Scientists think it's possible that the power of our subconscious mind could be as much as a million times greater than the conscious mind. Now, if we could harness that kind of power—considering the minimal effort required to make it work for us in an automatic way—what could we accomplish? It sheds a whole new light on the famous quote, "Our deepest fear is not that we are inadequate. Our deepest fear is that we are powerful beyond measure,"[16] doesn't it?

Here's what Catherine Collaut has to say about harnessing the power of *you:*

> At a power a million times greater, we might be tempted to regard our subconscious as 'the boss' from whom we have to get approval or permission in order to get things done. This is incorrect. You are the boss— at least, you're meant to be the boss. And part of your job as 'boss' is to give this most powerful, effective and efficient employee good and clear direction.
>
> Think of your subconscious as a computer: it's going to take its programming and run with it; it's your job to make sure that its programming is in functional, if not optimal, alignment with your goals by programming, re-programming and de-bugging, at regular intervals.[17]

---

16 Quote from A Return to Love, by Marianne Williamson.

17 Web cast interview of Catherine Collautt, PhD by Marie Forleo found at http://www.marief-

Making Sense of . . . Observing Your Thoughts

Here's an easy way to stop your thoughts dead in their tracks. Borrowed from the Emergency Breathing exercise you learned about in *Season of Renewal*, you'll want to take in three belly breaths; then ask this question silently within yourself:

I wonder what my next thought is going to be?

You'll notice a pause, a blissful silence before the next thought comes rushing at you. Just repeat the process, but this time, take one breath, then ask the question:

I wonder what my next thought is going to be?

If you are a visual learner, picture a tree or branch without leaves, a telephone wire stretched between poles, or a fence. Allow a thought to come. Identify the main theme of the thought and picture a bird(s) you've named with that theme landing. Then, ask the question:

I wonder what my next thought is going to be?

Visualize the bird(s) taking flight and hear the flapping of the wings as if startled by your presence.

Allow a space of silence to exist. Soon, with practice, you'll be able to stretch that brief moment of silence and stillness of thought into a longer and longer period of time. That's how powerful and effective being present is at dissolving the hold your thoughts have over you. This is the practice of presence.

REACT OR RESPOND: HOW TO DECIDE

When living under the weight of PTSD, being reactionary becomes a habit run by the automatic function of your brain. Like a knee-jerk reaction when the doctor tests your reflexes, you move very quickly from a stimulus (cause) to a reaction (effect). So quickly, as a matter

orleo.com/2012/09/your-subconscious-mind/

of fact, you don't even realize you've made a decision in the process. Think about it. The phone rings: you answer it. No pause to consider whether you want to, have time to or even know who's on the end of the line. RING! RING! RING! Hello? And while you're dealing with the interruption, everything else goes on hold. My bet is that there are other ways you're doing this same thing—reacting—in your life.

You don't have to be a slave to this kind of thinking. To be honest, you can't really call it thinking at all. Your mind is just habitually doing what you've allowed it to do for years. For that matter, how much choice or free will do you really have, when you've turned the management of your life over to:

- the automatic function of your brain

- old neural pathways formed by past experiences

- limiting beliefs placed on your Belief Window by yourself or others

THE EGO

There is a way out. By combining what you've learned about being The Observer with practicing presence, that moment when thoughts are put on pause, you will create enough space between cause and effect, stimulus and reaction to actually engage the intentional, thinking, creative part of your brain. Herein lies the power of choice.

Annmarie's Story

After one long day of mourning over feeling perpetually overrun by triggers, getting knocked down every time I tried to get back up, being victimized by my brain's chemical responses, and exhausted by the effort of trying to figure it out, my Healing Partner said, "You know, Annmarie, there's another way."

"What way?" I responded. "I've tried everything! Nothing's working!"

"It's called surrender. Have you tried that?" she said.

Surrender! That sounded like giving up to me. Waving the white flag. Maybe she was right.

She was; I was the one who was wrong. Many, many months later, I learned the lesson of surrender. It wasn't what I expected. Surrender was more like a gentle acceptance of the facts as I saw them at the time than a giving up or giving in. As a life coach, I had shown hundreds of people how to shift the way they view the "facts" of their life by engaging their power of choice. I had even used it myself, but I never dreamed how difficult it could be under the flood of emotion pouring into my body from the past. But I kept trying. Sometimes I would shift my perception before a trigger could jump on my emotions. At other times, I couldn't make the shift until the hijack of emotions subsided. Nevertheless, by mastering the skill of surrender (acceptance), I got my *yes* and my *no* back.

First, an explanation about reactions. You can understand a lot by looking at the word *reaction* itself. It's from Latin, meaning "done again." (Britney Spears' second album and title song could just as easily been, "Oops, I reacted!" I know, that stunk. That's why I'm a writer, not a singer.) You could easily think of it as recreating, once again, something you've done before. However, reactions are not limited to actions alone—remember, thought is an action performed by the mind, so don't limit your observations to external effects.

Experience is the best teacher. Recall a time when you were triggered. The easiest way is by referring to your InnerAction Journal. Taking the position of The Observer before you review the event, identify the trigger and your reaction to it. Did you write with enough detail to notice how quickly you reacted? Did you include any observations you made about your thoughts before you took action? If so, great! If not, stay in the loving detachment mode of The Observer and try to remember not only how long it took for you to react, but also what thought or thoughts prompted you to take action. Write down your observations. Now, reward yourself! Take a stretch break, perform a few breathing exercises or do some other sort of grounding activity that brings you back to the present moment. You've just witnessed your ego leveraging PTSD to keep you in old, limiting ways of thinking and believing. Now, what do you do about it?

As you become more aware of your body's cues telling you that a trigger has just appeared (upcoming Collaborative Healing Activities will help you with this), you'll gain the awareness necessary to practice going within and taking the place of The Observer. No need to focus on the trigger (cause) at this point, because of the Law of Cause and Effect. Let's review:

The Law of Cause and Effect, a Universal Law that applies to everyone and everything (whether believed in or not) states that for every effect there is an equal and opposite cause; however, every cause has a mysterious element that doesn't allow you to predict its effect with one-hundred-percent accuracy. The Universal Law of Cause and Effect doesn't allow you to predict the future, because of another Universal Law—free will.

What you can't predict, you can't change. Causes will happen in this life—accidents, mistakes, unintended consequences. However, because of the Law of Free Will and thanks to the dynamics of cause and effect, you have the power to change outcomes. In the case of interrupting PTSD pathways and changing your ways of thinking, you have to wait for what I call the first effect in order to divert those effects toward change. As soon as the effects appear, you can know the cause by analyzing your observations afterward. But isn't a different effect what we really want? Who gives a rip about the cause! It's like trying to steer your car. You can yank on the steering wheel all day, but it's not until the car starts moving that you're able to direct it where you want it to go.

Making Sense of . . . Deciding to Respond

Here you are, minding your own business, and you notice that you're feeling a little spacey. You close your eyes, take the position of The Observer and do a quick internal scan, discovering you also feel kind of nauseated and your heart rate has increased. A trigger has just come up on your radar. You divert your attention deeper within to hear what's going on in your mind. You hear the voice of the ego:

- You'd better run and find a place to hide.

- You're having a melt down and it could get embarrassing.

- What if you freak out?

You slip your shoes off, plant your feet squarely on the floor and initiate Emergency Breathing (some people find it helpful to keep their eyes closed). Keeping a safe, loving sense of detachment, you focus on staying in The Observer position, allowing the thoughts generated by the ego to come and go, not holding on to any of them. After each thought appears, you ask yourself:

I wonder what my next thought is going to be?

Sometimes, this is enough to alleviate your symptoms; if you were at home, you would be recording the details in your InnerAction Journal to examine later. Today your mind must have something it wants to resolve and let go of. You recognize this from your Observer position, so you switch tactics and ask yourself:

What wants to happen?

Right away, the ego dives into a fearful tirade. You continue grounding yourself and breathing properly, allowing tears to come if they want to as you sit by as the silent observer of your thoughts. Soon, the ego ramps up its effort to get you to react and its ranting turns into an angry temper tantrum. You do your best to monitor your physical state, remaining in the driver's seat, when you notice the ego is running out of things to say. Another round of Emergency Breathing, and you ask again:

I wonder what my next thought is going to be?

This time, a quieter, calmer "knowing" that's not really a voice introduces something more like an idea than a thought. It suggests, *Do what you need to do.* You feel hopeful and motivated at the suggestion and recognize this as your opportunity to change history by responding instead of reacting. You find that pause in thought, that silent space of clarity, then you ask:

What do I need right now?

An image comes into your mind of you laying on your back in the grass, enjoying the end of the yoga class you took last week. You ask:

Will this response move me closer to or further away from reclaiming a life of wholeness and healing?

It's obvious to you that excusing yourself from the room and laying in the grass for a few moments couldn't hurt, especially considering how exhausted you feel after this minor healing crisis. Of course, the ego tries to interrupt your decision, but as you've learned by now, it doesn't have your best interests at heart.

So, what do you do during that in-between pause? Up until now, you've (hopefully) been enjoying the silence of your thoughts, the oasis in the desert, a break from the tyranny of your chattering ego. It's a wonderful, safe place of refuge you carry with you and can retreat to whenever you need a break. Now, let's use it in a different way by taking advantage of the clarity it brings to ask a question:

Will my response bring me closer to or further away from…

Finish the question by repeating the Personal Healing Statement you created in the HomeWork section from *Season of Transformation: Let The Journey Begin!* You'll likely experience a similar brief pause before a thought arises. By now, you can probably recognize the voice of the ego. It may sound like either someone from your past (usually a person of authority) who was critical of you—a parent, a boss, a teacher, a sibling—or a harsh version of your own voice. The above exercise will teach you how to recognize that smaller, peaceful, legitimate voice of wisdom within you that we've been calling The Observer, but chances are, right now the voice of the ego is much louder. Let's examine some of its tactics and know thy enemy.

The intrusive thoughts produced by the ego are nothing more than illusions. Think about it. Don't intrusive thoughts usually deal with something that hasn't happened yet or has happened already? Whatever the ego is pestering you about, there's not much you can do either way, since all we ever really have control over is this moment. If you get caught up in the ego's busy-ness with non-essentials, you'll feel frustrated by problems that never seem to have solutions. Release yourself from the grip of fear and disconnect from fearful thinking by remembering that, like a magician, the ego tries to influence you with illusions.

Illusions aren't dangerous, because they're not real. Any effects that result from illusions exist because of our belief in the illusion. What has no effects doesn't exist. In other words, by denying the reality of the cause or withdrawing your belief in it, you can make effects disappear. Do you take some sort of action every time the ego jerks your chain? I'm willing to bet the effects or outcomes from your efforts are always unhappy ones. It's important to understand the ego has no power without your agreement.

Clarity undoes the confusion created by illusions, so my attempt here is to reveal a few of the mysteries behind the ego's magic show. Keep in mind that the ego doesn't want to be found out to be a horrible magician, so it is difficult to pin down. The more you try to explain how it works, the more elusive it becomes, leading you around in circles, but there are a few patterns to its way of operating. You can be confident that all its thoughts are ultimately fear-based at the core, but here are a few clues about how to tell if a thought is a legitimate idea or the voice of the ego.

Ego-Centered Thoughts:

TIME FOCUSED

Attempts to delay

A sense of being completely alone; on your own

Pain

Overlooks greater meaning

Becomes strong in strife

Judgement or labeling

Attacks

Inconsistent

Separation in all its forms—"isolation will save you"—dissociation

Punishment

Thinking or action not in line with your true nature

Sees dependency as threatening	Unaware of something greater than itself
Fragmented perception	Contradictory
Distortion; deception	Irreconcilable
A need to demonstrate proof	Learning is frightening
Confusion	Harsh
Unconnected to bigger picture; disconnected	Feels unnatural
Thoughts or actions make you feel tired, exhausted	A sense of needing more—teaching, evidence, money, information
Analyzes to breakdown or separate	Vulnerable to stress, meaning that when the thought is tested, it falls apart or leads in circles
Error focused	Comparisons
Avoidance of truth	Giving to get
Mistakes are exaggerated	Anything but a direct sense of fear—unbelieving, distant, emotionally shallow, callous, non-committal, uninvolved, even desperate
Variable, unstable	
Chaos	
Needing to defend or protect	

Legitimate Ideas:

DIRECT VERY SPECIFIC
Right-minded thoughts, meaning truth-focused, healing-oriented, creative (vs. left brain, logical thinking)

Only what you need to know

Separates truth from illusion

Looks beyond to what you were
before healing was needed

Perceived as painful by the ego

Perceives totally not selectively

Does not see error

Accepting

Equality

Charitable

A "knowing" sense that's
beyond perception

Found within a deeper
part of yourself

Interacting with others
increases the ideas

A permanent communication link;
the volume is either up or down

A sense of motivation at
the idea presented

Unity

Ego dissolves at its sound

Peaceful

Correction vs. error or punishment

Ideas or actions result in
feeling hopeful, joy-filled

Listening is the only require-
ment; doesn't demand action

Gentle

Dissociation falls away

Uses everyday life as a
teaching device

Calls you to remember, so you
can forget; a sense of undoing
the past in the present

Doesn't command or
demand, only reminds

Healing focused

Ideas are compelling

Direct opposite of the ego; brings
to mind a sense of the "other" way

Increases and/or strengthens as you share it

Reinterprets error by bringing understanding

Guides in making choices

Never produces fear

Cannot ask for more than

you're willing to do	Mediator between perceptions of the ego and knowledge of the truth
Recognizes a bigger plan; a sense of something larger than oneself	
	Miraculous effects

The ego's magic act doesn't change much. As a matter of fact, the ego sees change as something to be feared and avoided at all costs, so it tries to get you to believe in the illusion that no change is peaceful. That's why many survivors try so hard to control their environment and everyone in it. They want predictability, consistency and routine, so they can stop feeling afraid; no change is peaceful, according to the ego. Predictability, consistency and routine have helpful elements, but living life like the movie Groundhog Day is very hard to maintain over time and is impossible to achieve when needing to learn new ways of dealing with PTSD symptoms. The truth is, change is happening around you all the time. The question is whether it's making you better or bitter.

Our thoughts, like birds, fly through our mind and occasionally land for awhile. Healing begins when we are able to observe our thoughts with loving detachment, like watching birds land momentarily in a tree. It's when we allow the birds to nest and feed in our tree that we have crossed over into creating an identity as a bird house or bird feeder! That's not you! You're a tree, growing and healing over the course of the four seasons, remember? Yes, thoughts, like birds, will come and go. Allow them to do so and enjoy the variety that come your way. But don't get hung up on creating a story about who you think you are just because a thought happened to show up.

HEALING, RELIGION & SPIRITUALITY

Many (if not all) people revered for their wisdom and positive contribution to humanity have endured extraordinary suffering. Jesus was crucified. Buddha shed his princely trappings and lived as a pauper. Muhammed experienced being shunned, physically attacked and even stoned. Mother Teresa's sister and brother died young, and her father was murdered for his political affiliations, leaving her and her remaining siblings to be raised by a single mother. Nelson Mandela, who believed in democracy and racial equality, suffered twenty-seven years of brutality and near-starvation in a South African prison after having been convicted as a terrorist. Martin Luther King was frequently harassed, beaten and had his life threatened until he was ultimately killed. Did you know that Abraham Lincoln survived a near-death experience (by almost drowning) before the age of seven? Furthermore, his mother died when he was nine, leaving his older sister to care for him—then she died when he was nineteen; his first love died before he could marry her, three of his four children died between the ages of four and eighteen, his wife spent time in a mental asylum, and Lincoln himself suffered with life-long clinical depression and PTSD until his assassination at the age of fifty-six—oh, and don't forget the brutality and horrors he witnessed during the Civil War.

What got these people through? More than that, how did they eventually thrive to the point of altering how humanity marched into the future? One thing is for sure: they each had a deep sense of something at work that was bigger than themselves. You can call this "something"

God, the Universe, a creative spiritual force, whatever you choose, as long as you understand that by giving this "something" a label, you have attached meaning from your past to it and quite possibility, have unintentionally placed it within a tiny box, limited to your understanding of it. The reality is that we can't know all there is to know, or understand about the mysterious ways our spirit communicates with the Divine. However, we can see the results—the effects—and by experiencing the effects, we can know and understand the cause, even if we don't have the vocabulary to articulate it.

Thinking Things Through . . . Locus of Control

To what degree do you feel you have the power to make change happen in your life? People who feel as if life is going on around them, happening to them, or occasionally sweeping them into the flow tend to feel more stressed and have more stress-related symptoms. On the other hand, people who believe they have a direct result on how life goes for them feel more secure, confident, and embrace change more quickly, resulting in better over-all health. What may be surprising is how we sometimes remove the locus of control from ourselves. You can see it in thoughts and language such as:

- I don't care. Whatever you want.

- God will take care of it.

- What I don't know can't hurt me.

- There's nothing I can do about it. It's just the way it is.

How you perceive the effect of your influence on external events is directly related to how stressed out you'll feel. Check out the locus of control quiz on the *PTSD Self Help* website to determine just how much credit (or not) you're giving yourself for creating the life you're living.

Words are just symbols, signs or pointers to a larger, unspeakable truth. Words can direct you, get you close, even motivate you toward an experience, but it is up to the Divine to take the final step and bridge the gap bringing you knowledge of the truth. Here's where I'll reveal to you what I've come to know about how and why I was led away from a life of suffering and fear toward a life of miraculous wholeness and healing. I'll use words that come from my experience in the Christian religion, because it's the language I know. I believe the core of any healing experience is a deep spiritual journey that transcends any limiting beliefs we may individually hold as human beings, making the effect of that healing experience both a personal and universal truth—a miracle. Please engage that quiet stillness within you. Try not to get hung up on the pointers, but look beyond them to what they are pointing to.

Making Sense of . . . Religion and Healing PTSD

The rock icon Bono said, "Religion is what's left when Spirit has left the building." People struggling with the roller-coaster ride of PTSD symptoms have a difficult, if not impossible, time trying to control their emotions. Consequently, their behavior can seem erratic and out of control. Religious doctrines that over emphasize self-discipline and/ or strict behavior as evidence of moral or upright character are in danger of stigmatizing parishioners wrestling with PTSD symptoms, or worse. Consider that statistics gathered by the U. S. Congregational Life Survey[18] estimates that sixty-one percent of attending church members are women; then, understand that National Comorbidity Survey estimates show that fifty-one percent of women have experienced at least one traumatic event in their lifetime. That brings our total number of women potentially struggling with PTSD while sitting in church pews to thirty percent—conservatively. It is commonly accepted that women experience PTSD at more than twice the rate that men do, and U. S. Prevalence estimates of lifetime PTSD in women come in at 9.7%. That makes for a staggering potential number of women who could be exposed to secondary wounding by uninformed, well-intentioned religious leadership. And that doesn't take into account men, children, or veterans.

---

18 uscongregations.org, 2003

Many people turn to the church or faith-based groups as a last resort, seeking the help they so desperately need. When met with standards of behavior higher than the ones they are already imposing upon their fragile selves, they conclude if God/the church can't help, then there is nowhere else to turn, pushing a person toward thoughts of suicide. Instead of receiving a message of grace and acceptance (then careful assistance in moving them toward recovery with faith as a foundation), unhealthy standards of perfection and concepts of separateness—dare we say "specialness"—seep in. Sometimes subtle in nature, these obstacles to healing could be best described as *perscriptures*. Perscriptures are recitations of scripture, religious doctrine or inappropriately applied spiritual concepts that regardless of the intention, create obstacles to healing and leave the recipient feeling defeated, lost, confused, lacking or even hopeless. What does a perscripture sound like?

- You need to trust in God, not man (as a response to seeking psychiatric help)

- Behold, all things have become new!

- Faith it, 'til you make it.

- You just need to press in to God.

- You must have unforgiven sin in your life.

- You're being attacked by the enemy/Satan/a demon.

As opposed to practical, hands-on assistance (much like that of The Good Samaritan), these ideologies may have their place in religious training, but they are not only inappropriate responses to someone in the throes of full-blown PTSD—they are also dangerous. Those of us who adhere to religious practice and tradition would do well to remember the creative power God has given each of us and use our words with wisdom, not as a magic wand. Unfortunately, at the time of the publication of this book, there is no organized effort to educate the religious community about the special needs of PTSD survivors.

When God created, He did so by speaking words. In our own human experience, we understand that words come as a result of some thought we've had, and that we use our mind to think. We think, we speak (out loud or internally) and creation happens. Recall the Universal Law: you can know a cause by recognizing its effect. Thus, you can trace any creation backward through the process and discover its originating cause—its creator. Look around you. Everything in our world began as a thought or an idea. How do you think the chair you're sitting in, the cup you drink from, or the garden you look upon came to be?

To heal is to make happy. Healing is a thought—an idea. It happens when two minds connect, and in recognizing their unity in that thought, each becomes glad. The Bible says, "May the mind be in you that was also in Christ Jesus." Christianity uses this scripture as a blessing; *A Course in Miracles* acknowledges the scripture and calls it the blessing of miracle-mindedness. I've experienced its effect. The result was healing.

Annmarie's Story

After my mother died, I wondered where she went. I felt ripped off. In the last six months of her life, we finally started a friendship. Then she was gone. My only memory of church was grape Kool-aid, graham crackers and felt-board bible characters. However, my experience of God was a whole different deal. Throughout my childhood, I had a compelling sense of having a companion with me. At times, I felt drawn by this presence. Often, its guidance kept me out of danger and comforted my loneliness as an only child. I turned to this friend just hours before my mother passed, a few months after my first nervous breakdown. I remember a deep, heartfelt sorrow for what had become of my life. I felt overwhelmed by fear at passing disastrous habits on to my son. I literally cried out, "There's nothing left for me. I've made a mess of my life. I've lost everything. If you can do something with this mess, be my guest. I'm done. I'll do whatever you want."

Four years later, I found myself wanting to be around other people who were as curious as I was about God, what life means, and why we're all here. Those four years were spent in a blissful state of exploration, a deepening relationship with that friendly presence I had known as a child. I had read the Bible from cover to cover and the New Testament three times. I was still searching for something, reading between the lines to try to see more clearly the truths buried there. I didn't imagine I was the only person searching, so I got involved in a non-denominational Christian church. I learned a lot about myself, about others, about human behavior and the power of collective beliefs during the ten years serving in women's leadership. However, my personal experience of God had left my life, and I wanted it back.

Looking back, I'm grateful for people's ignorance about what PTSD looks like in the life of a person. It was painful to be told I was possessed by a demon, wasn't praying to or seeking God enough, or had sin in my life that was keeping God from healing me. Far too many survivors hear this from their "religion of last resort." Now, I can say with certainty that it's God who guides, heals, and gives happiness - not a building or movement, big or small. Because God dwells within us, we are the altar, and wherever we are, there is the church. When my life came crashing down the second time, I turned to the religion I'd been serving faithfully for so many years. When I leaned on its structure for support, it too came crashing to the ground. I was alone with God once again. And He didn't fail me.

So, what minds share the same healing idea? Clearly, at least one of the minds needs to belong to someone who wants to be happy or healed. What about the other mind? Who does that belong to? Scripture says that whenever two or more are in agreement about anything, it will be done.[19] Does that mean the person who wants to be happy needs to find another person who agrees with them? If so, that would limit God's ability to heal—especially His ability to heal survivors who have isolated themselves, have difficulty trusting anyone, and are afraid to tell a single soul about what's going on inside them. That's not the God I experienced. Let me introduce you to the One who connected with my idea of being happy.

The Holy Spirit is referred to as the Healer, the Comforter and the Guide. He is also described in scripture differently than God the Father and Christ the Son. He is the only part of the Holy Trinity that has a symbolic function. He is known as a wind, a dove, a flame, a light, a cloud, a seal, water, and in 1 Corinthians 2:16, the mind of Christ. Interestingly, the Holy Spirit is described as having a sword (Ephesians 6:17). This sword is a symbolic representation of words coming directly from God. Words, as we know, are a result of thoughts—in this case, God's thoughts.

---

19 Matthew 18:19

The Holy Spirit's symbolic activity and purpose makes Him difficult to understand. Why? Because symbols, like words, can have different meanings to different people. Think back to our discussion about the Belief Window and PTSD being like an opaque shade drawn over it. This state of mind makes it doubly difficult to see the reality of the world beyond. However, when your life and your very soul are hanging in the balance, suddenly a shift occurs. The pain of who you are becomes greater than the pain of becoming who you need to be, and you take the first step toward the truth. The truth is the pain of who you are being becomes greater than the pain of remembering who you are.

The Holy Spirit operates within God the Father and God the Son, much like our own spirit operates within us. At some point during our suffering, we become acutely aware that we are more than a body with a brain. The Holy Spirit is so close to the knowledge God and Christ have about you (and everything else in the universe!) that He calls it into view. He rolls up the PTSD shade for a moment, cleans off a grimy part of your Belief Window and/or in some cases, opens the window entirely. He is so much a part of the Holy Trinity and has such intimate knowledge of all truth that God Himself can flow across the little gap between you. You can block this flow of knowledge, but it's always there waiting for you. You can never lose your ability to access the knowledge of the truth.

Remember, the Holy Spirit is also called the Healer. His purpose is to heal or make happy. That's why scripture talks about the joy of the Spirit. The voice (or words) of the Holy Spirit, then, is the call to heal (also known as *Atonement*, an often-misunderstood word). Let's keep it simple by looking more closely at the word *Atonement* as a pointer or symbol: AT - ONE - MENT, is to be one, wholeness; a repair for a damaged relationship. Atoning means "undoing." The undoing of fear is an essential part of the atonement value of healing, also known and experienced as a miracle. So, the Voice of the Holy Spirit is the Call to Atonement, or the restoration of the integrity of the mind, bringing your mind and the mind of Christ together in agreement about your happiness, your healing. How does this happen? The Holy Spirit is the Christ Mind which is aware of what you really are, and calls it into your remembrance by suggesting what you were before healing was needed.

The truth is, I didn't come up with the idea of being happy. I had lived in such an unhappy state for so long that I couldn't remember what happy felt like. I had to trust that there was more out there for me. I had to trust the happiness other people saw for me could become real. I was the one who finally connected with the idea of being happy which had been waiting there all along in the mind of Christ. And I had to trust that the Holy Spirit would speak to me through my interactions with other people. At some point, the biggest question and ultimate lesson was would I listen?

RELIGION

There are elements of religious practice and tradition that are beautiful representations and reminders not only of God, but also of His nature, which is love. At the time of my healing journey, there was only one Christian author who dared write about the effects of child sexual abuse. Consequently, I had to look outside the Christian community to get the help I needed. This brought me into contact with people who thought and believed differently than I did. With the help of the Holy Spirit, I was able to take what was personally helpful and discard what wasn't. Surprisingly, the most difficult interactions I had in doing that were within the Christian community.

Learning how to turn down the volume of the ego was something I first began learning by practicing prayer. In taking a physical posture of sitting with hands folded and pouring out the contents of my heart (instead of my mind), I noticed moments of blissful silence. Then, I visited a Catholic church and experienced their tradition of the Rosary. I found that the tactile act of touching beads and reciting words accomplished the same thing. Once, I visited a friend's Buddhist meeting where I participated with a group of people who were reciting words (some were touching beads) and holding a heartfelt intention for peace in the world. I noticed the ego didn't have much to say then, either. Yet another time, during my healing journey, I began the physical practice of yoga to alleviate chronic muscle tension. The act of slowly moving my body into positions that felt strong and alive, while breathing deeply into the core of my being, brought up clear rantings of the ego; later, during quiet meditative poses, yoga inspired ideas that I'd never had before. This compelled me toward healing, something I didn't expect while practicing what I'd believed to be a non-religious activity.

It seemed there were elements of my religious experience that were common among people of other faiths. While I was undertaking the difficult journey of healing from PTSD, I chose to focus on these things we had in common, the guidance provided directly to me by the Holy Spirit and suggestions from people He brought along the way that were truly helpful in bringing me the relief I so desperately needed. Unfortunately, PTSD manifests many early warning symptoms through the body, and many religions have a difficult time with the subject matter surrounding the human body. We are taught that we are spiritual beings inhabiting a body, but we're not taught what the body is used for outside of procreation. It was through my PTSD healing experience, combined with my understanding of scripture and my relationship with Christ via the Holy Spirit, that I came to the truth—and it's this: the body is a means for communication.

When you are presented with an opportunity to react or respond, your alignment with the ego or the Holy Spirit will determine the outcome. The Holy Spirit bridges the gap between knowledge and perception, and He'll teach you how to know the truth by using things you are familiar with. What could you be more familiar with than your body? Or have you dissociated and separated from your body so much that you're no longer in control of it? The Holy Spirit can and will use it to teach you the truth about PTSD. Transformation, a shift in your thinking that brings happiness, comes through the body, like a message showing up through the device called your cell phone.

Annmarie's Story

My Healing Partner had three reminders she would speak at various times according to the need of the moment. They were:

- Stay in your seat.
- Tabula Rasa
- The only way out is through.

These life lines were very personal reminders of conversations we had about experiences I was having and revelations I received after working with other members of my Healing Team. Just the mention of stay in your seat reminded me that I was in the driver's seat of my mind and that any uncomfortable tactics of the ego or symptoms related to PTSD were temporary. It was my job to ride out the storm by finding that still, quiet place within until a healing crisis passed. Sometimes, fear would overtake me. I would literally be shaking, nearly crawling out of my own skin in response to the fearful memories that began to surface.

Looking back, it wasn't the visual pictures my memory was displaying on the movie screen in my head that frightened me as much as it was the emotions that came with them. Since my abuse began when I was very young, I hadn't developed the ability to understand or discharge the energy those emotions created in my body. I didn't even have the vocabulary to describe what I was feeling. I wanted to turn back away from my healing path, retreat into the numbness of dissociation and unplug from my mind and body. That's when I would hear "The only way out is through," and I would remember that what I wanted more than anything else was to stop running in fear from PTSD, to get rid of it once and for all, so I could have a chance at a normal life.

In the aftermath of a healing crisis, when I would feel emotionally bruised and beaten, Tabula Rasa was a gentle reminder that this process was an act of kindness: Tabula Rasa, a Latin phrase for clean slate. Although often painful, the entire three-year healing journey was the most gentle way of lancing a deep festering wound that hadn't healed - one that was crippling me as a result. Much like submitting myself to a necessary surgery, Tabula Rasa reminded me not to jump off the surgery table before the operation was over, and brought a cooling wash over my burning heart and mind; it was a reminder that this process was necessary, so healing could solidly root itself within my soul and make the illusion of fear disappear forever.

Making Sense of . . . Emotional Vocabulary

Do you have a difficult time putting your emotions into words? Many people who experienced trauma in childhood have a limited vocabulary to describe the flood of emotions brought on by PTSD. For those who experienced trauma later in life after a strong vocabulary was established, the tidal wave of emotions comes so quickly and changes so rapidly that they're almost impossible to pin down with a word. Try using this helpful feelings chart to teach yourself about the varied aspects of your emotional climate and to communicate it with others.

Are You AWARE of How You Are Feeling Now?

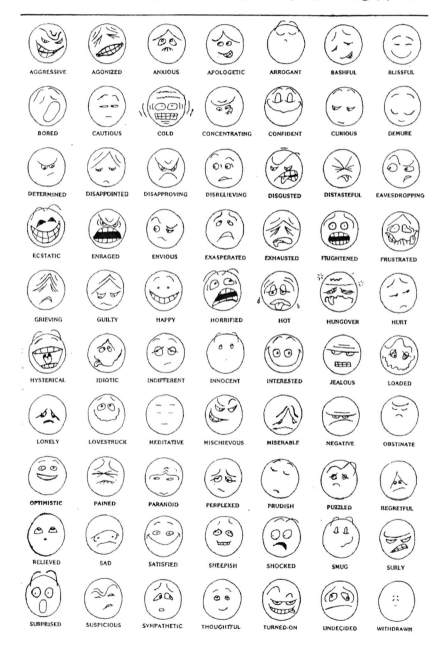

SPIRITUALITY

There's no doubt that, eventually, PTSD will bring you to a deep spiritual awareness. As we've learned through our study of the Belief Window and the ego, we must be careful about the meaning we attach to stories, the identities we create out of fear, and the power of words to limit our understanding of the world around us. Communication ends separation. Attack promotes it. And communication is what has happened here. The body is beautiful or ugly, peaceful or savage, and helpful or harmful, according to the use to which it is put. Misuse it and you will misunderstand it. The thinking mind, or what you could call your spirit, is not physical: the brain is. The thinking mind can, however, use the body to manifest results. Right now, is the ego still hijacking your mind and using your physical brain to manifest what we call Post Traumatic Stress Disorder? And isn't it just like the ego to separate you from all of "normal" humanity by helping you create an identity about being disordered? Don't give the ego any help. Focus on healing your body, which includes your brain. Learn the skills necessary to discern the voice of the ego from the Voice of God—the Holy Spirit. Remember who your Father and your Brother are, and that you can never be separated from Their very DNA, which resides within you. You are asked to do only one thing: offer the tiniest willingness to be happy.

BE GENTLE!
Do your words represent thoughts generated by the ego or ideas inspired by the Holy Spirit?

Do you know how to slow down your mind so you can choose one or the other?

Do you want to?

I'M OPEN!
Go back and review the section The Belief Window in *Season of Hope: Plan & Pack*. Specifically, consider any limiting beliefs you may have surrounding religious practice or tradition, as well as faiths and practices you may not be familiar with.

ALL IN!
Feeling resistant to this conversation about healing and religion? Have

other areas in your life that you want to accomplish but seem like you're constantly rolling a bolder uphill? Try Catherine Collaut, PhD's suggestions for getting your subconscious mind (the part the ego loves to use most) on board:

1. *Recognize Resistance:* It is always best to tune in and discover the slightest resistance, because if you aren't even aware of resistance you're not likely to do anything about it.

2. *Be Humble:* Don't assume you know everything, and certainly not everything about your resistance. Pretend for a moment that you don't know everything there is to know about your internal 'opponent.' Trust your subconscious long enough to learn from it. Trust that it has something important and wise to say. Because it does.

3. *Get Specific:* What exactly is the fear or fears? What are the associations you've made (beliefs) about getting or having what you want? What exactly is your subconscious looking out for or protecting you from? Interview yourself with curiosity and compassion. Let the subconscious make its case. You want it to! There's powerful information in it that's valuable to you. The key is having a childlike curiosity that has no agenda, a genuine desire to understand, and a compassionate heart. Come in like a know-it-all, and you'll get nothing in return, so get details and applaud (don't judge) whatever you get!

4. *Make a Promise:* Make a promise to yourself that you'll work it out with your resistance, not work against it. For example you could say, "Dear, dear friend, listen, if doing _____ means _____ I won't go for it. I don't want that either! I appreciate you looking out for me! If I have to choose between _____ and peace of mind and heart, I'll choose the latter. I promise. I promise I'll choose _____, only if that isn't what it means. Are we cool? Can we at least take a look then?" Of course, you'll want to be a good partner to yourself, one that you can rely on, and you will want to keep your promise.

5. *Find Exemplary Examples:* Now that we have an "Okay, I guess it wouldn't hurt to take a look," from your resistance, we want to see what's true. Evidently you must have some not-so-positive ex-

amples of what happens when you get what you want. Now, you want to see what else is true. Look to see if your fears can also *not* be true. Remember, your subconscious can and will do anything you tell it is possible. You want to douse your mind with positive examples, case studies and true stories of other people who have done *all* of what you want to do or have *all* of what you want to have. Get as many examples as you can that prove what you want is possible. They can be people you know or people you don't know. The more examples you get, and the more time you spend studying/learning from them, the more you reinforce the idea, "This is definitely possible."

6. *Solidify and Affirm:* Strengthen what you have learned, gleaned and now understand about your fears, the reality about how life can work, about what you want and what you're moving toward. Bathe yourself in your new found, harmonious, integrated and now possible truth. Remind yourself of the road, the only possible road in light of the promise you made above, that you are actually taking. The more ingrained your new perspective becomes in the subconscious, the more it uses its power and resources to facilitate and work toward your goal and effectively execute on your behalf—and the easier it will be for you to manifest or materialize it.

Now to affirm. Affirmations only work if you believe them. If you don't, they can have the opposite effect of what you're affirming. After completing the steps above, you have adequately shifted your beliefs about what you want. Affirmation statements will now become more of a reminder, a remembrance of what you've learned and saw to be true and possible. They will also bring back the feelings of hope and possibility, as well as a peaceful orientation, free of internal conflict, that gives you the sense of a light in the distance you may not know how to move toward, but are no longer afraid of getting to. You'll enjoy stating your affirmation! If you can't get behind your affirmation with a good feeling, leave it alone. Remind yourself as often as you'd like, but be sure to do so upon waking, right before sleeping and during any meditation activity.

A comment about timing. Trust—don't resent!—the timing of life. Trust that if what you want is standing right before you, it means you have the resources to deal with it. On the other hand, know that if what you're after hasn't made it into your field of vision, it is there waiting for you, and life is continuing to bring you the experiences you need to hone, develop, and acquire the strength needed to manage, contain, and enjoy what you want fully when it does show up. Enjoy where you're at right now! Be confident that by doing so, you're calling in the next level needed to get where you're going. Before long, you'll start enjoying the journey as much as the destination!

Want to discover more of what Catherine Collautt, PhD has to offer? Visit her site at www.catherinecollautt.com or watch an interview where Catherine talks about this process with socially conscious business and life strategist, Marie Forleo at www.marieforleo.com/2012/09/your-subconscious-mind/

COLLABORATIVE HEALING ACTIVITIES

The thought of adding exercise to your daily routine is probably about as attractive as taking a trip to the moon, and likely just as daunting. We've all heard the benefit regular exercise gives in decreasing the effect of stress on our body. I see the frowns and hear the moans already. So, forget about it. Don't add exercise to your already burdened schedule. Instead, add field trips. That's right—field trips. Remember the field trips you would take in grade school? It was so exciting to climb on board a bus with a special lunch packed and an entire day away from the school room to engage in a tactile learning experience. Collaborative healing activities, like the field trips you would take in grade school, are fun opportunities to engage in a tactile learning experience, and will challenge you to think outside the box and retrain your brain to think differently about triggers. Don't forget about using the practical application guides to ensure choosing an activity that's appropriate for your energy level, financial position and where you're at in the healing process.

Weighing the Evidence . . . Don't Be A Dropout

There are factors that will challenge your commitment to seeing the healing journey through to the end. Although healing is certain, it is up to you how quickly it shows up. By preparing for a few common obstacles to healing, you can ensure you won't abandon the healing journey at a time when you probably need it most. Here are some of the reasons people drop out of therapy:

- Low income

- Young age

- No insurance that covers mental health

- Thinking that it's not working

- Embarrassed to see a therapist

Just by reading *PTSD Self Help,* you're taking precautions against becoming a drop-out! You're learning what to expect, how to prepare, and best of all, a method for making sure you succeed. Survivors who receive both practical advice as well as therapeutic intervention are more likely to achieve the success they're looking for. By integrating healing activities into your overall lifestyle, it becomes more difficult to just walk away—you'd be unraveling your whole life! Another way to avoid the tendency to want to quit? Set goals. You could choose one trigger, one traumatic memory or one issue to work with until you feel a measure of resolution. You could set dates where you review your progress, comparing your symptoms and emotional climate to how you felt weeks or months before. You could focus on one element of the *PTSD Self Help* method at a time, until you're ready to try something new or add to your routine. Just having a Healing Team will decrease the possibility of your quitting. Don't forget to talk to your team members about how you're feeling about the process. They might have great ideas and solutions you've never thought of!

BODY ARMOR: WHY YOU NEED A MASSAGE

Did you know the body stores memories? Most people think memories are only stored in our mind, but that's not true. The body remembers what the mind chooses to forget. Sometimes people's muscles get locked tight from holding stress inside or trying to forget unpleasant memories. Chronic muscle tension is one of the many aggravating symptoms of PTSD.

The term *body armor* describes one way survivors cope with PTSD symptoms. It starts in the brain, which sends signals beyond our conscious awareness to the muscles, creating chronic holding patterns in the posture and tissues of the body.

How does this happen? A traumatic event causes the body to contract its muscles and harden to shield the inner self. Just think back to the last time something frightened you or someone treated you harshly. Do you remember your shoulders and neck tightening in response?

If the trauma is substantial enough, the brain will continue to send messages to the muscles, which will be reluctant to release their grip in an effort to protect you from "what's about to happen," even if "what's about to happen" already happened years ago.

Another explanation for body armor? The Herculean effort you are making to contain how out of control you feel or to resist memories from the past has created a cycle of tension that's hard to break without professional help. My massage therapist and yoga instructor friend who now lives in California says, "When I encounter a person on my massage table with a lot of body armor, the first thing I ask them is, 'Do you drink enough water?'" Surprisingly, drinking the recommended eight glasses of water a day is a great start toward loosening the hold tension has on your muscles. "If I can get a client to drink water, then more space is created between the cells of their muscle tissue. That's the focus of massage, to manually manipulate the muscles to create more space, blood flow and oxygen."

Energy and blood flow in your body can't circulate freely through areas of tension. One bad side effect is that your body may shut down those areas, causing physical ailments and emotional imbalances. A Tacoma mother whose adult daughter was molested as a child shares via email, "The emotional outbursts that occur, seemingly without provocation, and the physical ailments that no doctor can pinpoint make life for a young adult woman harder than it should be."

Physical symptoms and emotional turmoil are the body's way of responding to unresolved issues and events. If the tension and emotional residue left by the traumatic event are not dealt with together, symptoms can go on for years. Massage, as well as acupressure and chiropractic adjustments, can really help to loosen up those muscles and get you on the path toward emotional healing.

My massage therapist friend points out, "Knowingly or unknowingly, when we allow chronic muscle tension, we are keeping the memories associated with that tension from flowing freely through us. By unlocking the tension, you also release the emotional memories stored within the cells. Depending on what a client wants to accomplish, I can help them release those memories."

Remember, it all begins with the brain. Massage therapy alone won't take you very far toward walking away from PTSD forever. That's why you need a Healing Team! Using the natural healing arts of massage and acupressure has no adverse side effects and costs little or no money. All you need are two willing hands—yours or someone else's. Give these suggestions a try:

BE GENTLE!
Pay attention to your feet. Did you know that your feet have more than 7,000 nerve endings that can affect the entire body? Practice massaging your feet regularly. It's a great way to experience the calm, relaxing effect of massage, and you don't have to take your clothes off.

Check out books from the library about reflexology. This is a good one: *Hands On Feet*, by Michelle R. Kluck

I'M OPEN!
Make an agreement with your spouse/significant other or Healing Partner to exchange massages! An at-home massage given by someone close to you can make this a fun, trust-building experience. Do whatever feels comfortable at any given time. Remember, what feels okay one day may not be okay the next. Why not agree to a let's-take-turns seated or foot massage given by someone you trust and feel comfortable with? They don't have to be an expert, just any old rub will help increase your ability to feel at ease with physical touch and your awareness of how your body is feeling. Eventually, you can take it up a notch by scheduling a massage from a stranger or get comfortable with the idea of manual chiropractic adjustments.

ALL IN!

Schedule a deep-tissue massage every two weeks. More than that is too much for your body to process. Massage forces toxins into your blood stream, so it's important to drink plenty of water before and after a massage, as well as to give your body time to recover between appointments. Massage doesn't have to cost a lot of money, either. Ask for massages as gifts for special occasions! Mother's/Father's Day, birthdays, or holiday times are opportunities for you to enjoy the benefits of massage at least three times a year. Gift cards to local spas make great gift ideas from the ones you love.

YOGA

When I ask survivors to persevere in trying yoga for relief of their PTSD symptoms, they're always glad they did. Some poses are hard while you're attempting them, but in the end, accomplishing a pose through the use of relaxation, targeted muscle engagement and proper breathing technique brings a satisfying sense of accomplishment. But yoga doesn't have to be hard! You can accomplish many of the benefits of yoga right from where you're sitting. Because yoga is a non-competitive, highly personal practice, it is a wonderful way to overcome symptoms like body armoring, panic attacks and insomnia. There are two key elements of yoga that directly benefit your attempts to heal from PTSD:

1. Breathing techniques that cue your body to override the automatic fight/flight/freeze response

2. Having grace toward your body's limits as they shift from day to day and moment to moment

Try yoga just once, and you'll come away with the experience of having calm control over your body instead of beating it into submission. Annie Carpenter, a yoga instructor and mentor for other yoga instructors at Exhale Center for Sacred Movement in Venice, California, explains that yoga also " . . . teaches you the determination you need to meet a challenge and the perseverance to return to it repeatedly over time, despite its difficulty." This is a key concept to master while traveling along the PTSD healing journey. Whenever practicing yoga, always remember to listen to your body. Pain or discomfort is *not* the goal. A gentle stretching that feels good is the goal. Before you know it, you'll be challenging your sense of balance in tree pose!

Be Gentle!
Find a local yoga class and ask if you can watch one time. Check your local cable listing for a televised yoga class or borrow a video from a friend and just watch. Be sure to choose a beginner's practice! Don't freak yourself out by watching advanced sessions where participants wrap themselves up like pretzels. Be realistic. Watch a class you might like to try and take baby steps toward giving it a shot!

I'm Open!
Try visiting your local library (at the time of this printing, those are still available) for beginners videos or books about practicing yoga at home. If you subscribe to cable television, check your provider's menu for free on-demand exercise videos that include yoga as a selection. Also, don't forget about YouTube! There are hundreds of free yoga asanas (brief routines of only a few poses) to try just by searching beginning yoga.

All In!
Need time away from the kids? Check in to a local YMCA, yoga studio or other gym membership. They usually offer beginning or senior yoga, all the way up to more advanced levels. Plus, you'll be able to drop the kids off at the childcare center or enroll them in their own exercise program while you take time to focus on a healing activity. Another benefit is the use of their steam rooms and saunas! Think it might be too expensive? Ask them about special deals for military, seniors, or those with a limited income. You might be surprised how affordable it can be.

Karate

Traumatic events can make victims out of the strongest people. Survivors wrestling with the symptoms of PTSD often feel as if their everyday life is attacking them. When someone wants to learn how to defend themselves, martial arts come to mind. But not all martial arts programs are alike. It's important to discover a martial art that supports the calm and peacefulness you're trying to attain. Karate is just such a martial art.

One of the key elements in practicing Karate is to never use it to attack others. Instead, Karate teaches you to use the centrifugal force of your opponents blows against them. In other words, Karate could be thought of as the art of deflection. Through your body, Karate can teach your mind to respond to perceived attack in a calm, focused manner and use the negative energy coming at you as a force for your protection. When you use your body to apply this concept in re-training your brain to re-direct the negative energy produced by the ego and PTSD, suddenly symptoms like triggers and flashbacks are no longer opponents, but rather sparring partners who work with you to make you stronger.

Although Karate can be practiced as an art, as a sport, or as self-defense training, we will be using it for the purposes of healing from PTSD. Traditional Karate places an emphasis on self-development and the psychological elements that are incorporated into a proper attitude for practicing Karate (such as perseverance, fearlessness, virtue, and leadership skills). Practice styles vary, but you'll find most classes perform two important exercises. KIHON is the performance of a technique or a combination of techniques by an entire group in unison. KATA is a formalized sequence of movements which represent various offensive and defensive postures. You'll find these two exercises the most helpful in putting your physical body in a position that will help to retrain your brain.

Be Gentle!
Once again, watch a class! My favorite? Kid's classes. I figure if kids can do it, so can I. Just watching a Karate class makes you feel empowered. It really is easier than it looks.

I'm Open!
Maybe you feel Karate is a bit too aggressive for you, or you'd like to try something that moves more at your pace: try Tai Chi. Although the purpose is more meditative, the movements are similar and can serve to unlock chronic stress, cellular memory and body armor. You can start by watching a class (some classes meet in the park!), renting a video from the local library, or dialing in to your local cable television's exercise menu. Once again, don't forget YouTube! Search for beginning Tai Chi movements.

All In!
Dive right in and sign up for a beginner's class in your local area! Not enough challenge for you? Try going on a martial arts retreat. There are several retreat centers across the country that specialize in helping

people develop a passion for practicing martial arts. Just be sure to choose one that offers a beginner's option and follows a holistic approach, like including meditation, for instance. Remember, you'll want to communicate clearly to the registration staff that you're participating as an aspect of healing PTSD, so they can offer you added support on site should you need it.

BELLY DANCING (FOR WOMEN)

Did you know belly dancing was a sacred ritual to be performed only in the presence of other women? The greatest myth about belly dancing is that it is intended to entertain men. Known also as Middle Eastern dance, it was a ritual performed during rights of passage to mark seasons in a woman's life. Most notably, belly dancing was used to encourage a woman during childbirth. When a woman was ready to give birth to her child, women from her village would gather around her bedside, performing a familiar rhythmic dance, moving their bodies in a way that would remind the woman giving birth of the muscles she needed to use to accomplish her task. When the women of the village come together to support another woman in her femininity, men are not permitted.

Many historians say that belly dancing is the oldest form of dance, having roots in all ancient cultures from the Orient to India to the Mid-East. When nomadic tribes attacked villages, they would capture all of the women and, as a form of humiliation, require them to perform their sacred ritual in the presence of men—thus the myth of belly dancing as a sexual performance was born.

Belly dancing is natural to a woman's bone and muscle structure, with movements emanating from the torso, rather than in the legs and feet. The dance often focuses upon isolating different parts of the body, moving them independently in patterns, weaving together the entire feminine form—a form that many female PTSD survivors have lost contact with long ago. Belly dancing is generally performed barefoot, and this is thought by many to emphasize the intimate physical connection between a woman, her spiritual expression, and her grounded-ness to the earth.

Belly dancing's fine movements have the ability to put you in touch with parts of your body you've ignored for a long time and is especially helpful for women recovering from childhood sexual abuse. For a woman who has been victimized by men, and as a consequence has numbed herself to her entire body, belly dancing can reawaken who she is as a woman, re-establish her connection to her body, and become a powerful PTSD healing experience. Why not set aside time to explore this deeply private form of expressing love for yourself and invest a few moments in your schedule that are set aside for you alone?

BE GENTLE!
Have you lost track of your body? Take a good look at your feet. Are they cracked, dry, neglected? Or are they pink, vibrant and healthy? How about your back and shoulders? When you touch your skin, is it numb in places? Are the muscles tight and stiff? Try the collaborative healing activity Body Sketch (*Artistic Renderings: I'm Open!* practical application guide), and reacquaint yourself with parts of yourself that you've abandoned. Remember, awareness is the first step toward change. Then, come back to explore belly dancing as a fun way to reconnect with your body.

I'M OPEN!
Once again, make YouTube your friend and watch a few belly dancing videos! The best? You'll want to watch Suhaila Salimpour's YouTube channel, specifically the Margaret Cho docuality. Suhaila is a practitioner who gets it. She understands the disconnect twenty-first-century women are struggling with and the value of dance in reconnecting women to their femininity and their bodies. In the video, you hear from a variety of women who have experienced amazing transformations thanks to this ancient form of dance. Go on! Watch the video! You'll see.

ALL IN!
Find a belly dancing studio or gym that offers a fusion of belly dance and other forms of exercise, like Pilates or yoga. Of course, you could always check out videos from the library, buy Suhaila Salimpour's beginner video, or just follow along to videos on YouTube. Why not get a group of friends to join you, if you need a little fun in your life?

EQUINE ASSISTED PSYCHOTHERAPY (EAP)

Have you ever felt the bass from music you hear in a passing car? What you feel in your gut is called "resonance" or vibration. Did you know that's why the strings on a violin are often made of, you guessed it, intestines (called cat gut, though the strings are actually made from sheep intestines. Yuck!). And guess what else? Our emotions send out vibrations just like the music in that passing car! The funny thing is, you don't even have to be aware of your feelings to have this happen. Think about this: Horses have one of the biggest guts of all animals, giving them the ability to pick up even little vibrations. When a horse picks up vibrations, you can tell by their body language. Are their ears pointing backward? Does their skin "shiver" when you touch them? These are all clues that help people who are healing to discover more about their feelings. Besides, who wouldn't want to ride a pony?

Horses helping people is nothing new, but horses helping people understand how emotional energy shows up in the mind and body is just catching on. Animals in general have an amazing ability to put people in a healing state of mind. However, it's the horses' unique position as a prey animal that allows them to directly impact survivors struggling with PTSD. How is this possible?

On a deep level, horses find protection in the herd. Each horse in the herd plays a role in protecting the entire group. When a predator is apparent, a horse can send signals through body language and emotional energy to other members of the herd. Have you ever seen an entire herd of horses take off in unison, fleeing across an open pasture? It's as if they all move as one. It's because of this unspoken transmission that horses are able to protect themselves from predators. Similarly, people who are in a victimized state of mind are as sensitive as the horses. PTSD causes survivors to be hyper-vigilant to their environment, constantly alert to potential triggers. Because of this commonality between horses and survivors, spending time with horses can teach a survivor how to more accurately monitor their emotional environment.

SAFETY FIRST

Because horses are highly sensitive to their environment, it's important to understand how to be safe while working with and around them. Unknowingly, survivors who are in a heightened state of fear or anxiety could set off unexpected reactions in a horse's behavior. For this reason and in order to help you further connect to your body's communication system, it's time to learn about conducting an Inner Body Scan.

Once you're at the farm, ranch or barn, as you're standing next to your car, pause in silence for a moment. Close your eyes. Begin by bringing your attention to your feet (clad in heavy leather shoes or boots). How do they feel? Do they feel solid on the ground, powerful? Or do they feel as if they aren't touching the ground, hovering a small distance above it, perhaps? Make a mental note about how grounded you do or do not feel. Next, move your attention upward to your legs. Are they shaking, feel fatigued, ready to run away? Maybe they feel neutral. Continue your scan moving to your groin area. How does this space feel? What is this area of your body trying to tell you? How about your solar plexus? Does it feel hard, tense, guarded? Or maybe it feels relaxed and open. Make a mental note and move on, upward to your heart, your throat, your eyes, even to the top of your head.

With this quick assessment of your internal climate, you'll be able to share how you're feeling with the horse professionals and MHP you'll be working with. They will make sure to watch carefully for the horses reactions to being around you, keeping everyone including the horses safe during your EAP session. Whenever you feel a little out of sorts or overwhelmed by what you're experiencing while working with horses, conducting an Inner Body Scan is a good place to return. This way, you'll begin understanding how your body communicates and whether or not what you're noticing is energy that belongs to you or someone, something outside of you.

Have you ever walked into a room after an argument and felt the tension still in the room? This is an example of how our body can pick up on emotional energy that doesn't belong to us. Learning how to re-connect with this important skill will help you be better able to distinguish sensations you pick up as belonging to you (in that you're generating them in some way) or your external environment. With this knowledge, triggers and ego chatter become more obvious making it easier to know what to do about the symptoms they're whipping up.

When working with horses, be sure to follow these guidelines:

- Never approach a horse you don't know without it's owner or an EAP professional present.

- Always wear long sleeves, long pants and heavy shoes.

- Communicate your inner climate, fears and spontaneous thoughts to the EAP professional.

- Be quick to acknowledge your feelings and express your emotions (remember, don't be a lion in the grass: be who you are)

- Practice a soft gaze (also called soft eyes), soft (relaxed) belly and deep breathing when looking at or working around a horse.

- Use your tendency toward hyper-vigilance to instead, partner with your horse companion in monitoring the environment for the safety of both of you.

- Take it slow. Make your movements deliberate and within view of the horse (know their blind spots).

Annmarie's Story

Near the end of my healing journey, I almost gave up. Of course, I didn't know how close I was to the end. To me, it felt like I still had so much I didn't know about my past. I was still fearful that it might rear its ugly head later in life and take me down permanently. I'd been actively participating daily in healing activities for more than two years. I was tired. I wanted to be done. The exhaustion was drawing me back into depression. The evidence showed I was making remarkable progress, but I wasn't where I wanted to be. I started thinking, "Maybe this is as good as it gets for me. Will I be able to live the rest of my life with the measure of healing I have now?"

I told my therapist I needed a break. She strongly advised me not to stop therapy. That made me angry. Where before the PTSD symptoms were wiping me out, now the intensity of the healing process felt like it was doing the same. I asked my healing partner for help.

We put our heads together and came up with an idea: she would look for a retreat facility with a spa-like environment that had therapists on site, just in case I needed help while I was there. "While you're at it, could you look for one that has horses?" I asked. "I'd love to spend time with horses like I used to when I was a kid."

She discovered Leigh Shambo, a social worker with a love of horses who had figured out how to help people overcome their fears. I was sold. I told my therapist that I wouldn't take a break, but that I was adding Equine Assisted Psychotherapy to my recovery program. I asked her if she'd be willing to confer with Leigh, and I gave her permission to do so. Soon, I attended sessions that happened every other week over the course of six months. The ninety-minute drive to and from the sessions gave me the time I needed to absorb the revelations that came during my time with the horses. I can honestly say that the horses helped carry me the rest of the way to a complete healing from PTSD. Here's an example from one of my sessions:

Maggie - an extremely spirited horse - and I were locked together in a power struggle inside a round pen. I wanted Maggie to come to me, so I could pet her, feel her velvet nose and feel comforted by the smell of apples and grain on her muzzle. Maggie, on the other hand, wanted nothing to do with me. She wanted out to run free with her horse friends within view across the pasture. She paced back and forth at the opposite end of the pen.

Leigh said, "You seem frustrated by what's happening. What do you want to have happen?"

"I want her to come to me, but I can't figure out how to make her do that," I said as I moved toward Maggie with thoughts of grabbing her mane. Maggie shifted her weight and scampered away from my grasp.

"Come back to the center and tell me if how you feel right now reminds you of a time you felt like this before."

Alternately kicking the dirt and gazing at Maggie (who wanted so desperately to be anywhere but with me), I searched my memory banks.

"You know, I used to feel like this around my mom. She was always busy with something, anything, but spending time with me. She wouldn't even touch me or say she loved me. It was like I was invisible. But I wanted her attention! I tried to get it by pleasing her, being the good kid, but maybe it would've worked better if I had rebelled."

I noticed a huge smile break across Leigh's face as I spoke. That's when I realized that while I was being authentic about how I felt, instead of stuffing it and trying to "work" my way out of my feelings, Maggie had walked right up to me. I was absentmindedly caressing her neck when she moved around behind me, encircled her neck around my shoulders and rested her large cheek over my heart.

When a survivor comes into the presence of a horse, the horse will respond with body language to the survivors emotional state of being. If the survivor is anxious, uncertain, or fearful, the horse will perceive this in the human and interpret the human's communication as an alert to a potential threat in the area; they will respond accordingly with body language, such as pinning back the ears, shifting the weight from hoof to hoof, or wide, fearful eyes. These body cues can be helpful to an observant survivor working with a horse professional. It helps the survivor to become aware of how their emotional state of being impacts the world around them. It can also make for groundbreaking discussion with regard to whether or not the survivor was even aware of their emotional state of being at the time, and can provide real time experience in shifting their emotion to a more positive vibration.

Because the ability to pick up on subtle vibrational energy is part of the horse's natural ability to protect itself and the herd, they have also been equipped with the ability to discharge that energy quickly, something that PTSD survivors cannot do. By working with horses, survivors can learn how to discharge the adrenaline rush from a flashback, an unexpected trigger, or intrusive memory. The adrenaline that courses through the veins of a startled horse is the same adrenaline that courses through the veins of a PTSD survivor in the throes of their symptoms. Many times in therapy with survivors, I've watched horses walk away from a survivor to the opposite end of the arena and shake its entire body as if brushing off the dust from some major windstorm.

Additionally, working with horses helps to create new neural pathways in the brain of survivors by causing them to have to think of new ways to get a 1500-pound animal to do what they're asking it to do.

BE GENTLE!
Watch horses. Take a drive out to the country and park by a pasture where you can see horses. Just watching horses graze and seeing how they play with each other has an amazing effect on humans. You don't have to even get out of your car!

I'M OPEN!
Volunteer at a local barn. Many people who board horses are happy to have some extra help. Ask about exchanging some work for time grooming or playing with a horse. They may even exchange work for

riding lessons, if you're interested.

All In!

Participate in workshops or retreats that introduce you to horses helping people with PTSD. Many non-profits are popping up all over the country and have scholarships to cover the cost. You'll want to check out the Equine Assisted Growth And Learning Association's web site at www.EAGALA.org. They've been around since 1999 and are at the forefront of establishing Equine Assisted Psychotherapy (EAP) and Equine Assisted Learning (EAL) programs that operate safely, humanely and ethically for both humans and horses. You'll be able to search for an EAGALA certified program near you!

Barefoot Walk

You can tell a lot about a person by the condition of their feet. Hard, crusty heels, cold, numb toes, and cracked, discolored nails reveal a general disregard of these vital members of your body. Think about it—your feet carry more than 100 pounds on them every single day of your entire adult life. Your feet, like the tires of your car, are one piece of equipment that should not be neglected. Also, your feet are the points of contact with the earth. Psychologically this gives us the ability to ground ourselves in space and time. In other words, we know where we are, what season it is and where we're going by our ability to orient ourselves to the earth. If our connection with our feet is numb or nonexistent, then our sense of anxiety will be increased. A barefoot walk is just the thing! It's simple. Take off your shoes and socks, feel the grass between your toes, feel the pinch of rocks beneath your feet; all of these things come together to inform you about your world and what is real in it. This helps survivors discern the difference between reality and their state of mind.

Be Gentle!

Sure, you may walk around your house without shoes on, but when was the last time you went barefoot to the mailbox? Tune in to what you feel beneath your feet. Try to describe the textures and temperature of carpet, tile, grass or cement. Are your feet so neglected and calloused it still feels like you're wearing shoes? Move on to the I'm Open! practical application guide!

I'm Open!

Treat your feet! Give 'em a good soak (guys, this isn't just for ladies!), examine the nails and nail beds: give 'em a trim or a file here and there, if needed. Then, rub in (or get your spouse/significant other/healing partner to do it!) a lotion made especially for feet. My favorite is Aveda's Foot Relief. It smells great, is made of natural products and helps soften/eliminate calluses. Here's a great recipe for a revitalizing foot soak that will bring life back to those tired, old dogs:

> 1 C apple cider vinegar
> 1 C epsom salts
> 1/2 C baking soda
> 1/2 C dried lavender

Place all ingredients in a small tub large enough to comfortably submerge your feet up to the ankles. A twenty-quart Rubbermaid container with a lid works great and can store all your foot soaking ingredients when you're done. Just be sure to sanitize and dry it after use. Fill the container with comfortably warm water (don't burn your feet!) and throw in a few smooth rocks or a dozen marbles for your feet to play with. Sit back and *aaaahhhhhh* . . . relax.

All In!

Schedule time and money to enjoy a relaxing spa treatment for your feet every two weeks or once a month. The best treatments include a soak, a scrub, a massage and a paraffin wax dip. I like spas that use natural ingredients, like Aveda. That way, my senses aren't being bombarded by artificial fragrances or other treatments going on in the spa. But don't forget to soak and lotion up in between visits! You can spend a lot or a little money, so shop around until you find just the right price and treatment for you.

Playtime

What kind of things did you enjoy doing as a child? Swinging on the swings? Playing hopscotch? Roller skating? Getting back to what you enjoyed as a child is the quickest way to open up creative pathways that not only lead to intensely healing moments, but also honor what you've done to survive. It's by getting back to the innocence of childhood that creativity to invent your own healing pathway can thrive. Not only that, but actually participating in things you did as a child can serve to recall memories, both pleasant and traumatic, that can help you resolve your feelings in the present. Think about it—Western culture does not promote the idea of play. We work longer, harder, and at a frenetic pace not seen in other cultures. It's no wonder the United States is a stressed-out nation! For this reason alone, taking time to play can also serve as a wonderful restorative stop along your healing journey.

BE GENTLE!

Pick up a few inexpensive kids' games, like Jacks, Pick-up-sticks, Cat's Cradle, marbles or sidewalk chalk for hopscotch or drawing! Find a kid to borrow, or hang out with your own and play the games with them. Maybe you could teach them how to play tag, hot lava or hide-n-seek.

I'M OPEN

Get outside with your spouse/significant other/healing partner and throw a frisbee, a football or softball around. Trace each other's outline on the driveway with sidewalk chalk. Grab the dog or cat and trace them! And what about bubbles, water balloons and silly string?

ALL IN!

If you can, find a place in your yard to install a tire swing! Got room on your porch or deck? Find a fancy swing, make an old-fashioned one, or pick up a rocking bench at a garage sale. Or how about paying a visit to the local playground, park or schoolyard? Take your spouse/significant other/healing partner with you and push each other on the swings. Did you ever swing doubles? The first person sits normally on the swing. The second person sits on the first person's lap facing them, with their legs hanging out the backside. You end up looking kinda like a crab. Be careful and have fun!

ARTISTIC RENDERINGS

You've heard it said a picture is worth a thousand words. In the case of healing PTSD, this could not be more true. The emotional tidal wave caused by PTSD symptoms can defy explanation. Words, simple language, cannot go far enough to express the depth of pain, fear, and grief that a survivor experiences. Sometimes, a person's traumatic experience may have occurred at a time when they were developmentally not able to vocalize what was happening to them, or simply did not yet have the vocabulary to explain to the adults in their lives how the traumatic experience was affecting them.

As adults, we may continue lacking in emotional vocabulary and find it impossible to effectively communicate our experience to our Healing Team. When faced with this situation in healing PTSD, the act of drawing pictures can be helpful in working around emotional vocabulary and help articulate to others what is going on inside you. Finding ways to artistically express yourself can also give expression to feelings that don't seem to have any root in a particular memory, current event, or trigger. When feeling out of sorts and unable to put your finger on what's bothering you, finding an artistic way to express yourself can serve to move the healing process along. Pay a visit to Instagram, where you can follow @ptsd_selfhelp to see pictures other survivors have taken that represent their healing journey or show how they're using PTSD Self Help methods!

BE GENTLE!
Review the practical application guide *Making Sense of . . . The InnerAction Journal and Creativity* for the exercise that teaches you how to communicate when you're at a loss for words about how an event impacted your day. Experiment with drawing the progression of non-threatening events that are a normal part of your everyday life.

I'M OPEN!
Try an exercise I call Body Sketch. You'll need:

- A piece of butcher paper a few inches wider and longer than your body

- Colored (washable, unless you're careful) markers

- A helper

Lay the paper out on a hard surface. Lay on top of the paper. Have your helper trace an outline of your entire body with one of the markers. When you're able to be alone with your thoughts, perform an Inner Body Scan (See *Equine Assisted Psychotherapy - Safety First*). As you assess each area of your body, pause, returning to your outline to use your colored markers to artistically represent what you feel, sense or intuitively know about that area. Keep doing this back–and–forth assessment until you've covered your entire body. There's no right or wrong here! Don't judge. Allow your subconscious, even the ego, to share its information in whatever way comes to your awareness. If you'd like to take it a step further, jot down notes about what each area revealed to you on the reverse side.

ALL IN!

They can be difficult to find, but art therapy practitioners do exist. Your best bet for immersing yourself in something other than a self-guided exploration is to search the Internet for art therapy retreats. You will likely have to travel to California, Maryland, Tennessee, or Idaho. You can also find art therapy retreats off the mainland. How about Portugal, or heaven forbid, Maui? Don't want to get involved in a group thing? You'll need to search under the criteria *art therapy practitioners* to find a therapist, life coach, massage therapist or yoga instructor that offers art therapy as a supplement to their practice.

MUSIC

Hollywood spends billions of dollars on musical scores for the purpose of evoking an emotional response. Why not put all their hard work to use by tapping into music as a way to describe how you're feeling, or better yet, change it? Music has an amazing ability to bring a person to the verge of tears, and to bring back particular memories from their past—moments in time that are set so deeply that a person can recall what they were wearing, particular smells that were present, and the people they were with at the moment they heard a particular song. Music has also scientifically been proven to change our mood. Music can uplift you, inspire you, give you hope.

BE GENTLE!

Why not make a collection of music that describes how you're feeling about your PTSD? Can you find music that describes what happened to you? Can you find music that describes how you're feeling about it today? Create a collection of encouraging and uplifting tunes for those blue days when you're not quite feeling yourself. Don't forget—singing is music! Sing along with those songs. You'll be surprised at how effective singing is at shifting your mood or stirring the pot of your emotions when you're trying to work through something painful.

I'm Open!

Pay a visit to a symphony near you! Can't afford the symphony? Check out your local high school or college musical productions. How about the outdoor summer concert series at the park down the street? Many coffee houses and independent book stores occasionally offer acoustic sessions performed by local talent. Another easy way to get inspired with music is to take advantage of free YouTube videos or online radio/ streaming stations. Have you seen an inspiring movie lately? Why not pick up the soundtrack? Soundtracks are a great way to collect a variety of music that's all intended to play on your emotions.

All In!

Just listening to music not enough for you? Think about trying a drumming circle or working with a mental health professional who incorporates music therapy into their practice. Pick up that instrument you played as a kid—the guitar, the piano, the violin, the clarinet, and any other instrument you can think of can be rented from local music stores. Also, don't underestimate yourself as a living musical instrument! Get involved in a local choir or schedule karaoke nights in front of the television (cable television services sometimes offer karaoke music on their menu) or at a local gathering place.

Detox

Included in the concept of diet and food as medicine, detox activities will surprise you with how quickly they help remedy pesky PTSD symptoms and make you feel better fast. Much of the negative emotions, anxiety, and stress associated with attempting to live an everyday life under the influence of PTSD causes a residual build-up of toxins in your tissues, lymph nodes, and internal organs. The chemicals cascading through your brain are not always easily eliminated. For this reason, scientists and doctors are beginning to understand that stress can cause debilitating illnesses such as Syndrome X, fibromyalgia, and even cancer. For these reasons alone it's important to incorporate detox activities into your lifestyle, not to mention your PTSD healing routine. They're simple to accomplish, and involve changes in diet, hygiene habits, and routine. One thing they all have in common is the removal of toxins through the use of your body's elimination system. That means your bowels, liver, skin and kidneys will get a workout. It's best to work with a physician; at the very least, check with your doctor before jumping in to any extreme detox program.

Be Gentle!

Next time you relax in the bathtub, add detoxifying ingredients to the water and soak your way toward healing. Here's an inexpensive easy recipe:

1/4 C sea salt or Himalayan salt
1/4 C epsom salts
1/4 C baking soda
1/3 C apple cider vinegar
10 drops of your favorite essential oil (optional)

It's helpful to dissolve the salts and baking soda in boiling water on the stove, then add it to warm water you run into the tub. If you like your bath very hot, you can add the salts and baking soda directly under the spout as you fill the tub. Add the apple cider vinegar and essential oil. Soak for at least thirty minutes and drink plenty of room-temperature water. As with any detox bath, you might feel light-headed or tired when you get out; continue drinking room-temperature water into the next day. Reserve detox baths for just before bedtime; since they make you sleepy, you'll get the added benefit of a good night's rest.

I'm Open!

Everyday food ingredients like sugar, caffeine, artificial sweeteners, dairy or wheat products can build up in your body, making you feel sluggish, full of mucus, and achey. Taking a break from these foods can give your body a chance to address other toxins building up in your system, such as the ones produced by PTSD symptoms. There are many digestive cleansing products on the market, but one thing's for sure—if you don't follow the directions, you'll be uncomfortable. Doing a detoxifying cleanse isn't fun or easy. Be prepared to drink *a lot* of water, and to totally change up your eating habits. You'll probably experience a headache for a few days, either due to sugar and/or caffeine withdrawal or due to muscle tension as a result of mentally resisting the process. You could also feel tired or as if you're coming down with a cold. This is due to toxins flooding your system on their way out—a healing crisis of sorts. A safe and healthy cleanse will incorporate whole, high-fiber foods along with a supplement that helps remove toxins from your digestive tract. You don't want a cleanse that gives you abdominal cramping or keeps you close to the toilet. When researching cleanses online, read the reviews and choose one that not only acts in a gentle way, but also lasts no more than ten days.

ALL IN!

Make good use of the naturopathic physician on your Healing Team and ask him or her about prescribing a detox regimen. Be prepared. You'll likely work with your doctor over the course of several weeks and experience procedures such as:

A liver detox: With this detox, you lay back and relax while a set of electrodes attached to the right side of your body gently send low level currents of electricity through your liver, causing it to contract like a sponge, squeezing out stubborn toxic build-up (this should always be followed by a colonic).

A colonic: Your colon is the toxic waste dump of your body. Eating a high-fiber diet is very important for sweeping out the entire digestive tract and the colon, but it's not always enough. During a colonic, you recline in a comfortable "seat" that has a basin under your bottom area. While the doctor is out of the room, you insert a small, firm, lubricated tube just an inch or so into your rectum (the muscles of the rectum loosely grab on to it, keeping it in place until you remove it) and cover up with a warm blanket. The doctor returns, makes sure you are comfortable, and begins turnings dials and knobs on a machine that gently circulates warm salt water in and out of your rectum. The doctor will massage your abdomen and legs (maybe even your feet!) with a vibrating tool that looks like a car buffer to release toxins from your lymph nodes.

Near the end of the procedure, the doctor will add a dose of healthy probiotics to the water, which you hold inside your colon for a minute or so before releasing. Afterward, you'll likely spend a short time in the restroom releasing any water that wants to exit, thanks to gravity. This procedure is not for the faint of heart. There is no pain, but you will feel the need to "push" or poop, and that's okay (the special basin below you catches everything). You'll want to work with the cues your body gives you, or you'll feel uncomfortable during and after the procedure from holding the water inside your colon. The difficult part is "pooping" in front of a relative stranger. Even though your modesty is preserved at all times, you'll want to communicate clearly any anxiety you have and request that the doctor walk you through each moment step by step.

IV therapy: In the event your body hasn't been taken care of properly, or if there's a combination of genetics and chronic diseases, taking organic supplements orally may not be enough. Intravenous therapy infuses the body with an over-abundance of vitamins and minerals by way of the bloodstream to help bring back homeostasis and return the body's ability to absorb nutrients to normal. IV nutrition is helpful for people who need vitamins and minerals added directly into the bloodstream, bypassing lack of absorption and assimilation processes that may be deficient in the gut. IV nutrients can support your body rapidly and efficiently and in much higher doses than taking supplements orally. IV therapy is only used until your body can thrive with smaller amounts taken orally. The nutrients used include Vitamin C infusion, Glutathione infusion, anti-Candida (yeast) treatments, and other multivitamin and mineral infusions. Bring a good book (like this one!) and plan to sit for about an hour. Oh, and hopefully you're not afraid of needles!

Sauna therapy: The skin is the largest organ of the body and a major eliminative channel. In most people, their skin isn't working well as a detoxifying channel due to being congested and overwhelmed with the toxic effects of issues like ultraviolet sun exposure, use of synthetic clothing, bathing in chlorinated water, and exposure to hundreds of chemicals which damage the skin. Not only that, but excessive sympathetic nervous system activity (e.g., physical exercise) and emotions such as fear, anger and guilt cause blood to be withdrawn from the skin, contributing to inactivity of the skin as a part of the body's toxic elimination system.

According to the United States Environmental Protection Agency (EPA), toxic chemicals are the worst environmental problem in the nation, responsible for up to eighty percent of cancer deaths. However, medical studies demonstrate that most toxins can be eliminated through the skin with the help of an infrared sauna, relieving the burden on the kidneys and liver. How does this work? The infrared sauna gives us the gift of the sun without the damaging effects of ultraviolet rays. Infrared rays warm a person without warming the air around them, increasing blood flow in the body's tissues. This is the same technology used by the sun (the suns rays are eighty percent infrared). Infrared saunas are the most effective way to release unhealthy toxins like chemicals and heavy metals (e.g., mercury) from the body through perspiration, because of the direct heating process of infrared rays (1.5 to three inches deep). Also, infrared rays assist the release of organic chemicals (food additives and solvents) and biological toxins (fungi and bacteria) from fat cells. You'll find your infrared sauna experience will be extremely effective, comfortable and dry compared to traditional saunas. Plus, the FDA approves the sauna as a therapeutic device.

Color or Light therapy: Chromotherapy, also called color therapy or light treatments, is the use of color and light to gently bring balance to your body's systems. Color and light are applied to specific areas and accupoints on the body to assist in correcting imbalances, according to the Institute For Chromotherapy. Angelo Cammilleri is a certified practitioner and trainer in the use of color and light for deep healing. He also is certified in both Electro-Biology/Electro Ecology and Bau-Biologie. A Bau-Biologist is a person who can identify problem areas in existing buildings and propose non-hazardous solutions. For example, if a medical doctor suspects an environmental cause for a person's poor health, Mr. Cammilleri sees to it that the home of patient is inspected and cleared of health hazards. He is also consulted during the construction of a new building and can, as an architect or builder, design and build healthy structures. Here's what Mr. Cammilleri has to say about color therapy as a piece of the overall healing puzzle:

> The earth, the oceans, in fact every living thing, is dependent upon light for its very existence. A recent scientific study disclosed that each cell in the body emits light. We live in a sea of energy and our bodies are composed of energy. Color works through and in us, in every nerve, cell, gland and muscle. Within our body, our organs, muscles, cells and nerves all have a level of vibration. When our body becomes out of balance, disease occurs. Each color has its own frequency and vibration. Through extensive research, we know that color and light will help bring our physical and emotional systems into balance.[20]

---

20 http://www.light-color-therapy.com/about-chromotherapy/

Want to know what color can do for you?[21]

Orange: Orange is warm, cheering, and non-constricting. It stimulates creative thinking and enthusiasm.

Yellow: Yellow helps strengthen the nerves and the mind.

Green: Green is the color of nature and the earth. Green affects blood pressure and all conditions of the heart.

Turquoise: Increases intuition and sensitivity. Works to disinfect or as an antiseptic. Tones the general system, builds the skin and relaxes sensations of stress.

Blue: Blue is cooling; electric, astringent. Cools down inflammation (including rheumatic inflammation), fevers, high blood pressure. Stops bleeding, relieves bursting headaches, calms strong emotions like anger, aggression or hysteria.

Purple: Purple is a color of transformation. This color slows down an over-active heart, stimulates the spleen and the white blood cells (aids immunity).

Red: Brings warmth, energy and stimulation making this color good for energy, fatigue, colds, chilliness and strengthens passive people. Red energizes heart and blood circulation, it builds up the blood and heightens a low blood pressure. It energizes all organs and the senses.

ACUPUNCTURE

Acupuncture is an ancient form of Chinese medicine developed more than 2,000 years ago that uses very small needles inserted into the skin at key points to address the primary cause of symptoms. It is one of the oldest and most commonly used medical procedures in the world. It's important to remember that the needles used are not used as "medicine." Rather, think of an acupuncturist as a facilitator who inserts needles to stimulate your body's natural ability to heal itself. Ultimately,

---

21 http://psychology.about.com/od/sensationandperception/a/colorpsych.htm and http://greenwavefamilywellnesscenter.com/wp/services/infrared-saunas-with-light-therapy/

you are doing the work of healing. If you suffer with painful symptoms associated with PTSD, such as back pain, chronic tension, numbness or tingling, and haven't found relief through traditional methods, consider giving acupuncture a try. Although not recommended as a primary treatment for anxiety, depression or PTSD, it does work well in conjunction with additional therapies.

Be Gentle!
Check out Amy Guinther, M.S. (Master of Science) on YouTube—she'll explain what acupuncture is, how it works and what all those needles are about. Then, wander around watching other videos that demonstrate acupuncture treatments.

I'm Open!
Pay a visit to a practitioner near you. Interview them about the procedure. Ask if they'd be willing to give you references to patients who'd be willing to share their experience with you. Also, ask around; you might be surprised to find out who you already know that have used acupuncture to treat all kinds of health problems, even to quit smoking.

All In!
Be brave and overcome your fear of needles all in one shot (oops, I should say *in one fell swoop*)! Here's what you'll want to look for in an acupuncturist:

Education and Credentials: Licensed Acupuncturists practice internal Chinese medicine, which focuses on the underlying source of the problem, rather than just treating symptoms. As a result, their treatments go beyond simple pain relief offered by chiropractors and medical acupuncturists. Also, most Licensed Acupuncturists must have a Masters degree in either Acupuncture or Oriental Medicine. The distinction between the two is that a practitioner with a Masters in Acupuncture is trained primarily in acupuncture. A practitioner with a Masters in Oriental Medicine is trained in acupuncture as well as diagnosis and treatment using traditional Chinese herbs.

Area of Specialty: Some acupuncturists treat everything, while others treat primarily specific conditions. Be sure to ask what their specialty is or what kind of results they've had in treating PTSD and its physical symptoms.

Method: Where on your body will the treatments be performed? How often? How many treatments will there be in total? Will they offer other kinds of treatments besides acupuncture? A practitioner should never be able to answer these questions over the phone. Only after a thorough examination, review of your health history, and preliminary diagnosis will you get the answer to these questions.

Payment: Check with your medical insurance to see if they cover part or all of your acupuncture needs. If you have to pay a portion or all of the cost out of pocket, you deserve to know how much the bill will be. Don't be afraid to ask how much they charge for initial treatments and follow-up visits.

THE CENTER FOR HOPE & RENEWAL:
PTSD TRANSFORMATION FOR SURVIVORS & FAMILIES

What if there was a place you could go to experience all you've read in *PTSD Self Help?* Originating in the evergreen rich environment of the Pacific Northwest, The Center for Hope & Renewal could be just such a place. The only organization of its kind offering PTSD workshops and Healing Intensives to survivors and their families in an experiential learning environment, The Center for Hope & Renewal would exist to achieve the following three goals:

1. To facilitate PTSD education and recovery plan development for individuals, families and industries

2. To provide alternative wellness services in conjunction with traditional, trauma-focused psychotherapy for individuals diagnosed with PTSD

3. To develop nationwide collaborative partnerships with agencies, healthcare/wellness providers, universities and PTSD programs to collect and report statistics related to the study of alternative PTSD treatments

Everyone who visits The Center for Hope & Renewal for help would begin their journey by participating in an orientation that explains the dynamics of PTSD and equips participants in developing a recovery plan or a support strategy—in the case of family members of survivors—based on the *PTSD Self Help* method. Most importantly, orientation participants will be guided in the formation of a Healing Team. Through partnerships with professionals who understand PTSD and how it impacts their clients, as a result of the *PTSD Self Help* training and certification program, The Center will offer participants high-quality, holistic Healing Team referrals to practitioners in their local area.

What Would I Learn?

You already know the damage it has caused; now learn exactly how PTSD keeps tripping you up and how to begin the healing process. The Center's PTSD Orientation will be a two-hour opportunity open to anyone who suspects they might be struggling with PTSD, has been diagnosed with PTSD or cares about someone with PTSD. You'll discover:

- How PTSD consistently interferes with life

- Practical ways to help healing begin

- Opportunities to partner with The Center to accelerate healing

This orientation will be a solid foundation upon which to begin creating your recovery plan, and a first step and pre-requisite for future participation in all workshops, programs, studies and intensives offered by The Center for Hope & Renewal. You can be confident of understanding exactly what to expect from the healing journey and what to do to ensure healing success!

Healing Intensives

The only thing intense about this program is the relief you'll feel! Designed to plug you into resources that will help you feel better fast, the Healing Intensives are experiential learning immersions. You'll enjoy an extended stay in The Center's lush retreat environment, consume the highest quality organic foods harvested locally and prepared by expert chefs, explore your senses in the serenity of the Ayurvedic Spa, and cocoon in the luxurious comfort of individual mini-suites, where you'll surrender to deep, restful sleep in our renowned Heavenly Beds. Healing never felt so good!

By day, as you walk out the Healing Plan developed during the PTSD Orientation, you will be:

Actively doing. Experience practical collaborative healing activities and alternative wellness therapies in an environment created to accelerate your healing process.

Actively learning. Gain an education from respected professionals who provide services that alleviate PTSD symptoms.

Actively connecting. Journey along with other survivors who are dedicated to achieving not only a life free from PTSD, but also a life of triumph!

Thanks to you, the dream of creating The Center for Hope & Renewal is already underway. A portion of the revenue from the purchase of this book goes toward building not only this amazing facility, but also an interactive, virtual reality version of it on the *PTSD Self Help* website. That way anyone, anywhere can visit The Center for Hope & Renewal from the comfort of their own space 24/7. But healing won't stop there! With plans to open regional facilities and programs across the United States, hopefully one day there will be a Center for Hope & Renewal near you!

SEASON TO ENJOY A
LIFE WORTH LIVING

TRYING ON THE NEW YOU!

ENDING YOUR WORK WITH A MENTAL HEALTH PROFESSIONAL

She's been there for you when you needed someone the most. She's been real with you, held you accountable and challenged you. She knows everything—your secrets, flaws, fears, hopes, and dreams. She knows your past and your present. You started seeing each other every week at first, then every two weeks, then once a month. You let her in. It's been the first healthy relationship you've had in a long time. Even though you paid her to care (it was a professional relationship, after all) you're surprised by how much you genuinely like her. And now that you're feeling better and have achieved what you set out to accomplish together, it's time to move on. This is the first test of your newfound confidence—breaking it off with your therapist.

Therapists call the end of their work with you *termination*. It's harsh technical lingo that should be reserved for insurance paperwork, but nevertheless, it reminds you of the professional boundary between you and this crucial Healing Team member. Remember that you hired them to guide you at a time when you needed it—thus it's your decision to end the relationship when you choose to do so, for any reason. Understandably, ending your sessions with an MHP can bring on vulnerable feelings, so let's talk about what you need to know when finalizing this part of your PTSD healing journey.

Why Will It End?

There are a number of reasons why you'll be ready to end your sessions, and only a few reasons why your therapist might end the relationship. Optimally, you began your search for an MHP with a clear goal in mind after reading *Season of Hope* where you did the foundational work of envisioning what successful healing would look like in your life when you achieved it. If you've done this important work in the beginning and shared your vision with your MHP, ending your sessions will come naturally to both you and your therapist. Each of you will know when the goal has been reached, since the evidence will be there in the life you've been examining together. Here are other reasons why it might end:

- You or your therapist moves away

- You can't afford to pay and/or lose your health insurance

- Your therapist retires or is transferred to another agency

- Your MHP recognizes you have needs outside of their training or expertise

- You've completed a contractual program in which the MHP played part

- Your MHP has countertransference issues (countertransference means a therapist has an emotional reaction to the contribution made by the client that causes the therapist to no longer remain objective—therefore, further work together is unsafe for the client)

- Your MHP is acting unprofessionally (e.g., being rude, belittling, has broken your trust or confidentiality agreement, makes sexual advances or comments, brings their own personal issues to your sessions, tries to see you outside of their office)

How Does It End?

Even though you may leave therapy for any reason (or no reason at all), it's best to leave in an honest and straightforward way. Some things to consider before making the move to end your sessions are:

- Has your life improved since you first started seeing your MHP?

- What have you learned?

- How have you grown?

- Are you clear about your weaknesses? Strengths?

- What still needs to be done?

- Do you have a plan for dealing with future problems?

- Have you developed strategies and skills to overcome or cope with the unexpected?

After careful review, if you can honestly say you're ready to move on and give your newfound healing some wings to fly, the only way to end your relationship is to talk with your MHP about it. Here's where you get to try on your new skills! Don't be afraid. The reason for ending the sessions is more important for you to understand than it is for your MHP. The way termination happens is very important legally and ethically to the MHP. There must be clear communication and specific procedures the therapist must follow.

Doing the hard work of healing can seem to take its toll, but more often than not, when you're thinking of throwing in the towel, a major breakthrough is right around the corner. Don't be premature about ending your work with this member of your Healing Team! Here are some misguided reasons to end your sessions:

- Your circumstances and feelings have improved, but you haven't really solved any deeper issues (e.g., You started unemployed and depressed, but now you're working and feel better).

- You don't have time or it's inconvenient.

- You get angry at your therapist and quit instead of dealing with your feelings during sessions.

- You allow "lesser" priorities to take over.

For some people "good enough" is all they're after, but it would be a shame to only come half-way and not get what you deserve; remember what you started this journey for—an amazing life! The best time to end your sessions is when you've come to a conscious realization about how your life works (and doesn't) and understand your unconscious motivations so well that you feel you have what it takes to guide yourself; when you no longer feel your therapist is a necessary part of gaining a greater awareness or understanding; when you have, to some degree, dissolved your illusions and feel capable of finding your identity within yourself.

WHAT CAN YOU EXPECT?

Once you bring up termination, you and your therapist will probably discuss your thoughts and answers to the questions above, then agree on where you're at in the overall treatment process and consider a time frame for completion of your sessions. When the termination conversation becomes more concrete, you can expect to have one to four additional sessions and the option for entering into treatment again in the future, or coming back for a one to two session "tune-up," should you need it. You can ask your therapist to share their thoughts about what work you may still have ahead, signs or symptoms you should look out for, and if they will continue to be available to you by phone or email (ask if they'll charge you for this!).

Even after your sessions have been terminated, you can still expect the benefits of confidentiality. They cannot reveal anything about your sessions without your permission and are required to keep your file on hand for anywhere from three to twelve years. If you decide to enter into treatment again with another MHP, you can ask to have your treatment records transferred. As a side note, if a person dies while undergoing psychotherapy, or after psychotherapy, privilege (a legal term)—including the ability to view the psychotherapy records—usually passes to the deceased person's estate. However, legal advice is required to make that happen.

Leaving your therapist can feel a bit like breaking up an intimate relationship, and in a way, it is. You've relied on this person to guide you at a time when you were vulnerable and shared intimate aspects of your life you've likely never revealed to anyone else. It's understandable that you'd be reluctant to detach. You might even feel a sense of loss or grief. This is why MHPs have standards of care that include an honest discussion and clear plan for ending their work with clients. Those last few sessions will focus on any last-minute feelings of uncertainty, vulnerability and insecurity, so make the most of them! You want to start the rest of your fabulous life in a healthy way.

LIFE AFTER HEALING

By the time you reach the end of your PTSD healing journey, a fair amount of time has likely passed. You have different people in your life. Hopefully some relationships have deepened as a result of their commitment to your healing work. You may be ready to re-establish relationships with others who have been watching from the sidelines, or those you've lost connection with. You've discovered practices and developed habits that have served you well. Most of the peace and wonder of life you're now enjoying is a result of those practices. Why give them up? Continue to explore activities that bring you new, healthy lessons about yourself and how you engage your world. You've made huge changes and the payoff has been worth it. Keep the momentum going! Maybe you'll decide to go deeper into learning more about nutrition and how it affects your body. Exploring a greater commitment to exercise in some form could do nothing but help you maintain clarity and groundedness. Everyone is complaining about stress these days, but you've found a way out from the worst kind of stress there is! Don't succumb to the idea that stress is "normal." You have more control over everyday stress than you think, and you've already got a great start on managing it, so keep up the good work!

Weighing The Evidence . . . The Stress of Everyday Life

In 2012, the American Psychological Association (APA) conducted a study about stress in the United States and found that seventy-three to seventy-seven percent of Americans regularly experience physical and psychological symptoms caused by everyday stress. They struggle every day with:

- Fatigue

- Headache

- Upset stomach

- Muscle tension

- Change in appetite

- Teeth grinding

- Change in sex drive

- Feeling dizzy

- Irritability or anger

- Feeling nervous

- Lack of energy

- Feeling close to tears

With our economy still recovering from the recession and people trying desperately to balance home, work and health, it's no wonder our personal and family lives are falling apart. You might not think your stress affects your kids, but if you ask them, they'll tell you it does. Here's what the APAs *Stress In America Study* (2010) found out:

- 69% of parents say their stress has only a slight or no impact on their children

- 91% of children know their parent is stressed because they witness yelling, arguing, and complaining

- 47% of tweens and 33% of teens say they feel sad about their parents stress

- 36% of tweens and 43% of teens feel worried about it

- 25% of tweens and 38% of teens feel frustrated when their parents are stressed[22]

There are so many benefits to healing from trauma, and learning how to manage stress is just one of them. You can enjoy *all* the benefits every step along the way toward a full recovery. You don't have to wait! Look for these gifts along the pathway of your own healing journey:

- An abiding awareness and appreciation for your inner strength

- Priorities that are meaningful and satisfying

- Trust in your ability to take care of and protect yourself

- A comfortable assurance when facing fears, the unexpected, and the unknown

- An appreciation for the ease of everyday life

- New philosophies about tragedy, suffering and wellness

- An assurance that although life is complex, its lessons bring about the best in you

- A deep spiritual awareness

- A rich and healthy emotional life

22 http://www.apa.org/news/press/releases/stress/national-report.pdf
http://www.statisticbrain.com/stress-statistics/

- Strong, supportive relationships

- The ability to experience and give love in all its forms

It may be hard to imagine living life, enjoying these gifts, and knowing they'll be there every day. If while you're working your way through the healing process you can look for evidence of them—no matter how small—you'll find the journey less painful and more exciting.

UNRESOLVED ISSUES

We have a tendency to separate the various aspects of our lives instead of integrating them. We forget that who we are at home follows us to work, to church, to our friend's house and so on. During this journey, we've focused on your complete healing from PTSD, in a sense, separating it from other possible issues that need resolution in your life. This was necessary, since PTSD had created a chronic neurological cycle of anxiety that needed to be broken. Now, you have the tools you need to differentiate between organic, run-of-the-mill emotions and any remaining residue associated with your originating trauma. Pay close attention to the energetic weight of thoughts and emotions, while acknowledging that although you've defeated PTSD, you may have some more work to do. . . if you choose to allow the PTSD healing journey to be the catalyst for a complete personal transformation. In other words, as a result of your work with *PTSD Self Help* you have the opportunity, the skill and the stamina to dump all the psychological baggage you've been carrying, if you want to.

Certainly, now, the end of your PTSD healing journey, would be the time to take a break. When bringing your relationship with an MHP to a close, consider asking them if they'd be interested in working with you on other topics in the future, should you feel you need their assistance. Then, enjoy the freedom of engaging life! Surely, there are things you may want to address in the future that you don't currently see as being a part of your PTSD journey, but journeys never cease. Maybe you have another journey to take. Maybe you don't. Either way, trust in the wisdom of your own internal guidance, your ability to remember when and how to use your new skills, and your mind's way of bringing to light anything that needs to be healed *in its own proper timing*, so that you can have the abundant life you deserve. Remind yourself:

I am normal.

I will do what works.

I already have everything I need.

Annmarie's Story

Ultimately, everything I've told you about my past has been my story. What you've learned was my view of the people and events as I saw them through my belief window. The meaning I attached to that perspective became my story, and after having lived that story for more than half my lifetime, it became my identity. It's true that PTSD played a part in who I became. It was the catalyst for change - for my metamorphosis, for my transformational healing. Now, it's not only a boulder incorporated into the deep root structure of my life, but also a doorway through which I enter into the lives of others, bringing the gift of healing and wholeness.

To each and every person who played their part, I am eternally grateful. To those who robbed me of my freedom to choose, you showed me the value of choosing for myself. To those who insisted on controlling and manipulating me, you helped me see the futility of control and manipulation and to embrace change as life brings it to me. To those who were stead-fast and patient, believing that somehow, some day, I would find my way, you helped me to believe in myself. To those who brought their expertise, knowledge and willingness to learn about PTSD, you taught me the value of collaboration and allowing others to use knowledge as a platform for gaining personal experience. And to those few who loved me uncondition-ally, you released the power of love in my life so completely that the only possible outcome was an abiding love in myself and others. Thank you, each and every one.

Enjoy ♡

FREEDOM AND VULNERABILITY

Healing from PTSD is much like the growth of Jung's metaphorical tree mentioned at the beginning of this book. The tree is always growing. You are always learning. The tree has seasons when outwardly it doesn't seem like much is happening. So do you. The tree also has seasons when it produces fruit, then drops its fruit to move on to the next season. You too will experience moments when you enjoy quantum leaps in healing and bask in the newness of the freedom you've found. Then, you'll return to the hard work of healing another area, another memory, another wound. But this time, when you return to the work of healing, it's with a new sense of strength and purpose. You've got a few successes underneath you, and although you may feel a bit apprehensive about digging in again, you no longer really fear the journey.

This is where many survivors make the mistake of thinking they've gone backward, lost the healing they worked so hard to achieve, or feel betrayed by the whole healing experience. It can feel like a three-steps-forward, two-steps-back kind of journey. So when that season comes along where you are relishing freedom from flashbacks, nightmares, triggers and painful physical symptoms, enjoy it! Get out and do some fun activities that have nothing to do with healing. Reconnect with supportive family members and friends. Then, when your season of enjoyment passes, remember the tree. The tree is still growing. It hasn't died, isn't shrinking in size or strength, and hasn't been uprooted. In truth, the tree is preparing itself for the next season. In your case, that season is likely a return to *Season of Hope* where you might need to re-commit yourself to seeing the journey through to the end. Look back at the *Season of Renewal* and ask yourself if there's someone new you need to add to your Healing Team. Try some of the collaborative healing activities you passed up in *Season of Transformation*. You've traveled this path before, and although there will be new sights and lessons along the way, you're sure to pass through each upcoming season more quickly than before. And each time you pass through the *Season to Enjoy a Life Worth Living*, you collect a bit more wholeness, strength, stamina, health and knowing the truth about who you really are.

When you least expect it, a time will come when you enter into the *Season to Enjoy a Life Worth Living* again, and you'll recognize a sense that you're close to ending your journey and it'll come with a new feeling: vulnerability. You'll wonder how you'll ever make it living in a world where you can genuinely feel your emotions. You're plugged in! Life is all at once beautiful and full, yet you still lack the confidence to contain all the joy and wonder it has to offer. You feel exposed, unable to return in good conscience to your old, unhealthy ways of coping, but not yet comfortable relying on your newfound wellness skills. You wonder if it will last. This is the point of no return. The choice is up to you. Will you go back to the comfort of what you once knew—though it gave you pain and misery—or will you keep moving forward, believing the strength that brought you this far will carry you through to the happy ending you deserve?

I'm here to tell you that it's true, it's real, it's lasting. I'm living proof that you can walk away from the effects of PTSD for good. Don't turn back now! You've been given the gift of life, a second chance, and it's meant to be lived, so you can share it with those you love. It doesn't matter how long you've struggled with PTSD or where your healing journey has taken you. All that matters is that *you did it*. Not only are you *alive*, you've transcended mere survival. You now have a solid foundation upon which to build whatever your heart desires. Join me here. Welcome to wholeness. Welcome to a life worth living.

Making Sense of . . . Wholeness and Emotions

Here you are minding your own business, enjoying the vibrant health and wholeness of body and mind you so deserve. That's when it happens. Instead of PTSD triggers or symptoms sneaking up behind you, real, authentic emotion washes over your senses. Maybe it happens when you're watching a movie. More likely, it'll happen when you've encountered the raw emotion of relationship. Whether it's heart-pounding joy and excitement or crushing remorse and sorrow, you'll notice a strong wave move through your soul. This experience is different from what you remember as a struggling survivor. Instead of feeling overwhelmed, flooded and pummeled by the energetic surge, you realize a comforting flow that carries you. Emotions are a normal part of the human experience. As you learned already, emotions are caused by a chemical release in the brain and are felt throughout the body. What caused those emotions and where they're carrying you are worlds away from where you used to live on a daily basis. In a state of wholeness, emotions are preceded by the witnessing of emotion in others, recalling states of emotion from the past but with a loving perspective or being moved to emotion as a result of being "in the moment," present, just to name a few. Allow emotion to flow in and out of your awareness, like a river you walk along side during your healing journey. There's nothing to fear. It's the damming of emotion by restricting it, stuffing it or dismissing it (or damning it by placing blame, resourcing guilt feelings and rehearsing the past) that causes it to become a stagnant, smelly pool of something which was intended to bring life and sustenance. Be cautious about applying meaning, since doing so will attach perspectives to your Belief Window, all the while welcoming and allowing emotion to have a place in your new life!

APPENDIX A:

Practical Application Guides

THINKING THINGS THROUGH
Post Traumatic Stress Disorder 22
The Ego 28
Stigmatization.. 32
Fight, Flight or Freeze 44
Are You Closed or Open?...................................... 52
Symptoms... 57
Healing as a Release From Fear............................... 80
Ranking the InnerAction Journal Risk Factor................. 85
The Power of Our Mind.. 193
Locus of Control... 206

WEIGHING THE EVIDENCE
The Financial Cost of PTSD................................... 23
Visual Motor Rehearsal....................................... 30
Flashbacks... 39
Healing Childhood Sexual Abuse 42
Secondary Wounding 53
Hypervigilance... 60
Knowledge Is Power 68
Relearning How to Breathe 104
Don't Be a Dropout... 221
The Stress of Everyday Life 260

MAKING SENSE OF . . .
Triggers... 25
Mental Health Professionals.................................. 40

Successful Healing 67
The InnerAction Journal in Action 82
The InnerAction Journal and Creativity 86
Enlightenment 100
Emergency Breathing 102
Chiropractic Benefits 130
Secondary Wounding 149
Practical Application Guides 165
Overlays. 178
Observing Your Thoughts 194
Deciding to Respond 197
Religion and Healing PTSD. 207
Emotional Vocabulary 214
Wholeness and Emotions 265

APPENDIX B:

Summary Of Exercises

Hello, Ego. Who Asked You? 28

Counting the Cost 33

Being The Observer 43

Warning! Do Not Heal! 55

What is a Success Story? 65

Making Sense of . . .
Successful Healing 67

Thinking Things Through . . .
Ranking the InnerAction Journal Risk Factor 85

Making Sense of . . .
The InnerAction Journal and Creativity 86

Making Sense of . . .
Enlightenment 100

Tools for Your Backpack
– An Emergency Plan of Action (EPA) 101

Making Sense of . . .
Emergency Breathing 102

Making Sense of . . .
Chiropractic Benefits 130

Scavenger Hunt: A Look Through the Belief Window 184

Personal Healing Statement 187

Making Sense of . . .
Observing Your Thoughts 194

Collaborative Healing Activities (all) 221

Season of Transformation: Let the Journey Begin! (all practical application guides)

APPENDIX C:

Resources For A Dynamite Trip!

BOOKS FOR YOU
HEALING CONCEPTS
Stillness Speaks, Eckhart Tolle
The Power of Now, Eckhart Tolle
The Language of Letting Go, Melody Beattie
Co-dependent No More, Melody Beattie
A Course In Miracles
I Can Make You Confident, Paul McKenna
The 7 Habits of Highly Effective People, Stephen R. Covey
The 10 Natural Laws of Successful Time and Life Management, Hyrum W. Smith
Welcome to Your Brain, Sandra Aamodt, PhD and Sam Wang, PhD
28 Days: A Daily Horoscope for Your Hormones, Gabrielle Lichterman
The Path, Laurie Beth Jones
The Blue Day Book: A Lesson in Cheering Yourself Up, Bradley Trevor Greive

HEALING HOMEWORK
Life After Trauma (2nd ed.): *A Workbook for Healing,* Dena Rosenbloom, PhD and Mary Beth Williams, PhD
The Complete ACOA Sourcebook, Janet Geringer Woititz, EdD
After the Tears: Helping Adult Children of Alcoholics Heal Their Childhood Trauma, Jane Middleton-Moz and Lorie L. Dwinell
The Tao of Equus, Linda Kohanov
Attacking Anxiety and Depression, Midwest Center for Stress and Anxiety
Freedom from Depression Workbook, Carter & Minirth
Now Discover Your Strengths, Marcus Buckingham & Donald). Clifon,

PhD
The Path, Laurie Beth Jones

COLLABORATIVE HEALING ACTIVITIES
Key Poses of Yoga, Long
Chakra Foods for Optimum Health, Deanna Minich
The Sevenfold Journey: Reclaiming Mind, Body & Spirit Through the Chakras, Judith & Vega
AVEDA Rituals, Horst Rechelbacker
Hands On Feet, Kluck
The Busy Person's Guide to Reflexology: Simple Routines for Home, Work and Travel, Ann Gillanders
Healthy Eating's Detoxification Programs to Cleanse, Purify & Renew, Linda Page, PhD
Hatha Yoga Illustrated, Kirk, Boon, & DiTuro
The Tao of Equus, Linda Kohanov

PTSD EDUCATION
The Courage to Heal, Ellen Bass and Laura Davis
The Sexual Healing Journey, Wendy Maltz
Secret Survivors, E. Sue Blume
I Can't Get Over It! A Handbook for Trauma Survivors (2nd Ed.), Aphrodite Matsakis, PhD
Outgrowing the Pain, Eliana Gil, PhD

BOOKS FOR TEAM MEMBERS
MENTAL HEALTH PROFESSIONALS
Handbook of PTSD: Science and Practice, Friedman, Keane & Resick
Transforming a Rape Culture, Butchwald, Fletcher, Roth
Moving a Nation to Care, Ilona Meagher
Helping the Healers Not to Harm: Iatrogenic Damage and Community Mental Health, Ruth B. Caplan and Gerald Caplan
Eastern Body, Western Mind: Psychology and the Chakra System as a Path to the Self, Anodea Judith

SPOUSE
Loving the Adult Child of an Alcoholic, Evans
The Language of Letting Go, Melody Beattie
Getting To Yes: Negotiating Agreement Without Giving In, Roger Fisher and William Ury

Boundaries in Marriage, Cloud & Townsend
The Five Love Languages, Chapman
Life Strategies: Doing What Works, Doing What Matters, Phillip C. McGraw, PhD
Relationship Rescue, Phillip C. McGraw, PhD
Ghosts in the Bedroom, Ken Graber, M.A.
Allies in Healing, Laura Davis
I Can't Get Over It! A Handbook for Trauma Survivors (2nd Ed.), Aphrodite Matsakis, PhD

HEALING PARTNER
The Language of Letting Go, Melody Beattie
The Courage to Heal, Ellen Bass and Laura Davis
I Can't Get Over It! A Handbook for Trauma Survivors (2nd Ed.), Aphrodite Matsakis, PhD
Allies in Healing, Laura Davis

NATUROPATH
Transforming a Rape Culture, Butchwald, Fletcher, Roth
Moving a Nation to Care, Ilona Meagher
Helping the Healers Not to Harm: Iatrogenic Damage and Community Mental Health, Ruth B. Caplan and Gerald Caplan

CHIROPRACTOR
Transforming a Rape Culture, Butchwald, Fletcher, Roth
Moving a Nation to Care, Ilona Meagher
Helping the Healers Not to Harm: Iatrogenic Damage and Community Mental Health, Ruth B. Caplan and Gerald Caplan

MASSAGE THERAPIST
Acupressure for Emotional Healing: A Self-Care Guide for Trauma, Stress & Common Emotional Imbalances Michael Reed Gach, PhD and Beth Ann Henning, Dipl. A.B.T.

WORK WITH A. E. HUPPERT

343 SOULUTIONS

Annmarie has combined her extensive experience in life coaching, psychology and change management to form 343 Soulutions, an organization that exists to unearth and ignite transformational healing though advocacy, coaching and consultation.

343 Soulutions has made the healing of Post Traumatic Stress their top priority through the following:

- Speaking and writing publicly in support of the survivor's healing experience

- Giving instruction to individuals or teams of people dedicated to serving PTSD survivors

- Sharing professional, expert advice to industries seeking to implement programs, policies and/or procedures impacting PTSD recovery

Want to work with A. E. Huppert to eliminate PTSD from our human experience?

Tell us about it!

A. E. Huppert
3110 Judson Street, PMB #21
Gig Harbor, WA 98335
(253) 228-9843
hello@343soulutions.com

ABOUT THE AUTHOR

A. E. Huppert (Annmarie Esther Huppert) is an advocate for survivors struggling with Post Traumatic Stress Disorder (PTSD), author of non-fiction articles and books on transformational healing, cofounder of 343 Soulutions, and visionary of The Center for Hope & Renewal – an experiential learning facility designed to empower people with a holistic approach to emotional healing.

Annmarie's practical, self-help perspective comes not only from 20 years studying PTSD, its therapies, and obstacles to healing, but also from being a recovered survivor. She partners with health care professionals, government officials and everyday people to provide PTSD education and healing as a motivational speaker, consultant, and strengths-focused healing coach. With an emphasis on securing citizens' equal access to accurate PTSD diagnoses and quality recovery options, Annmarie works collaboratively with legislative officials and public policy makers as a voice for those struggling with PTSD – veterans and non-veterans alike.

Annmarie passionately delivers relief and a reason for hope through her writing found on blogs, websites and in-print media. Directed at survivors and their families, Annmarie delivers relevant, practical how-to information. As a professional outside government administration, she is respected and trusted by veterans for giving real world guidance in developing a workable healing plan. Specializing in low/no cost alternative methods, Annmarie's natural healing advice brings proactive transformation and enlightenment to all health conscious readers.

Annmarie's unique and effective approach for educating survivors and their families about PTSD, empowers them to initiate an individualized plan for healing. Her foundational methods incorporate concepts such as making a life style change and embracing a proactive, holistic approach that includes body, mind and spirit. A supporter of Equine Assisted Psychotherapy (EAP), she acknowledges the ability of animals to assist humans in the healing process and promotes best practices that protect both. Annmarie has coined the terms healing partner, healing plan, and healing team in connection with her work.

Annmarie holds a B.A. in Psychology/Public Policy and specializes in recovery from childhood sexual abuse. She practices many of the life style changes she recommends but loves yoga, being in her garden and hanging out with Friesian horses best. Annmarie lives on Puget Sound in beautiful Gig Harbor, Washington with her spouse and two pugs.

CPSIA information can be obtained
at www.ICGtesting.com
Printed in the USA
FSOW01n0021170617
35327FS